David James Burrell

For Christ's Crown

And Other Sermons

David James Burrell

For Christ's Crown
And Other Sermons

ISBN/EAN: 9783337116965

Printed in Europe, USA, Canada, Australia, Japan

Cover: Foto ©Lupo / pixelio.de

More available books at **www.hansebooks.com**

"For Christ's Crown."

"For Christ's Crown"

AND OTHER SERMONS.

BY

DAVID JAMES BURRELL,, D.D.,

*Pastor of the Collegiate Church at Fifth Avenue and 29th Street,
New York.*

NEW YORK:
WILBUR B. KETCHAM,
2 COOPER UNION.

COPYRIGHT, 1896,
By WILBUR B. KETCHAM.

CONTENTS.

	PAGE.
"For Christ's Crown,"	7
The Unspeakable Turk,	19
Mors Janua Vitæ,	33
The Form of Godliness,	42
The Story of an Outcast,	51
The Story of an Outcast—The Sequel,	63
The Ascent of Man,	74
Loose Him and Let Him Go,	83
The Genealogy of Jesus,	92
Armageddon,	104
The Story of a Wayward Youth,	120
The Part of the Hand That Wrote,	132
The Conspiracy Against The Liquor Traffic,	144
The White Solar Ray,	156
The University of Jerusalem,	167
As the Hart Panteth,	182
The Cleansing of the Temple,	191
Come and See,	202
Protestantism,	213
King Saul at the Witch's Cave,	224
How Jericho Fell,	235
Tom Brown of Rugby; Or, Manly Christianity,	244
The Prophecy of Palm Sunday,	254
How to Read History,	264
The Boundless Prayer of Faith,	276

THE EPWORTH SINGER,	285
THE SUNDAY NEWSPAPER,	297
THE FIRST AND GREAT COMMANDMENT,	305
AND THE SECOND IS LIKE UNTO IT,	314
ESTHER IN SHUSHAN,	322
ORTHODOXY,	331
HE IS APPREHENDED IN THE GARDEN	341
HOW DAVID THOUGHT OF THE FORGIVENESS OF SIN,	351
THE GOLDEN WEDGE,	361

"FOR CHRIST'S CROWN."

"Now unto the King eternal, immortal, invisible, the only wise God, be honor and glory for ever and ever." Amen.—I. TIM. i. 17.

The ideal form of government is the Jewish theocracy. In it were combined all the advantages of all other forms of government whatsoever. It was a republic, in that all men were free and equal before the law. It was a sovereignty, in that God was recognized as King, sole and absolute. It is scarcely possible to conceive a better order of things. Far enough have the nations departed from that original fabric, but in the final restitution they will surely return to it. The millenial glory will be established in the commonwealth of God.

It was natural, however, that the children of Israel should be impatient under these conditions. They saw the neighboring tribes and nations prospering in the magnificence of fleets and armies and royal establishments, while they themselves had only the simplest forms, with no rulers save priests and prophets who administered in the behalf of God. Wherefore they demanded a king: "Make us a king to judge us like all the nations." And God was pleased to yield to their importunate weakness. Howbeit he solemnly protested against their folly. He admonished them that in time to come their kings would whip them with whips of scorpions and lay on them vexatious and intolerable burdens. Nevertheless they insisted: "We will have a king to rule over us!" Therefore Saul was chosen; and there was not among the children of Israel a goodlier person than he. In due time he was inaugurated with much pomp and circumstance, and the people offered sacrifices and peace offerings unto the Lord and rejoiced greatly. "If now," said the prophet on this occasion, "ye will fear the Lord and obey his commandments, then shall both ye and your king continue to follow him; but if not, his hand shall be against you. Now, therefore, stand and behold a sign, that this is the Lord's doing!" It was the dry season of the wheat harvest; nevertheless, on a sudden the heavens were darkened, black clouds marshalled themselves and amid rolling thunder copious rains poured down all day. Thus ended the theocracy, and thus amid awful omens and admonitions began the sovereignty of Israel. The outcome—is it not written in the chronicles of the nation, from the time of Saul until the sceptre passed from Judah, and the King whose right alone it was to reign sat over upon the slopes of Olivet and mourned: "O Jerusalem, Jerusalem, how often would I have gathered your children as a hen doth gather her brood under her wings and ye would not"?

All powers and dignities whatsoever—didactic, pontifical and political—centre in Christ. He is our Prophet, Priest and King. The administration of this world's affairs is committed to him. The ancient line of prophets, a mere temporary makeshift and expedient, moving through history, comes at length to Bethlehem and vanishes in the glory of him of whom it had been written, "A prophet shall the Lord your

God raise up from among your brethren; him shall ye hear in all things whatsoever he shall say unto you." And he alone is Prophet since that day. In like manner the priestly line came down through the centuries, kindling the altar fires on either side to symbolize the atonement of Calvary, until it also came to Bethlehem and lost itself in him of whom it had been written, " He is an high priest forever after the order of Melchizedek"; who was to offer himself once for all as a sacrifice for the world's sin, to lift the veil and enter with blood-stained hands into the Holiest of All, where he ever liveth to make intercession for us. And there has never been a priest, save by usurpation of authority, from that time until now. So all the kings of the earth, the Sauls and Cæsars and Alexanders, are mere signs and silhouettes of Christ's Kingship, pointing on to the glory of that ultimate reign when the revolted kingdoms and dominions of this world shall become the kingdom of Christ. "Now unto the King eternal, immortal, invisible, the only wise God, be honor and glory forever and ever!"

The Kingship of Christ runs like a golden thread through ancient prophecy: "For unto us a child is born, unto us a son is given, and the government shall be upon his shoulder; his name shall be called Wonderful, Counsellor, the Mighty God, the Everlasting Father and the Prince of Peace." He was seen in the visions of Isaiah clothed in regal splendor and marked with the tokens of a glorious triumph: "Who is this that cometh from Edom, this that is glorious in his apparel, travelling in the greatness of his strength?" "I that speak in righteousness, mighty to save." "Wherefore art thou red in thine apparel, and thy garments like him that treadeth in the wine-fat?" "I have trodden the wine-press alone; and of the people there was none with me; for the day of vengeance is in my heart, and the year of my redeemed is come."

This was "the hope of Israel." All through the centuries of her sin and suffering she looked for the coming of her King. He was David's son, and his reign was to be marked by a magnificence beyond that of Solomon in all his glory. The song of the procession that wound around the spur of Olivet, leading the man of Nazareth to the Holy City, was an historic song: "Hosanna! hosanna! to the Son of David; blessed is he that cometh in the name of the Lord!"

And Christ in his Messianic character claimed this regal authority: "Ye call me Lord and Master, and ye say well for so I am." He had much to say of "the kingdom." This is the key of his preaching. He came to set up, amid the chaos and confusion of earthly principalities, the kingdom of truth, the kingdom of righteousness, the kingdom of heaven, the kingdom of God. He came to restore the simple glory of the theocracy, the Commonwealth of God. The charge brought against him for which he was haled to judgment and ultimately dragged to Calvary, was that he made himself a king. His judge took him aside from Gabbatha and gave him an opportunity to clear himself of this accusation. "Art thou a king?" he asked. And Jesus answered, in the strongest form of affirmation that was possible in the Aramaic tongue, "Thou sayest it." And this accusation was written over his head: *Iesu Nazaret Rex*

Iudæorum—Jesus the man of Nazareth, the King of the whole Israel of God!

And here runs the party line—the line of separation between citizens of the kingdom and aliens from the household of faith. The human race is divided in twain along this line, the acceptance or rejection of the Kingly claim of Christ. The Jews and their Roman confrères committed the unpardonable sin. They reviled his royalty, placing a crown of thorns upon his head, throwing about him the cast-off purple of a Roman magistrate, putting an impotent reed in his hand, bowing before him and crying in derision, "Hail, O King!" The same sin is committed still by those who reduce the dignity of this eternal King to that of a mere man, dispossessing him of his scepter and degrading him to the level of the creatures of his hand, as well as by those who reject his authority with a sturdy disclaimer, saying, "We will not have him to rule over us."

But, blessed be his name, there is a vast and ever increasing number of such as acknowledge his benignant sway. They believe that he, being the only-begotten Son of the Father, came into this world to set up a kingdom whose cardinal truth is righteousness, laying its foundation in the great atonement of the cross. And they count it their highest joy to pass under his yoke and call themselves citizens of the commonwealth of which he alone is ruler.

How came they into this citizenship? By faith; an implicit, appropriating, obedient faith in the Messianic claims of Christ. By an absolute surrender to his authority and a joyous acquiescence in his word, "If any man will come after me, let him deny himself, take up his cross and follow me."

But while faith in this sovereign Christ marks the birth of a sinner into the kingdom and so assures his deliverance from sin and death, it is only the beginning of his citizenship; that is to say, of his spiritual life. Two things now follow, not so much because they are enjoined as because they naturally and inevitably proceed from loyalty to the King:

I. *Confession.* He who truly believes in the sovereignty of Jesus as King of kings and Lord of lords will obviously not hesitate to acknowledge him.

Did you ever hear an assembly of Englishmen sing "God save the Queen"? Not long ago I was in a company of Scottish gentlemen at a banquet reaching into the wee sma' hours, and when they closed their conference with that inspiring hymn, my Anglo-Saxon blood was quickened by the enthusiasm of their devotion to Her Majesty. She is neither tall nor fair. Not by the largest stretch of the imagination can she be called beautiful. But you will speak a word against her on British soil at your peril. Ashamed of Victoria? Not they. She represents the greatness of that empire on whose dominion the sun never sets. She represents in her own person the armies and navies of the realm. She stands for the history of five centuries of political splendor and for the hope of brighter glories and nobler conquests yet to come. Ashamed of Queen Victoria? O no!

Followers of Christ, up with your hearts, up with your voices alway, "God save the King!" "Long live the King!" He hath upon his vesture and his thigh a name written, King of kings and Lord of lords. Behold his diadem of stars. What are the crown jewels of the nations to this? Behold his girdle of almighty power, his vesture like the snow, his eyes like flaming fire. Think of his conquests, the hearts he has subdued, the evil powers he has vanquished, the Cæsars he has scourged to their tombs, the empires he has touched and they have crumbled into dust.

> Jesus! and shall it ever be,
> A mortal man ashamed of thee?
> Ashamed of thee, whom angels praise,
> Whose glories shine through endless days?
>
> Ashamed of Jesus! sooner far
> Let evening blush to own a star;
> He sheds the beams of light divine
> O'er this benighted soul of mine.
>
> Ashamed of Jesus! yes, I may,
> When I've no guilt to wash away;
> No tear to wipe, no good to crave,
> No fears to quell, no soul to save.
>
> Till then—nor is my boasting vain—
> Till then, I boast a Saviour slain!
> And, oh, may this my glory be
> That Christ is not ashamed of me!

II. *Obedience*—frank, implicit and absolute. Obedience in all things. Obedience unquestioning. Obedience joyous and unto death.

All the problems of life are solved for Christian people in this word obedience. These are the matters of supreme moment to us: truth, character and service. And these are the three great problems: What shall I believe? What shall I be? and What shall I do? All these are solved at the footstool of the King.

(1) *What shall I believe?* Believe what the Master says. His word is the final dictum for the formulation of our creed. He himself is the court of last

appeal in all matters pertaining to truth. When our Sovereign speaks there is an end of controversy. Let infallible popes and councils and ecclesiastical courts stand out of our light. Tradition must yield to his *ipse dixit*. In our quest for truth we have been sent forth like sailors in a staunch ship over a great sea and our Lord has provided us with a trusty pilot and a trustworthy chart. Our chart is the Bible, as he said, "Search the Scriptures, for in them ye think ye have eternal life and these are they which testify of me." Our pilot is his Spirit, as he said, "If I go away, I will send unto you the Comforter; he shall lead you into all truth." If we fall into error, it is because we doubt his word or deny his Spirit.

(2) *What shall I be?* Be like Christ. His character must be our rule of character. To imitate him is to grow unto the full stature of a man. Here again, for our guidance, he has given us his word and his Spirit. In that word we have his portrait—the ideal Man, the chiefest among ten thousand, the one altogether lovely. We attain unto perfection just in the measure in which we copy him and in that effort we have the assistance of his Spirit. The fruit of that Spirit is love, joy, peace, long-suffering, gentleness, goodness, faith, meekness, temperance. The effort of our life, as royal subjects of the King, is to make that bundle of graces ours. "Add to your faith virtue; and to virtue knowledge; and to knowledge temperance; and to temperance patience; and to patience godliness; and to godliness brotherly kindness; and to brotherly kindness charity. For if these things be in you, and abound, they make you that ye shall neither be barren nor unfruitful in the knowledge of our Lord Jesus Christ."

(3) *What shall I do?* Do what the King commands. This is the secret of a successful Christian life. And the King's command is this, Seek ye the kingdom. Seek ye *first* the kingdom. Seek ye *first of all* the kingdom. As citizens of this divine Commonwealth it is our business to do our utmost toward the extension of our Sovereign's realms. And we have our instructions in that word, " Go ye into all the world and evangelize, beginning at home."

The work of the kingdom begins at home; in the narrow circle of your immediate environment. If you love the King, see that his name is honored by your intimate friends and associates. "Go down to your own house," said Jesus to the man of Gadara, "and tell what great things the Lord hath done for thee."

Then the broader provinces—the city, the commonwealth, the nation, the world. Oh, for an enlargement of our hearts ; for it devolves upon every true follower of Christ to extend his influence to the very uttermost. This is involved in loyalty to the King. His purpose is to subjugate the world ; he is setting up the kingdom which shall ultimately extend from the river to the uttermost parts of the earth. To this end the campaign has been marked out and as loyal and obedient servants of Christ it is not for us to presume to criticise his methods. It should be enough for us that he has said, " Go ye."

In view of the recent massacre of missionaries in China, the question has again been broached, "Do missions pay?" It is discussed in labored editorials in our secular newspapers. Do missions pay? Pay! Who said anything about paying? Look to your marching orders! If every missionary that ever set out to preach the glorious gospel in the habitations of cruelty had been murdered in cold blood; if there were not one native convert to show for the great expenditure of wealth and energy from the time of William Carey, the consecrated cobbler, until now; it would still remain the indubitable duty of the Church, calmly, unquestioningly, without hesitation and with implicit faith, to push the propaganda to the remotest corners of the globe. The word of the King has gone forth; who are we that we should reply against him?

But missions do pay. Let the question be looked at from any standpoint whatever; commercial, scientific, industrial, moral or spiritual. Missions do pay. The history of the last one hundred years, the one hundred years of missionary enterprise, is the history of modern civilization. The King's blessing has been placed upon the obedience of his faithful people in the conversion of multitudes, the enlightenment of nations and the opening up of the whole world to the benignant grace of the Son of Righteousness. The royal standards onward go!

And the ultimate triumph is sure. "Let the kings of the earth set themselves, and the rulers take counsel together. He that sitteth in the heavens shall laugh: the Lord shall hold them in derision." The battalions who were seen going forth on their white horses in the vision of the Apocalypse, are already returning from conquest: One riding at their head in garments stained with blood. "Worthy art thou!" is the cry of the veteran host, and "Worthy art thou!" is the response of angels and archangels at heaven's gate, "to receive honor and glory and power and dominion for ever and ever."

Thanks be to God for the honor of serving the King! A brave word was that of the wounded Spartan who, having distinguished himself in battle, was asked by his king, "What wilt thou? A wreath, a noble title, a lucrative province? What wilt thou?" And he answered, "Let me march, O king, in the van of the army." There is no higher distinction than that. Let us push to the front, O followers of Christ; close to the royal banner, close to the person of the King.

Not long ago in the Gallery of the Luxembourg I saw a picture called, "The Return of the Martyr." The scene is in the catacombs. Yonder through the door-way, seen by the flickering light of torches, the mangled body of one slain in the amphitheatre is being carried in. Friends are weeping; some are gazing with a sorrow too deep for tears. The minister stretches forth his hands in welcome to the dead. A mother lifts her babe that the shadow of the bier may fall in blessing over it. Yonder is the niche in the wall awaiting its treasure of dust. A palm-branch is ready to be placed beside it. And as I looked upon that picture I thought, what if some artist could paint the entrance of yon martyr's soul into the heavenly glory? Ah, that were a theme to make a man immortal. But who shall show the rolling back of the pearly gates, the rainbow arch, the crystal sea, the waving palms, the dazzling splendor of the throne? And who shall paint the glow upon the faces of those who press forward to salute the veteran, or the majesty of him who stretches forth his hands, saying, "Well done, good servant. Enter into joy"? All heaven is in that word. "Be thou faithful unto death, and I will give thee a crown of life." Oh, to come thither and enter into the eternal peace of that benediction! Oh, to behold at last the King in his beauty! "Now unto the King eternal, immortal, invisible, the only wise God, be honor and glory for ever and ever. Amen."

THE UNSPEAKABLE TURK.

"There is Elam and all her multitude round about her grave; all of them slain, fallen by the sword, which are gone down uncircumcised into the nether parts of the earth, which caused their terror in the land of the living; yet have they borne their shame with them that go down to the pit."— EZEK. xxxii. 24.

The land of Elam here referred to lay west of Persia and south of Assyria and was, therefore, in part, identical with the "Turkey in Asia" of to-day. It was a mighty power as far back as the time of Abraham. There is a set of tablets in the British Museum taken from the royal library of Assurbanipal on one of which is a war bulletin signed by Assurbanipal himself, in which he says: "I directed the march against Elam. I overwhelmed Elam from end to end. I cut off the head of the king Te-umman, who was ever devising evil. I slew a multitude of his soldiers. I swept over the land for a month and a day." This was about B.C. 650. The bloody and barbarous land of Elam has a worthy successor in the Sublime Porte; and the kings of Elam, from Te-umman down to His Majesty the present Sultan Abdul-Hamid II., have ever been "devising evil." The face of Abdul-Hamid tells its own story—the low sensual brows, the cunning eyes, the sinister lips. The government of Elam has suffered the usual vicissitudes of time; but king and people remain as cruel and barbarous as ever.

The Armenians also are an ancient nation. In Xenophon's "Retreat of the Ten Thousand" he refers to them as a courageous people devoted to industrial pursuits. They may be still characterized in that way. The Armenians are the leading merchants, skilled artisans and farmers of the Turkish Empire. They are, moreover, a deeply religious people. It is claimed that the Armenian Church is the oldest Christian Church on earth. The story runs that King Abgarus sent a letter to Jesus of Nazareth enquiring as to the new religion which he was introducing among the Jews. He received a courteous reply through Thaddeus and Bartholomew, who preached the gospel to Abgarus and his people. It may be asserted, without passing judgment upon the truth of this venerable legend, that the Armenians have stood for their ancestral religion as far back as runneth the memory of man.

The Turk stands as the pre-eminent representative and champion of Islam. Turk *versus* Armenian is but another phrase for Mohammed *versus* Christ. The relation of these two neighboring peoples has been for centuries a story of continuous strife and oppression. It was back in the fourteenth century that Timour the Tartar celebrated the triumphs of his crescentade by piling up outside the gates of Baghdad a pyramid of Christian skulls.

The narrative of this conflict is in two chapters. (1) Conversion. For some hundreds of years the effort of the Turks was to win over the Armenians to the Mohammedan faith. The sword was the constant instrument of this propaganda aided by tyrannies and oppressions of every sort, including the imposition of unjust taxes and burdens greater than any people could bear. (2) Extermination. Failing in the endeavor to convert the Armenians by even the strongest methods of force, the Sublime Porte has apparently resorted to the plan of wholly destroying the Armenians as a people. The Kurds—a wild nomadic people without industry, devoted to plunder and unscrupulous in slaughter—have been organized for the accomplishment of this purpose. A faint parallel to this may be found in the appeal made by Gen. Burgoyne at the beginning of the American Revolution to the Mohawk and other Indians, urging them to march against the American colonists,—an appeal against which Pitt remonstrated in a speech in Parliament in 1777, saying, "Such abominable methods are equally abhorrent to religion and to humanity." The Sultan has organized these Kurds into cohorts of cavalry, which have, during recent years, committed dreadful outrages against the Armenians under his authority and with the open support of the Turkish army.

I. This condition of things is a belated fact in the history of civilization. The world has moved on magnificently since the rising of the Day-Star at the beginning of the Christian era; the light has been diffused everywhere. But here, in the Turkish Empire, is a deep, dark corner of hell still remaining in the midst of the general progress of the race.

The massacre of Sassoun, which occurred two years ago, was but an episode in this policy of extermination. With the approval of the Sultan, an army of three thousand Kurds was let loose upon the Armenians. For two horrible weeks they plundered and killed. The details are too harrowing for words. Men, women and children were slaughtered until the air was foul with the stench of the unburied dead. No less than seventy villages were wholly or in part destroyed. The Kurds, during this fortnight of inhuman slaughter, carried aloft upon their spears the heads of the slain and the bodies of unborn children torn from their worse than murdered mothers. A company of sixty young women and girls having suffered beyond all possibility of portrayal were, on one occasion during this march of devastation, offered life on certain indescribable conditions if they would abjure their faith. "Our fathers and brothers," they answered, "lie yonder dead; we are no better than they. In mercy, kill us!" I know of nothing better than that in the chronicles of heroism. It is estimated that more than ten thousand victims fell in this massacre. Their blood crieth from the ground!

"The massacre of Sassoun," says Dr. Dillon, who speaks from personal observation as special commissioner of the London *Daily Telegraph* to Armenia, "sends a shudder to the hearts of the most callous. But that butchery was a divine mercy compared with the hellish deeds that are being done every week and every day of the year. The piteous moans of famishing children; the groans of old men who have lived to see what can never be embodied in words; the piercing cries of violated maidenhood, nay, of tender childhood; the shrieks of mothers made childless by crimes compared with which murder would be a blessing; the screams, scarcely human, of women writhing under the lash; and all the vain voices of blood and agony that die away in that dreary desert without having found a responsive echo on earth or in heaven, combine to throw Sassoun and all its horrors into the shade."

It thus appears that the story of Sassoun was a mere incident in the continuous effort of the Turkish Government to exterminate this people. An eyewitness of a more recent massacre at Trebizond writes as follows: "On October 8th, all danger seemed to be over and shops were opened and people walked in the streets. Suddenly, at 11 A.M., people in the streets were shot down. Men standing or sitting at their shop doors were dropped with a bullet through their heads or hearts. The aim of the Turks was deadly; I have heard of no wounded men. Some were slashed with swords until life was extinct. Generally, the Turks allowed the women and younger children to live. For five hours this horrid work of inhuman butchery went on, the cracking of musketry, sometimes like a volley from a platoon of soldiers, but more often single shots from near and distant points, the crashing in of doors, and the thud, thud of sword blows sounded on our ears. Then the sound of musketry died away, and the work of looting began. Every shop of an Armenian in the market was gutted, and the victors in this cowardly and brutal way glutted themselves with the spoils. For hours bales of broadcloth, cotton goods and every conceivable kind of merchandise passed along without molestation to the homes of the spoilers. So far as appearance went, the police and the soldiers distinctly aided in this savage work. They were mingled with the armed men, and, so far as we could see, made not the least effort to check them. Not one of the perpetrators of these outrages has been arrested or disarmed, but all have moved about with the utmost freedom to accomplish their nefarious purposes. On the other hand, many of the Armenians are in prison. There is no telling how many have perished in this outbreak. Four hundred is a moderate estimate."

Time and again they have appealed to the nations of Christendom for help. A petition signed by three hundred and six of the principal inhabitants of Armenia runs as follows: "We now solemnly assure you that the butchery of Sassoun is but a drop in the ocean of Armenia blood, shed gradually and silently all over the empire since the late Turko-Russian war. Year by year, month by month, day by day, innocent men, women and children have been shot down, stabbed, or clubbed to death in their houses and in their fields, tortured in strange, fiendish ways in fetid prison cells, or left to rot in exile under the scorching suns of Arabia. During the progress of that long and horrible tragedy no voice was raised for mercy, no hand extended to help us. That process is still going on; it has already entered upon its final phases, and the Armenian people are at the last gasp. Is European sympathy destined to take the form of a cross upon our graves?"

The suffering and destitution of this people have touched the hearts of the Christian Churches in America, who have sent contributions of food and clothing to be distributed by their missionaries among them. A telegram from Constantinople bearing the date of October 31st,* reads as follows: "The Turks demand that the American missionaries, who are distributing relief to the suffering people of Sassoun, withdraw from there in three days, otherwise, they say, they fear there will be a repetition of the mas-

---

* This sermon was preached on November 3, 1895.

sacres. In view of this critical situation, the United States Ambassador, Alexander W. Terrell, has advised the American missionaries to withdraw temporarily from Sassoun. The Kurds are held in check by the missionaries, fearing to commit excesses in their presence." Withdraw from Sassoun under such circumstances? Our missionaries withdraw from Sassoun for the accommodation of the Kurds who desire to continue their work of blood and violence? The good God forbid! The mere suggestion on the part of our national representative is suggestive of cowardice most contemptible. The followers of the crucified Christ, who uphold the banner of his cross in yonder land of persecution, can ill afford to preserve their lives at such a cost. Let them stand there in the spirit of their Master, like Aaron in the plague-stricken camp of Israel, waving their censers between the living and the dead!

II. To what shall we trace the origin of this dreadful tragedy? To the Oriental blood? Nay. The Turks stand almost alone among the Oriental nations in this murderous policy. To the fact that they are only semi-civilized? Nay; barbaric nations are not all cruel. The trouble lies deeper down and further back than this, in the religion of the Turks. They stand as sponsors and defenders of Mohammedanism. We hear it said that the Turk is on trial. True. The Turk has been on trial for long centuries and was found guilty of crimes nameless and intolerable long centuries ago. But Islam is on trial! The Turk is what his religion makes him. "By their fruits ye shall know them" is true of religions as of individuals. If it be answered, "Has not Christianity also drawn the sword?" We answer, "Yes; but never in the spirit of Christ." Note the following facts:

(1) The policy of blood is ingrained in the very fabric of Islam. The Lord Christ came as Prince of Peace. He said to Peter: "Put up thy sword into the sheath, for they that take the sword shall perish by it." He marked out the plan for the propagation of the Christian faith in the peaceable preaching of the gospel of good will. But Mohammed at the very outset declared a crescentade of blood. He sent forth eight of his followers from Medina to waylay a caravan in the valley of Nakhla; they returned with the announcement that they had killed one and taken two prisoners. "Allah be praised!" said the prophet. The tiger had tasted blood and his appetite was whetted for more. A Jewish tribe entrenched in its stronghold was presently besieged and overcome; eight hundred prisoners were led out in companies of sixes and butchered in cold blood, while Mohammed stood by, praising God. The sword of Islam has never been sheathed from that day to this. It is written in the Koran: "Fight against the unbelievers until the true religion stands alone upon the earth." Those who are accustomed to believe that one religion is as good as another, who speak kindly of Islam, may well ponder the following prayer—the official prayer of Islam, which is repeated daily in the great university at Cairo by ten thousand theological students and is used throughout the Turkish dominions; "I seek refuge with Allah from Satan, the accursed. In the name of Allah the Compassionate, the Merciful! O Lord of all Creatures! O Allah! Destroy the infidels and polytheists, thine enemies, the enemies of the religion! O Allah! Make their children orphans, and defile their abodes! Cause their feet to slip; give them and their families, their households,

and their women, their children and their relations by marriage, their brothers and their friends, their possessions and their race, their wealth and their lands, as booty to the Moslems, O Lord of all Creatures!"

(2) The shedding of blood—occurring in Christian history at intervals as an outburst of human wickedness and in distinct contravention of the mind and injunction of Jesus—is the settled policy of the Mohammedan religion, and has been the continuous method of Islam from the beginning until now. The Jehad, or Holy War, is a sacramental observance. To perish in the Jehad is better than to make a pilgrimage to Mecca. He who dies with his sword drawn against an unbeliever goes straight to Paradise, to receive the most splendid rewards and to be waited upon forever by beautiful houris. It is estimated that the number of Christian subjects massacred in Turkey since 1820 is above ninety-three thousand. In this connection it will be profitable to recall the words of Gladstone, uttered with reference to the Turkish massacres in Bulgaria in 1876: "I entreat my countrymen, upon whom far more than perhaps any other people of Europe it depends, to require and to insist that our government, which has been working in one direction, shall work in the other, and shall apply all its vigor to concur with the other states of Europe in obtaining the extinction of the Turkish power in Bulgaria. Let the Turks now carry away their abuses in the only possible manner—namely, by carrying off themselves. Their Zaptiehs and their Mudirs, their Bimbashis and their Yuzbachis, their Kaimakams and their Pashas—one and all, bag and baggage—clear out from the province they have desolated and profaned. This thorough riddance, this most blessed de-

liverance, is the only reparation we can make to the memory of those heaps on heaps of dead; to the violated purity alike o matron, of maiden, and of child; to the civilization which has been affronted and shamed; to the laws of God, or, if you like, of Allah; to the moral sense of mankind at large. There is not a criminal in a European jail, there is not a cannibal in the South Sea Islands, whose indignation would not arise and overboil at the recital of that which has been done; which has too late been examined, but which remains unavenged; which has left behind all the foul and all the fierce passions that produced it; and which may again spring up, in another murderous harvest, from the soil soaked and reeking with blood, and in the air tainted with every imaginable deed of crime and shame. That such things should be done once is a damning disgrace to the portion of our race which did them; that a door should be left open for their ever-so-barely possible repetition would spread that shame over the whole. Better, we may justly tell the Sultan, almost any inconvenience, difficulty, or loss associated with Bulgaria,

> 'Than thou reseated in thy place of light,
> The mockery of thy people and their bane.'

We may ransack the annals of the world, but I know not what research can furnish us with so portentous an example of the fiendish misuse of the powers established by God 'for the punishment of evil-doers, and for the encouragement of them that do well.' No government ever has so sinned; none has proved itself so incorrigible in sin, or, which is the same, so impotent for reformation. If it be allowable that the executive power of Turkey should renew, at this great crisis, by permission or authority of Europe, the charter of its existence in Bulgaria, then there is not on record, since the beginnings of political society, a protest that man has lodged against intolerable misgovernment, or a stroke he has dealt at loathsome tyranny, that ought not henceforth forward to be branded as a crime."

(3) It should be observed also that the attitude of the followers of Mohammed in these persecutions is one of open defiance. No denial is offered; no apology is made. When the foreign Consuls took it upon themselves to remonstrate with the governor of Erzeroum in behalf of the suffering Armenians, he replied in substance as follows: "Would you presume to interfere with the affairs of my harem? Would you question my right to strip and starve and beat my wives? The relation of the Turk to the Armenian is that of a husband to his wife, and you must not presume to interfere with it."

In view of such considerations we are justified in the assertion that the responsibility for these deeds of violence must be laid upon the Mohammedan religion. For hundreds of years its representatives have carried on their propaganda with sword in hand and fortified on either side by the harem and the slave market. These are the three historic forces of Islam: the sword, slavery and licentiousness. Back of these lies the two-fold doctrine of the system: there is one God, and Mohammed is his Prophet. The doctrine of the one God has been characterized as the infinite truth. Let us go one step further and characterize the other doctrine, "Mohammed is his Prophet," as the infinite lie. It is in the spreading of this falsehood that the Turks have manifested their most fanatical intolerance. The Sublime Porte is what Islam has made it.

III. As to the remedy. We have reached a point in the history of civilization where the responsibility for the solution of a problem so momentous must be laid upon all nations and all the children of men. A mere expression of grief or anger or sympathy goes for naught.

Shall we look for a political solution of the difficulty? One would think that France and Germany and Russia and England—great Christian nations all—would somehow solve the problem. But there is one insuperable difficulty in the way—the "Balance of Power." The Turkish Government has, for a quarter of a century, been called the "sick man," and this "sick man" would have died long ago but for the fact that the great powers of Europe dare not let him die. England is afraid of such a result—a consummation otherwise most devoutly to be wished—because Russia would, in all probability, become the residuary legatee. England stands sponsor, therefore, for Turkey's power in Asia; pledged to the integrity and perpetuity of her dominions there. Nay, furthermore, forty-one millions of the one hundred and seventy millions of Mohammedans on earth are subjects of the English crown. Wherefore it may be said, with little fear of question, that England stands sponsor for the perpetuity of Islam. Under these conditions it is well nigh hopeless to look for deliverance toward the great powers of Europe; unless, indeed, in God's providence, a war should be precipitated for the settlement of the Eastern Question, in which event the God of battles would in all likelihood put an utter end to the government of the unspeakable Turk.

In the meantime, is it too much to hope that America, the youngest of the Christian nations, and the only great nation which is unhampered by considerations of the "Balance of Power," should make her influence felt? We may at least demand that our missionaries and their native protegés, their churches and schools, with the Armenian children gathered in them, shall be protected in their life and liberty and possessions. It may be that in God's providence our nation may yet be able, by the use of a courageous policy in the defense of its own foreign rights, to accomplish what has seemed to be impossible to nations involved in the perplexities of the Eastern Question.

But the ultimate solution of this and all kindred difficulties lies in the calm and sure processes of the gospel of Christ. It was the word spoken by Paul from the Mammertine prison that destroyed the power of the Roman Empire and ushered in the Christian Italy of to-day. It was the gospel from the lips of Boniface, in the eighth century, that blasted the oaks of Odin and transformed the barbarism of the Northland into the Christian civilization of the Germany of to-day. It was the gospel from the lips of Irenæus, who met a martyr's death in the reign of Marcus Aurelius, that dissipated the darkness of pagan Gaul and made the Christian France of to-day. It was the gospel preached by St. Augustine among the Druids of Britain that shattered the Cromlechs and prepared the way for the splendid civilization of the England of to-day. So, in process of time, will the religion of Christ make itself felt in the dominions of Islam. Up to this time, however, the number of missionaries sent into Turkey for its evangelization would scarcely make the one-half of a regiment in our American army. And the total expenditure on Foreign Missions among the Mohammedans since the beginning of the Christian era is estimated at less than ten millions of dollars—less than we spend upon one of our great metropolitan hostelries; a mere fraction of the money spent on our East River Bridge. Is it not true that we are "playing at missions"? When the Church sets about the conversion of the Moslem world in earnest, the work will be done. Meanwhile the kingdom of Christ in that distant land, as everywhere, is like a mustard seed planted in the ground, which indeed is the least of all seeds; but when it is grown, it becometh a tree, and the fowls of the air lodge in the branches of it.

MORS JANUA VITÆ.

"But God forbid that I should glory, save in the cross of our Lord Jesus Christ, by whom the world is crucified unto me, and I unto the world."—GAL. vi. 14.

Here is a statement of a great truth—Life out of Death. "He that loveth his life," said Jesus, "shall lose it; and he that hateth his life for my sake and the Gospel's, shall keep it." And again, "I, if I be lifted up, will draw all men unto me."

It is the law of the acorn, of the chrysalis, of the graveyard; life out of death, and out of death only. "Except a corn of wheat fall into the ground and die, it abideth alone; but if it die, it bringeth forth much fruit." What is this that the husbandman scatters over his ploughed field? Bread. The bread which is necessary to sustain his own life; bread for his children's hunger. Why then, O husbandman, do you thus broadcast it? Why throw it away?—Lift up your eyes and see. The fields are white unto the harvest. The loaded wains come groaning to the granaries. The family gathers about the generous board. The corn of wheat died, and lo, it has passed into an infinitely vaster life.

This is the occasion of Paul's glorying. In these triumphant words he furnishes a threefold illustration of the great law. Here are three deaths and three resurrections to newness of life.

I. *The cross of Jesus Christ.* He died, not only that he might deliver the world from its penalty of death, but that through the portals of his self-renunciation he might himself enter upon a more glorious life.

The Lord Christ is dead. See him yonder upon the cross, his limbs distorted in the last anguish. No need of any death certificate here. "Is he quite dead?" asked the Centurion of his guard. "Aye, this is the spear which I thrust into his side but a moment ago; and when it was withdrawn, it gave sure token that his heart had ceased to beat." The Jews, Priests and Rabbis passed by, and, noting the pallor of his face, they said, "The Man of Nazareth is dead; we shall hear no further of his doctrines and wonderful works. He will trouble us no more." The disciples as they loosed him from the tree felt of his hands, and they were cold; and of his pulse, and it was still. "We hoped," they lamented, "that it was he who should deliver Israel; but, alas! he is dead."

Dead! Then why all this commotion? Why this controversy among the children of men? Is it possible that the world is still moved, troubled, about a dead man—one who died and was buried eighteen centuries ago?

What does this mean? There are some hundreds of millions of people who gather at intervals about a table where a frugal repast is spread. They break the bread and say, "Lo, thus his flesh was bruised." They pour the wine and say, "Lo, thus his blood was shed." And then they lift their hearts and voices and speak with him as a living Christ, laying all their plans and purposes and hopes before him.

And what means this ever increasing multitude

of men and women who declare that he, with a mighty hand, has lifted them out of the miry pit and set their feet upon an everlasting rock? He said to the paralytic in Capernaum, "Son, thy sins be forgiven thee"; and he has been loosing paralytics from their infirmity and forgiving their sins from then until now. He said to the sinful woman who anointed his feet with oil of spikenard, "Daughter, go in peace; thy sins be forgiven thee"; and through all the centuries he has been saving Magdalenes and restoring them to self-respect and to divine peace. He said to the dying thief on Golgotha, "To-day thou shalt be with me in paradise"; and there are multitudes of malefactors as guilty as poor Dysmas, who are prepared to testify that just now he met them with the same message of pardoning grace.

And how is it that the name of Jesus is to-day the most potent name in war and diplomacy? His figure towers aloft in the affairs of nations like the Brocken of the Alps. What has become of other magnates who ruled the earth in centuries gone by?

"Imperial Cæsar, dead and turned to clay,
May stop a hole to keep the wind away."

But Christ is the most influential arbiter in the affairs of men and nations. Let Napoleon speak from his lonely retreat at St. Helena: "You speak of Cæsars, of Alexanders, of their conquests, of the enthusiasm which they kindle in the hearts of their soldiers; but think of the conquests of this dead Man. Can you conceive of Cæsar as the eternal Emperor of the Roman Senate and from the depth of his mausoleum governing the empire, watching over the destinies of Rome? Yet here is an Arm that for eighteen centuries has protected the Church from the storms which have threatened to engulf it."

It may be that Macaulay's vision will come true, and at some future time a New Zealander will stand upon a broken arch of London Bridge to sketch the ruins of St. Paul's. If so, however, it will be because the New Zealander himself will be the last consummate fruit of Christian culture; a man of higher attainments in moral power than those who reared the fabric of St. Paul's. For Christ is a living and omnipotent force moving the world, through each succeeding sun, into a clearer light; and this will continue until, in the restitution of all things, every knee shall bow before him and every tongue confess in the full glory of his millennial reign, that he alone is King over all.

II. *I am crucified with Christ.* Who is this "I"? In the philosophy of St. Paul, man has a dual personality. The lower nature and the higher nature are ever struggling for the mastery. The "old man" grapples with the "new man who is created in Christ unto righteousness and true holiness." The antagonists are elsewhere characterized as "flesh" and "Spirit." As where it is written, "There is, therefore, now no condemnation to them which are in Christ Jesus, who walk not after the flesh but after the Spirit; for to be carnally minded is death, but to be spiritually minded is life and peace."

It is this lower *Ego* or self which is crucified with Christ. But from the death and burial of this lower nature, the truer self rises into newness of life. "I am crucified with Christ, nevertheless I live, and yet not I, but Christ liveth in me."

I live now as never before for the true advantage

of self. So long as my carnal nature had the mastery, the story of my life was constant degeneration. But now that my better nature has triumphed, I enter upon a process of progressive sanctification. I shall never cease to grow in character, but will continue to increase from grace to grace and from glory to glory, ever approaching the full stature of a man.

I live now more than ever toward others. The lower nature is selfish. The "old man" was given over to self-gratification, but the "new man" follows close in the footsteps of him of whom it was written : "He went about doing good." The influence of one whose sordid self has perished on the cross is an ever-increasing influence for good. The close of his earthly career does not end it. "Fear not, Brother Ridley; we do light a candle in England to-day which by God's grace shall never be put out."

And I live now more than ever towards God. The unregenerate man who lives after the flesh and not after the Spirit, is of little or no consequence in the kingdom of truth and righteousness. He bears to the household of faith the same relation that a scapegrace son does to any family circle. But as I come forth out of the death of the flesh into the life of the Spirit, I assume a new and vital relation toward the kingdom of God. The King counts me now a loyal subject and condescends to work through me for the casting down of the strongholds of wickedness and the building up of truth and righteousness on earth. I am living on a higher level and breathing a new atmosphere; as one who stands upon the summit of a mountain looking down on those who plod along the lower paths. What mites and midgets they are, who bustle to and fro in quest of things that perish with the using! Up here are life and immortality. I died down yonder on the cross to live up here with God. I buried all and have all. I was crucified, yet I live; nay, Christ liveth in me.

III. *The world is crucified to me.* What is this "world" which is impaled on yonder cross—the world that is dead to me? It is the habitat of those who live in the flesh, who spend their energies in sordid pursuits. This is the world that ever comes between a man and his own eternal life. This is the world of which it is written, "The friendship of the world is enmity against God." This is the world which was in the mind of Jesus when he said to the young ruler who had great possessions, "Go, sell all thou hast and come, follow me."

But the world which thus dies to the spiritual man has also a glorious resurrection. It lives again. It lives to me in all that makes life worth living; in all the dear pursuits which legitimately belong to this beautiful world in which God has placed me.

I am free as never before to pursue wealth. It is the business of every follower of Christ to acquire wealth so far as is possible by honest methods, because in so doing he shall increase his power for God. It takes money to print Bibles, to equip churches, to build schools and hospitals and reformatories, to charter missionary ships and propagate the gospel in distant lands. But let it be observed that the spiritually quickened man is urged to the acquisition of wealth by a motive far higher than that which previously prompted him. He is now the servant of the Lord Jesus Christ, and whatever he gets or gains is to be used wholly for the advancement of his cause. He is no longer an owner, but a trustee. He acquires, not for the sake of getting, or of hoarding, or of spending; but that he may with his substance glorify his Lord. And in all this he is amassing for himself a great treasure—not here, but all in bags that wax not old. He is putting all his treasure beyond the reach of rust that corrupts and of thieves that break through and steal. He is making himself rich forever toward God.

I am free also to pursue pleasure. It is not fair to say to a young Christian, "You must surrender all the pleasures of this world when you enter on the higher life." It is wiser and truer to say, "You now enter upon the enjoyment of all innocent delights with tenfold zest." "Rejoice, O young man, in thy youth; but remember!" Remember that as a servant of the Lord Christ you must needs keep your conscience pure and sweet. No amusement is lawful now that comes between me and the complacent smile of my new Master. No amusement is banned that does not dull the fine edge of the moral sense. Keep your heart sweet, your conscience clean. Let all your pleasure be as merry and as harmless as the laughter of a child. Get all the good out of this blessed world that God intended for you. Go down with Jesus to the marriage supper at Cana and make merry there with him. Away with passion, gluttony, sensual excitement, mad dissipation, the laughter like the crackling of thorns; and welcome the smiling peace of a conscience in harmony with the purposes of Christ. Let the tranquil satisfaction of doing your best, and the generous pleasure of kindly deeds, be ever yours. And, withal, remember that the milk and honey are beyond the wilderness. The sweetest pleasures of this present world are but clusters from the vineyards of the better country. "At the right hand of the Lord are pleasures forevermore."

And I am free also to pursue honor—not for its own sake indeed, but I ought to make the most of myself and enlarge my influence to the uttermost, because I am serving the Lord Christ. The man who realizes that all earthly honors and emoluments are merely a trust to be used for the highest good, is the man who, in the long run of history, gets the greatest honor. Not long ago, one of our fellow-citizens was appointed to a place of authority and straightway, in pursuance of his oath, set out to enforce the laws without fear or favor. The beasts of Ephesus, with the foam of malt-madness dripping from their lips came, out against him. To his honor be it said, he has stood consistently for the sanctity of law; and to-day, despite all cavil and malignant opposition, there is no man in America held in higher honor than he. The blessing of heaven rests upon all who wear their laurel wreaths as servitors of truth and justice and who care more for God's "Well done, good servant," than for what is called, popularity. It is for such as these that the promise is given, "To him that overcometh will I give to sit with me in my throne."

So then in Paul's manifesto we have the apologue of a noble life. Here are three crosses. On one hangs Christ the Author and Finisher of our faith, dead; but we look beyond and see his majestic presence, potent among all nations and the children of men, and we hear a voice saying, "I am he that liveth and was dead, and behold I am alive forevermore; and have the keys of death and hell." On the second cross I am crucified with Christ. Dead, also; dead to the world. Yet here am I thrilled through and through with the life of the risen One. Entering into fellowship with his death, I have also come into fellowship with his resurrection. My life that seemed to have passed away is hid with Christ in God. On the third cross the world is impaled—the world of shame and selfishness and wrong ambition, dead. But beyond it, see another world; harvests ripening from the wheat that died; mountain slopes whereon the soul stands surveying great truths and vast possibilities; rivers where we stoop to drink of living water. It is a royal demesne, and the King stands yonder, crown in hand, ready to welcome us.

These are the visions that strengthened the heart of Paul awaiting his departure. These are the visions that moved him to say, "All things are yours; Paul, Apollos, Cephas, things present, things to come, the world, life, death; all are yours; and ye are Christ's, and Christ is God's."

THE FORM OF GODLINESS.

*"Having a form of godliness, but denying the power thereof."—II. Tim. iii. 5.

The best definition of religion is in the word itself which is said to be derived from *religare*, meaning "to bind back." Religion is godliness; that is God-likeness. It is the binding back of the soul to God.

There is a "form of godliness." All substantial things indeed have both essence and form. God himself is the only exception, he being without "body, parts or passions." There are frames for pictures, trellises for climbing plants and cups for wine. Religion finds expression in outward forms; towards God in praise and prayer and faithful service, towards man in the reflection of the divine character.

But while essence without form is unthinkable, the obverse is to be found on every side. There are frames without pictures, trellises without honey-suckles, and empty cups. There is art without the artistic instinct, poetry without the divine afflatus, music without a soul. In like manner we note the form of godliness with none of its power. The correspondence is that of a manikin to a man. Here is the form of the eye, but no seeing; the form of the ear, but no hearing; the form of the heart, but no throbbing pulse; the venous system, but no flowing blood; the nervous system, yet you may tread with impunity on this manikin's foot, for no sympathetic thrill will fly to its finger tips. What is needed? Life. Power; the power to feel, to think, to act.

We have various kinds of formalists in the world.

I. *The aboriginal formalist.* The prophet Isaiah pictures him going out into the forest to hew him down a cedar: "And he taketh a part thereof to burn; he kindleth it, and baketh bread; he roasteth roast, and is satisfied; yea, he warmeth himself, and saith, Aha! I am warm, I have seen the fire. And the residue thereof he maketh a god, even his graven image; he worketh it out with a line, he fitteth it with planes and the compass and maketh it after the figure of a man. He falleth down unto it, and worshippeth it, saying, Deliver me, for thou art my God." Poor soul; he surely knows better than this. He must be aware that a lie is in his right hand. He cannot for a moment believe that the dull eyes of this image behold him as he prostrates himself before it; or that its carven hands can be stretched forth to help him. Here is formalism of a base and vulgar sort indeed. But who shall show to this bond slave of superstition the wiser and better way?

II. *The philosophic formalist.* The Apostle Paul portrays him in his best estate in cultured Athens: "I observe, O men of Athens, that ye are exceedingly devout." The instinct of worship expressed itself here in numberless shrines. It was a proverb that in Athens gods were more numerous than men. There were gods and goddesses for every episode of life. Lucina presided at the birth; Rumina attended to the nursing; Nundina was invoked at the christening; Potina prescribed the drink and Educa the food; Statina directed the first step; Farinus unloosed the tongue and Locutinos taught the child to speak.

There were lares and penates; gods on domes and pedestals, worn as armlets about the neck or carried in the girdle. There were avenues of gods. If the king put his left sandal on the right foot a score of pontiffs must be summoned to rectify the blunder. If a crow lighted on the Parthenon, the sacred men of all Greece must join their supplications to avert the evil omen. Aye, the men of Athens were exceedingly devout; but withal, they were notoriously ungodly. Their piety was wholly divorced from life.

Then came the philosophers; they were the Protestants of Greece. It was their purpose to get beneath the surface of things. By the banks of the Ilyssus they walked in solemn converse searching for truth. In no spirit of disloyalty to their gods, they still believed that there was a kernel of life in the form of devotion; but alas! they failed to find it. Socrates, the best of all that goodly fellowship, divided much of his time between the home of the courtesan Aspasia and the temple of his god, Æsculapius. Bad morals were the rule upon the banks of the Ilyssus as elsewhere in Athens. Those were the days of frivolty, of dishonesty, of sensuality, of fashionable infanticide. Those were the days when women counted their divorces by the rings upon their fingers which they flaunted before the public gaze. Greek culture was attended by a carnival of vice. The form of godliness was there, but there was a universal denial of the power of it.

III. *The Jewish formalist.* The palmiest days of Jewish ceremonialism were the ungodliest. The temple service was elaborated to the utmost, while the whole head was sick and the whole heart faint. "Bring no more vain oblations, saith the Lord; your incense is an abomination unto me; your new moons and your appointed feasts my soul hateth; they are a trouble unto me; I am weary to bear them. Your hands are full of blood; wash you, make you clean. Cease to do evil; learn to do well."

Then came the Pharisees. They were the Protestants of Israel. The meaning of their name was separatists. But they lapsed presently into the common error. With respect to doctrine they were strict constructionists. As to the proprieties of worship they were scrupulous to the last degree. On their garments they wore four tassels of blue; on their phylacteries and on the frontlet between their eyes were passages of Scripture, such as, "Hear, O Israel, the Lord your God is one Lord." They fasted twice in the week—more than the law required. They paid tithes, not only of the common products of the field but of their garden herbs—mint, anise, and cummin. They were extremely careful as to their ablutions —the cleansing of cups, platters and couches. They had a rigid rule of hand-washing; the water must first be poured into the palm of the right hand, then the left, then the palms must be turned upside down and left to drip. They were conscious of a superior righteousness, insomuch that they drew aside their garments from common sinners, saying, "Stand by thyself, for I am holier than thou."

It was against these religionists that the Lord complained, saying, "They honor me with their lips, but their hearts are far from me." It was upon these that his severest anger fell: "Woe unto you scribes and Pharisees, hypocrites! who strain out a gnat and swallow a camel. Ye make long prayers and devour widow's houses. Ye are like whited sepulchres;

fair without, but within full of dead men's bones and all uncleanness." Here was form without power. Here was a show of godliness but no life.

IV. *Christian formalists.* "And unto the angel of the Church at Laodicea write, I know thy works. Because thou sayest, I am rich and increased with goods, and have need of nothing; and knowest not that thou art wretched and miserable and poor and blind and naked; I counsel thee to buy of me gold tried in the fire that thou mayest be rich; and white raiment, that thou mayest be clothed, and that the shame of thy nakedness do not appear; and anoint thine eyes with eyesalve, that thou mayest see. I know thy works, that thou art neither cold nor hot. I would thou wert cold or hot. So then because thou art lukewarm and neither cold nor hot, I will spew thee out of my mouth."

They were church members, and, so far as we know, in "good and regular standing." In all probability they were sticklers for orthodoxy, regular in their attendance on the sacraments, devoted to the institutions of the church; but alas! there was nothing to correspond with this scrupulosity in their outward lives. Their walk and conversation were not such as became the avowed followers of Christ.

A recent traveller tells of a scene which he witnessed in a gambling house in Madrid. A company of men were shuffling cards and casting dice and indulging in profane and unholy jests, when the tinkling of a bell was heard without. A procession of priests was passing through the streets, bearing the consecrated wafer to the bed-side of the dying. At the sound all in this iniquitous place fell upon their knees and muttered their prayers. The bell ceased and they resumed their pleasure. Here was Christian formalism at its worst and basest; but at its best, there is something abhorrent in it.

We complain of the criticisms which the world passes on those who have made a religious profession. But indeed religion invites scrutiny. Thanks to the critics, the cavillers, the fault finders. Turn on the lights. If there are counterfeits, shall not the government itself be most interested in exposing them?

V. *Non-Christian formalists.* For Christians are not alone in making professions. There are multitudes of excellent people as the world goes—who pay their debts, comply with all the requirements of the civil law and are blameless in their outward life—who profess to be so self-sufficient as to need no church, no support of Christian fellowship, no atonement of Christ. They are like the young ruler who came to Jesus desiring to know the way of life, and on being enjoined to keep the commandments, protested in all sincerity, that he had kept them all from his youth up. "One thing thou lackest," said Jesus. One thing. A new heart; a changed nature; regeneration. For without this all apparent goodness is mere veneering. "Verily, verily, I say unto thee, except a man be born again he cannot see the kingdom of God."

But why should we discriminate between these various classes of formalists, when in truth there is no difference? They are all of one family; all having the form of godliness, but denying the power thereof. All dying for the one thing needful, namely, life; the life that can only come through the regenerating touch of God.

No sort of formalism can please God. He looketh on the heart. The fig tree that put forth leaves but bore no fruit, was placed under the ban of eternal barrenness: "No man eat fruit of thee forever." This is the curse which is ever laid upon a profession void of life.

No sort of formalism can satisfy the soul. "Wherefore do ye spend your money for that which is not bread and your labor for that which satisfieth not?" An eminent Churchwoman on her death bed lamented that, with all her good works, her devotion to church and charity, hers had been a Christless Christianity and she had never truly known God. To live thus is to sit at a Barmecide feast and to warm one's self at a painted fire.

> "Not all the blood of beasts
>   On Jewish altars slain,
> Can give the guilty conscience peace,
>   Nor take away its stain."

And, saddest of all, a formal profession is impotent to save. The five foolish virgins stood knocking at the door of the marriage hall, crying, "Lord, Lord, open unto us!" But the door was closed against them. They had lamps in hand, but because they had no reserve of oil in their vessels for their lamps, their lights had gone out. "And many shall say in that day, Lord, Lord, open unto us. We have eaten and drunk in thy presence and thou hast taught in our streets. We have cast out devils in thy name. But he from within shall answer, I know ye not whence ye are; depart from me."

The woman of Samaria was divided betwixt the claims of Zion and Gerizim. Her mind was running wholly on the respective claims of Jewish and Samaritan forms of worship. And the Master said, "Woman, believe me, the hour cometh when ye shall neither in this mountain nor at Jerusalem, worship the Father. The hour cometh and now is when the true worshippers shall worship the Father in spirit and in truth; for the Father seeketh such to worship him. God is a Spirit and they that worship him must worship him in spirit and in truth."

The only escape from the bondage of formalism is in the baptism of the Holy Spirit. The bones in the valley of Ezekiel's vision were "very dry"; insomuch that the prophet could scarcely believe that life was possible to them. But the voice said, "Come from the four winds, O breath, and breathe upon these bones that they may live." And there was a noise and a shaking, and the bones came together and the sinews were knit upon them. And again the voice said, "Come from the four winds, O breath, and breathe upon these slain. And the breath came into them and they lived, and stood up upon their feet."

O Spirit of God, come, and with quickening energy, awake us to newness of life! Lay thy vivifying hand upon our Bibles till their pages glow, and we see the living Christ walking through them like a king through the colonnades of his palace! Touch our pulpits until they shall seem transformed into temple courts where Christ himself shall stand, as in the great day of the feast, crying, "If any man thirst, let him come unto me and drink; and the water that I shall give him shall be in him a well of water springing up into everlasting life!" Touch our communion tables until every crumb of bread shall quiver like bruised flesh and every drop of wine shall say, "He died for thee"! Touch the mercy-seat where we kneel at morning and night till it shall sound, like a harp string, the promises of him who ever liveth to make intercession for us! Touch our eyes until they shall see apocalyptic visions of God and heaven and truth and righteousness and all eternal verities! Touch our lips until they shall burn to speak the gospel story as if kindled with a living coal from off the heavenly altar! Touch our hands until they thrill with longing to do those greater works which are possible to those who are baptized with power from on high! Touch our feet until they ache with eagerness to go about in the Master's steps, doing good! Touch our wills until they cry "Amen" to every word of invitation and command! Touch our consciences that they may be quick to discern between the evil and the good! Touch our hearts until they throb and yearn with the unselfishness of the great heart that broke on Calvary for us! Touch our souls through and through until they live and love and long forevermore for the life and love that dwelt in infinite fulness in the heart of the Lord Christ! And the honor and glory shall be thine for ever and ever. Amen.

THE STORY OF AN OUTCAST.

"And they came over unto the other side of the sea, into the country of the Gadarenes. And when he was come out of the ship, immediately there met him out of the tombs a man with an unclean spirit, who had his dwelling among the tombs; and no man could bind him, no, not with chains: because that he had been often bound with fetters and chains, and the chains had been plucked asunder by him, and the fetters broken in pieces: neither could any man tame him. And always, night and day, he was in the mountains, and in the tombs, crying, and cutting himself with stones."—MARK v. 1-5.

It had been a busy day. The Lord had been teaching in parables to the people on the beach at Capernaum and had wrought many miracles of healing. He was weary. As the day wore on he looked across the lake to the green slopes of Gadara and longed for rest and a breath of the country air. "Let us go over," he said to his disciples, "to the other side." Not without misgivings—for there were signs of an approaching storm—they pushed out. The Master lay down in the stern of the little boat with his head on the pilot's pillow and fell asleep. Look at him now. "We have an High Priest that can be touched with a feeling of our infirmities; he took not on him the nature of angels, but of men."

On a sudden the wind came roaring through the deep ravines on the eastern side of the lake and whipped the water into a foaming tempest. The fishermen sprang to the shrouds. Only one was unconcerned—the sleeper. They wakened him. "Carest thou not, Master, that we perish?" He arose, looked into their scared faces, then out upon the troubled sea. He lifted his hands and with the quiet voice of one conscious of power, said, "Peace be still." The winds went moaning to their caverns; the waves fell sobbing asleep!

It was a wondrous thing. Who but the Almighty Son of God could have wrought this miracle? Canute, the Dane, attempted it; standing on the heights, when the storm was beating against the rocks beneath, he cried, "Be still!" and the tempest laughed at him. Xerxes, the Persian, tried it; commanding his courtiers to place his throne upon the beach, he said to the flowing tide "No further"; but it drew nearer, nearer until it lapped his feet and they carried him back and proceeded by his orders to lay a penalty of three hundred lashes on the irreverent sea. Akbar, the Saracen, thought to do it; he spurred his horse down into the water calling out defiance to old Neptune; fetlock deep, knee deep, now to the saddle girth, when the horse, wiser than his rider, turned and fled shoreward and old Neptune roared after him. But Jesus of Nazareth calmed the stormy sea with a word.

However, we are to see a greater miracle than this. The little boat has touched the strand. The stern anchor is thrown, the bow made fast. Look yonder! What creature is that? A man? a demon? his hair flying, his clothes torn from him, his face distorted, foam issuing from his lips; muttering, shrieking out blasphemy, rattling a broken chain from his uplifted arms! Let us fasten our eyes on him as he runs furiously this way—for here is the power of sin—the monstrous power of sin!

Time was when yonder demoniac was a babe on his mother's breast; she fondled his chubby hands, kissed his lips, looked down into his sweet blue eyes, and dreamed a mother's dreams. Then he was a merry lad; his laughter ringing clear as he mingled with his playmates in the village street.

> ——Life went a-Maying
> With Nature, Hope and Poesy,
> When he was young.

And then a young man with all a young man's hopes and aspirations. What possibilities of honor and influence awaited him! But some evil power met him. Was it a siren with a sweet alluring voice? Was it a fiend with a crimson cup in hand? He yielded and fell and yonder he is. In him let us behold what sin can do. Nay, rather what sin in its approach to ripeness is ever bound to do.

We need in these days a deeper apprehension of this awful truth. The reason why men do not all hunger and thirst for salvation is because they are not sufficiently sensible of sin. The truth with all its dread significance is not pressed upon them. The sick must know their malady before they are willing to call a physician. Conviction precedes conversion. The needle of the law must enter the soul before the thread of the gospel.

It will not be unprofitable for us, therefore, to study in this miserable victim the full effects of sin.

I. *Sin had unlawed this man.* "He could not be bound, no, not with chains. He could not be tamed." In the controversies of the early Church a word was used to characterize sin which has since passed out of use and we have no other which precisely takes its place; to wit, *anomia*, which may be rendered, "unlawry." Sin and law are opposites. Sin is trespass, transgression, climbing a fence, intruding upon a preserve, breaking open a bolted door, a protest against restraint in any form.

Man was originally created under law; he was a normal being. He lived in an atmosphere of obedience. He moved in calm conformity with the laws of his own being. In such condition he was absolutely and ideally free. For freedom is defined to be perfect obedience to perfect law.

He fell. Fell from what? From law. He lost something. What? His freedom. And what did he gain instead? License, lawlessness, aversion to restraint; that is to say, sin. Some are fond of characterizing this acquisition as personal freedom; meaning by that, the liberty to defy God and the rights of one's fellow-men. It is in pursuance of this perverted sense of freedom that assaults are made upon our Sabbath laws, our temperance laws, our marriage laws, and all rules and regulations which are intended to conserve our happiness and prosperity in social life. Here the demon of sin clothes himself in the name of freedom and appears as an angel of light. He pours forth philippics against law and order. His other name is Anarchy. He was seen at his worst and ripest in that famous Haymarket meeting in Chicago where, amid the hissing of bombs, the cry arose, "Throttle the law!"

II. *Sin had unshamed this man.* His clothes were torn from him. He was heedless of the common decencies of life. There is a form of sin which one is reluctant even to mention to polite ears; but it must needs be.

It stares at us from the dead walls in painted placards, and from the windows of photographers' establishments along the thoroughfares. It looks us boldly in the face from our illustrated periodicals, and utters its vile pleasantries in the daily papers. It assumes the form of advanced culture on the walls of our art galleries. This is nothing new. It is as old as Satan. The same sort of "culture" frescoed the walls of Pompeii with cartoons that made that city the reproach of the old-time world. And God looked down upon it with eyes of flaming fire. At his command the ashes of Vesuvius were belched forth over that iniquitous city and buried it from the sight of men.

This form of sin is conspicuous in much of our current literature. It is estimated that more than one-half of the English novels issued during the past year have presented, as their heroines for public consideration, a class of creatures so disreputable that no self-respecting man or modest woman would for a moment think of saluting them if they were to spring into life and pass along the street. What a procession of "living pictures" with Trilby at their head! And many of us, the followers of the meek and lowly Jesus, men and women professing to honor the things that are pure and lovely and of good report, have welcomed them into the sanctity of our home-life!

And the drama? It is not necessary just now to advert to the question whether or no it is right to attend the theatre. Let it suffice to say that at this moment, by common consent, there are almost no plays presented in New York which can be witnessed with impunity by people of clean character. The contagion has seized not only on the concert halls and vaudeville resorts, but upon the two or three theatres which have hitherto assumed to be respectable. Within a stone's throw of this pulpit, in the play-house which has hitherto been assigned to the highest place of virtuous trustworthiness, there is a play on the boards of such a character that a man or woman witnessing it, while able to preserve an "anatomical virtue," can by no stretch of the imagination remain morally pure. One such spectacle as that rubs off the bloom of the peach.

In answer to such observations as this it is customary to remark, "To the pure all things are pure." Flat and nauseous sophism! Dirt is dirt anywhere and everywhere. Obscenity is obscenity. No admixture of antiseptic can change a dish of offal into a lemon-ice. It is impossible to take pitch into the bosom and not be defiled. Avoid it, therefore; pass by on the other side; go not near it.

III. Furthermore, *sin isolated this man.* "He made his dwelling among the tombs." Here were ghosts gibbering by moonlight; but he was not afraid. His proper home was among the dead. Here were the sepulchres of hope and promise and noble aspiration all about him. Dust and ashes of the past. A place of solitude and barrenness. He could see the village just yonder, hear the echo of its laughter and the hum of its industry. But he had no part nor lot in it. By night he saw the lights kindling in the windows. One light yonder in the window of his own home where wife and children were; but he had no business there. That was a village full of honest folk; he had ruled himself out. Sin always rules us out, robs us of the sweets of fellowship, shuts us up to selfish envy and jealousy, drives us alone to our own place. The sorrow of perdition lies in those words, "outer darkness." The soul exiled to wander there is not excluded from heaven by closed gates, for heaven's gates are always open ; he is shut out by his own character—fixed, formulated, crystallized in his earthly life. He is here among congenial associations. There is only one place in the universe that would be more dismal than hell to him, that is heaven ; because he has disqualified himself for it. If he draws near to an open gate he hears the voice of prayer, but prayer is not for him ; he hears the voice of singing,

> "All hail the power of Jesus' name
> Let angels prostrate fall."

But what sympathy has he with that coronation song? If God were to send forth his angels and archangels to constrain that poor soul to enter in, he would run shrieking to the furthest caves of night. He can never be at home save in his own place. "For without are dogs and sorcerers and whoremongers and murderers and whosoever loveth and maketh a lie."

IV. *Sin made this man injurious to himself.* "He cut himself with stones." We are accustomed to say of a man who is under the dominion of some tyrannical passion that he is his own worst enemy. But the sin in any man antagonizes his best interests; it robs him of all that makes life worth living and, in the long run, when it is finished it bringeth forth death.

A plant flourishes so long as it lives in harmony with the laws that environ it ; the moment it disobeys, refuses to assimilate the dew or sunlight or turns aside from any of the rules of its being, it begins to wither and fade. A star lives so long as it regards its orbit ; if it deviate an inch, it loses its place in the universal system, whizzes through space, and enters upon a career which means ultimate ruin. The soul that defies the moral laws that are interwoven with its very being, proceeds along the same path. Any form of transgression is self-injurious, as it is written, "He that sinneth against God, wrongeth his own soul." It is not easy to perceive in the earlier stages of sin when it assumes the form of stolen pleasure, this sure tendency towards death. But the tendency is there; and as sure as gravitation in the natural world. I recall five scenes in the life of a young man whose face comes to me from the days of my early youth. I saw him first with his sleeves rolled up, at work in the hay field. He was the only son of his mother and she was a widow. He was pointed out as an industrious young man, but with wild ways. I saw him again as I looked through the windows of a gilded gin palace; he was standing with a group of well-dressed men before the bar; his matted hair fallen upon his forehead, his hat thrown back, a half empty glass before him. I saw him again reeling through the street, out at elbows now, reeling along the downward way. I saw him again with his face against the barred window, his eyes red and wild, seeing phantoms. He had reached *mania a potu*. I saw him once more laid out for his burial; his face black and bloated, his mother bowed down with both her arms around him, kissing that poor face. His sin was "finished"; it had killed him.

V. *Sin made this man injurious to others;* as Luke says, "Travellers could not pass that way." We are all depending upon one another in this world. We are all travelling along by the way of the tombs, hoping to reach some better place. It is our business to help each other to bear one another's burdens, to relieve one another of pain and weariness, to make life tolerable and, if possible, happy for all. But, alas! sin makes us selfish and envious and injurious. Under its malignant power we are unsafe friends and comrades. We hurt where we should help. We increase the burden where we should lighten it.

If a man could die unto himself alone ; if he could waste his life, squander his energies and go out alone into the eternal night, that would be sufficiently dreadful—but that is not the worst. No man can die unto himself. A train follows after him. The sins of which he has been guilty are as stumbling blocks over which other souls fall and perish.

On last Thursday a man under the influence of liquor came to his home on Fifty-third Street. He was not a bad man ordinarily as drunkards go, but, being out of work, he had for weeks yielded to his besetting sin. His wife not being at home to welcome him, he walked up and down the room in anger. His only child, an infant of nine months, lay sleeping on the couch. His wife who had gone out perhaps to earn a little bread threw open the door and faced him. He began to curse her, and in a moment seized his child and threw the little one at its mother with such violence that it struck her and fell upon the floor dead ! It is bad enough that he should now be shut up in a prison cell to contemplate his awful crime under the shadow of a gallows tree. But think of the consequences that his sin entails ; a deserted home, a murdered child, a wife broken-hearted, worse than widowed, doomed to shame wherever she goes. If he die upon the gallows tree, will that end it ? Nay, the ghost of his iniquity will still live, to drive, as with a whip of scorpions, other souls to follow in his steps.

We shall all agree probably that the case made against sin in the person of this demoniac is bad enough. It is not with sin in him, however, that we have to do. It is of no profit to look on sin yonder at a distance as an objective thing. The theft of the little ewe lamb did indeed arouse the indignation and wrath of King David when he heard it; but a conviction deeper than that and more salutary came when the prophet pointed his finger and cried, "Thou art the man!" We have practically to do, not with sin in this demoniac of Gadara, but with sin as it is in ourselves, in you and me; for there is not one among us who can plead innocence. The best we can say is, that sin, as yet, is not finished in us; but we all shall fall upon our knees to-night if we are honest men and women, and confess before God "I have sinned and done evil in thy sight." If sin have indeed in itself such potency and possibility as we have been contemplating, shall we not cry out "Who shall deliver us from the body of this death? Who shall deliver me?"

The little boat has been waiting during this meditation by the beach at Gadara. The demoniac with hideous cries hastens this way. The Man of Nazareth, concious of his power, is not affrighted. He faces the sinner and his sin and cries "Come out of him!" A moment later, the man lies sobbing before his feet. We shall see him presently clothed and in his right mind.

It is glorious to think in the presence of such an awful scourge as sin, that there is One mighter than sin. One that has power on earth to forgive sin. Nay, more he has power to deliver from the bondage of sin. If ever there was a desperate case it was that of this demoniac. All entreaties and remonstrances had been vain. Law, penalty, fetters, and manacles had been futile. His friends had given him up. But did you never observe how Jesus loved to deal with desperate cases? If a paralytic were brought to him, it was only when all the poor victim's money had been wasted on physicians, and his last strength and resource were all gone, and he could by no means lift himself up. If a leper presented himself, it was in the last stages of his disease when his fingers were dropping from their joints. Or, perhaps, Jesus was called to a desolated home, from which the dear one had been carried out four days ago to his burial, so that corruption had already seized upon him. But here lay his great strength. He knew no hopelessness. Nothing was impossible to him. He healed them every one. O his name is The Mighty to Save! If there is a man who feels himself so wholly under the power of a long-cherished habit that he has surrendered all hope of deliverance, to him the Lord Jesus speaks the word of hope. If there is a mother whose scapegrace boy has gone off into the far country and wasted his substance, whom no maternal love or entreaty has been able to reach, to her this Omnipotent Son of God speaks the word of hope. Bring your loved one to Jesus; he is able to save unto the uttermost.

The old cobbler who laid his hand upon the shoulder of an inebriate, who was staggering through the streets of Nantucket long ago, saying, kindly, "John, there is One that can help you," wrought better than he dreamed. For those words had in them the ring of new strength and comfort, and John B. Gough lived to testify for forty glorious years to the power of the One that had helped him. There is help here. There is help nowhere else. Jesus is master of sin. All others are in less or greater measure servants of sin. He has power to forgive. He has power to deliver. "He is able to save unto the uttermost all that come unto God by him."

THE STORY OF AN OUTCAST.—THE SEQUEL.

"And they see him that was possessed with the devil, and had the legion, sitting, and clothed, and in his right mind."—MARK v. 15.

It is said that when the demoniac came into the village and told the strange thing that had happened "all men did marvel." And no wonder. If a man is disposed to reject the supernatural, he will find difficulties innumerable in this narrative.

(1) There, to begin with, is the suggestion of a personal devil. There are many excellent people who decline to believe anything of the sort. Sin, indwelling corruption, an evil principle; aye, by all means. But a personal devil, they will have none of it. There was a time when I disbelieved in that particular form of highway robbery known as "garroting." But one morning an old acquaintance came in to tell me that he had been garroted on the previous night, and showed me in evidence a purple mark around his neck. There was no reasoning against that. In like manner there are multitudes of people who bear about in their bodies the marks of a personal devil,—stigmata that can scarcely be traced to an impersonal principle.

(2) Demonianism or demoniacal possession. Here is another difficulty which some are disposed to cir-

cumvent by assigning this phenomenon to the category of mere physical maladies. But this will not answer. The Lord Jesus Christ had come into the world to deliver it from the bondage of sin. In other words, he was making an invasion upon the realms of the Prince of Darkness. Was it to be expected that the ruler of this world would allow his sovereignty to slip out of his hands without making a desperate effort to retain it? Demonianism was the outward token of this tremendous conflict at close quarters. The Son of God stood alone as the knight-errant of the fallen race; his adversary summoned all the hosts of the nether world to his aid. As God was expressing himself in the incarnate form of Jesus of Nazareth, so the Prince of Darkness must needs oppose him through mortal agency. Therefore the emissaries of evil entered in and took possession wherever the door of a human heart lay open. All heaven and hell stood looking on. And whenever this Jesus met his adversary hand to hand, it was as when Samson met the lion on the way to Timnath; "He rent him as he would have rent a kid."

(3) There is a difficulty also in the matter of the swine. Yet nothing in the narrative is more reasonable than this. Where else could the unclean spirits have found a refuge so congenial? See the swine yonder seeking their sustenance among the offal heaps. At the word of commission the unclean spirits take possession of them; then a sudden panic in the herd. They are rolling in the mire, uttering strange half-human cries, jostling one another, plunging headlong down the declivity and so into the water. Then a mighty commotion; they are struggling, strangling, drowning. They have left naught behind them but bubbling con-

fusion and widening, vanishing circles. All is over. The unclean spirits have gone to their own place and they have gone in their own way. It is an exquisite touch of nature. This was their fitting end.

(4) The most serious difficulty of all, however, in the narrative is the strange transformation in this man. There is nothing so marvellous in all the metamorphoses of Ovid. An hour ago we saw him running down the cliffs toward the lake, naked, hands uplifted, rattling a broken chain, foaming at the lips and shouting forth obscene blasphemies. Now here he lies, bound as chains never could bind him; tamed as laws could never tame him; transformed by the power of the Son of God!

We saw him under the power of sin—a hard taskmaster. It is related of Scirion, the robber, that he kept his captives always four days. On the first they were entertained with lavish hospitality at his table; on the second they were required to wash his feet and those of his robber band; on the third they were confined in a prison cell; on the fourth they were brought to the edge of a precipitous cliff and pushed into the sea. And therein we mark the downward steps of sin. It begins with self-indulgence; the feast of stolen pleasures.

> "Haste thee, nymph, and bring with thee
> Jest and youthful Jollity,
> Quips, and cranks, and wanton wiles,
> Nods, and becks, and wreathèd smiles,
> Sport that wrinkled Care derides,
> And Laughter holding both his sides!"

Next come the menial services of vice—the loss of self-respect, license, the gratification of the lower nature and sensuality. Then bondage; "For, whosoever committeth sin is the servant of it." And finally death; the cup is drunk to its dregs; there remains only enough to betray the fact that all along we have been partaking of slow poison. Death; spiritual and eternal death. Come Shame, Regret, Remorse, Despair, Retribution and push him out into the night! Probation is past; eternity begins. "He that is unjust let him be unjust still." *Aion ton aionon*—forever and ever!

The demoniac of Gadara had reached the last and most portentous chapter of his guilty life and was being pushed by all the furies headlong down to death, when he met—O, would to God that all who are in like extremity might meet him too—the mighty Son of God. At his word of command the furies fled and the unclean spirits abandoned their prey. Mark now the stupendous change; he lies prone before Jesus trembling in every sinew and sobbing out his mingled grief and gratitude. "John, Peter, lend a hand! Wash his open wounds and anoint them. Break off this clanking chain! Andrew, cast thy tunic over him and give him a little parched corn from thy girdle, with a drink of cool water from the lake! Now raise him up!"

This is conversion. The schoolmen might call it regeneration, but regeneration is the divine side of the great change and we have practically nothing to do with it. But conversion is a turning about. We turn about under the power of God. Our backs to the darkness; our faces to the light. Our backs to the world, the flesh and the devil; our faces toward God and the endless life. This is a revolutionary change. It is not a mere veneering, but runs through and through the human fabric. The old colonial clock that stands in your hallway is adjusted every morning by the turning of its hands, nor will it ever keep time in a trustworthy way, until you have summoned an expert to heal its constitutional infirmity. A man may turn over a new leaf, but as to his being made over again, that can only be done when he submits himself to God. A heart disease cannot be healed with a fly-blister. "Not by might, nor by power, but by my Spirit, saith the Lord." The change in this demoniac has been wrought from above. He is a new creature in Christ Jesus; new will, new heart, new conscience, new life. Old things are passed away, behold, all things are become new. Observe some of the tokens of this change:

I. *He is "clothed."* That is to say, he has regained his self-respect, and with it a respect for the courtesies of social life. Yesterday he would have declaimed loudly about personal liberty; his right to be clothed or unclothed according to his pleasure. But to-day he thinks not of himself only, but of his fellow-men.

II. *He is "in his right mind."* He was previously wrong-minded as to all important things. God was not in all his thoughts. Immortality was nothing to him; he lived for the present hour. His philosophy was, "Let us eat and drink for to-morrow we die." As to the beauty of holiness, this was repugnant to him. He was accustomed to think of religion as mere sanctimoniousness—a straight-laced melancholy. Perhaps he had seen it misrepresented in the lives of professed religionists and he had no desire for it. Now he longs for holiness; it seems the most delightsome thing in the world to him. And then as to the person and character of Christ. If he knew

Christ at all, it was only to hate and despise him. He was a root out of a dry ground and there was no form or beauty in Him that this man should desire him. Now there is no other in the universe so dear as Jesus. No other face like his; the chiefest among ten thousand and the one altogether lovely. And with respect to duty. Duty! What had he formerly to do with duty? Now it is the principal thing. Duty is destined henceforth to be the largest word in his vocabulary—larger than sympathy, larger than honor, larger than pleasure, larger than life. This conviction marks the beginning of the spiritual life. "What wilt thou have me to do?" cried Saul of Tarsus, under the great sun-burst from heaven. "Let me be with thee," cries the demoniac of Gadara. "Let me sit at thy feet as a disciple; let me follow in thy steps." "Nay," said Jesus, "go down to thy home and tell thy friends how great things the Lord hath done for thee."

III. *At home.* This man wanted to go with Jesus; but there were reasons why he could accomplish more in the narrow circle of his acquaintances than by joining the group of followers who accompanied Christ in his missionary work.

The home-coming of this saved man was most pathetic. It may be that an old mother had for years been praying for his return and hoping against hope. God bless the dear faithful mothers who never give up their wayward sons and daughters; who never forget the covenant and never lose hope! There she sat, her withered hands folded in her lap, when he stood in the door-way. Who shall tell the gladness in her heart? Who shall paint the brightness in her dimmed eyes? . . . It would appear that a wife awaited him. Time was when at the altar she passed with him under an arch of flowers out into the joys and cares of wedded-life. He had promised to love, honor and protect her. But as time passed there came a cooling of love, neglect, a remaining from home far into the night, a returning with red eyes and angry words, and oh! the horrible breath of the wine cup. Then one night, when he did not return at all, where had he gone? Some of the neighbors had seen him out in the tombs yonder, gashed and bleeding and muttering to himself. On stormy nights she lay awake and thought of him. God be praised for conjugal life; the love of the faithful wife that weathers all gales; the patience of hopeful wives that holds fast to early vows and the memory of former joys and the hope of a better time coming. He sees her standing yonder by the door. "Wife, I've come back," he says. "I've come back to begin again. I've seen Jesus of Nazareth and he has cast out the demons. I've come back to you and the children; to life and God." . . . And his children, how they dreaded his approach. They knew his savage ways. They had been accustomed to run and hide when he drew near, waving his hands and uttering his angry blasphemies. Now they stand at a distance awe-struck and wondering; they had never seen it on this fashion. "Come here," he says, "little daughter, I will not hurt you"; and the eldest reluctantly approaches. He parts her hair from her forehead and with sad, loving words makes his confession; "I've been a bad father, dear; but I've met Jesus of Nazareth and the demons are gone." His other children sidle near, wondering. At what? At the same mystery of regeneration which puzzles the older people. And they allow themselves to be taken upon his knees. He kisses them one by one and the past is gone.

Up yonder on the wall is a chain hanging. "Let us take it down, good wife. Please God, you shall never call in the neighbors to bind me again." And as he looks this way there is something glistening on his cheek,—a strong man's tear. Aye; and there is a rainbow of promise in it. "The sacrifices of God are a broken spirit; a broken and contrite heart, O God, thou wilt not despise." So the new life begins. There are scars on the man's face, his cheeks are still white and thin, and he will long carry about with him the marks of that awful nightmare in the tombs. But here with wife and children about him, ah, this is heaven begun on earth!

Is that all? Oh no. On the evening of that day he gathers his wife and children about him and tells them the whole story, how it all happened. How he saw the little boat upon the lake and ran down with curses to meet it. How the strong Man looked who, standing in the bow of the little boat, boldly faced him. How, with a ring of conscious power in his voice, He uttered those words, "Come out of him!" And then the awful struggle for a moment when life and death tugged for the mastery within him; and how life won. "The Lord bade me," he continues, "return here to the old home and live down my past and do good as I may have opportunity, by a holy and helpful life. But I can't do that without prayer. I am helpless and hopeless except as I have strength from above. Let us kneel down, therefore, and pray, 'Have mercy upon me, O God, according to thy loving kindness and according unto the multitude of thy tender mercies blot out my transgressions. Purge me with hyssop, and I shall be clean; wash me, and I shall be whiter than snow. Open thou my lips that my mouth shall show forth thy praise.' A long pause, and then : 'Bless the Lord, O my soul, and all that is within me bless his holy name. Bless the Lord, O my soul, and forget not all his benefits; who forgiveth all thine iniquities and redeemeth thy life from destruction. The Lord is merciful and gracious, slow to anger and plenteous in mercy. As far as the east is from the west, so far hath he removed our transgressions from us. Bless the Lord ye his angels that excel in strength ; that do his commandments, hearkening to his voice. Bless the Lord, all his works, in all places of his dominion. Bless the Lord, O my soul!'" And thus the changed man has changed his poverty-stricken home into the very gate of heaven. There may have been no tapestries or pictures there ; little meal in the barrel, or oil in the cruise ; but there was love and there was the family altar. It was like the house of Obed-edom with the Ark of the Covenant in the midst of it.

And was that all? The next morning his neighbors dropped in to see ; old friends who had known him in earlier and better days ; some who had joined in his revels and tarried with him long at the wine. And they marvelled. His earnest face, his evident sincerity, his interest in their welfare, won for him a hearing. There was no gainsaying his word. He told his simple story, keeping Jesus always in the center of it. He was never weary of sounding the praises of his friend. "He published throughout the whole city what Jesus had done for him."

Nor was that all. One chapter more remains. So far as we are aware this man never saw Jesus again. Nor did the Master ever return to Gadara. The people, immediately after this miracle and before they knew its whole bearing, had implored him to depart out of their coasts. It was a dreadful thing to do on the impulse of the moment. And he had gone. They stood and watched the little boat as it crossed the lake, and knew not what they were losing. Farewell, O Christ; Saviour, Helper, Friend of sinners,—farewell! The little boat has vanished and the light of a great possibility has gone with it. Nay, not wholly so; for Christ in leaving had provided for the need of these Gadarenes in his instructions to this man. He required him to abide among them a living epistle respecting His power to save. He was true to that commission and went about doing good, preaching the gospel in his humble way; and at length he fell on sleep. One moment he closed his eyes on earth; the next he opened them in heaven. Yonder on the throne sat One like unto the Son of Man. O light and glory unapproachable! He was the same, yet not the same. His hands were stretched out in welcome, and the demoniac fell down before him, as once before he had fallen before him at the lake-shore, and cried, "Oh Jesus of Nazareth, let all heaven hear! I am the demoniac of Gadara. I am he that dwelt among the tombs. I am he that broke the silence of the night with cries of blasphemy, and thou didst restore me to hope and manhood and life. Thou are worthy to receive honor and glory and power and dominion; for thou hast brought me into the land of everlasting peace!"

And this is the gospel which I preach unto you,

the gospel of a glorious salvation, of a Christ able to save sinners of the deepest dye,—a mighty gospel; to the Jews a stumbling block and to the Greeks foolishness; but to them which believe, the wisdom and the power of God!

THE ASCENT OF MAN.

"I will make a man more precious than fine gold; even than the golden wedge of Ophir."—Isa. xiii. 12.

We come upon these words in a prophecy respecting the fall of Babylon. Babylon stands for the world-power; for wealth and arrogance; for carnal pleasures and selfish pursuits. It stands for fleets and armies; for the subordination of the people to princes, of the many to the few. The overthrow of Babylon means the restitution of all things, the building up of the kingdom of heaven on earth, the uprooting of envy and jealousy and inordinate ambition, the ushering in of the Golden Age. Of the tokens of the approach of this millenial epoch none is more significant than this, that manhood shall be placed at its true value. "I will make a man more precious than fine gold; even than the golden wedge of Ophir."

The two ever-present thoughts of Scripture are God and Man. We say, "I believe in God the Father Almighty." How easy it is to utter the name, but who shall tell what infinite universes of meaning are in it? God;—infinite, eternal, unchangeable in his being and attributes. God;—omnipotent, omniscient, omnipresent! And along with this runs the thought of Man,—Man, who borrows all his greatness from his relations with God. "*When I consider thy heavens, the* work of thy fingers, the moon and the stars, which thou hast ordained; what is man, that thou art mindful of him? and the son of man, that thou visitest him? For thou hast made him a little lower than the angels, and hast crowned him with glory and honor. Thou madest him to have dominion over the work of thy hands; thou hast put all things under his feet: all sheep and oxen, yea, and the beasts of the field; the fowl of the air, and the fish of the sea, and whatsoever passeth through the paths of the sea." The apostrophe of Edward Young is but a paraphrase:

> "How poor, how rich, how abject, how august,
> How complicate, how wonderful, is man!
> How passing wonder He who made him such!
> Who centred in our make such strange extremes,
> From different natures marvellously mixed,
> Connection exquisite of distant worlds!
> Distinguished link in being's endless chain!
> Midway from nothing to Deity!
> A beam ethereal, sullied, and absorpt!
> Though sullied and dishonored, still divine!
> Dim miniature of greatness absolute!
> An heir of glory! a frail child of dust!
> Helpless immortal! insect infinite!
> A worm! a God!"

The subject of our thought is the Christian doctrine of Man. The Scriptures are very definite as to three points:

First. The divine origin of Man. We are introduced into a council of the ineffable Trinity in which we hear the several persons of the Godhead saying, to one another, "Let us make man in our image, after our likeness." Here is God's masterpiece, the crowning work of his creative hand.

Set over against that Scriptural statement the words of Charles Darwin: "Man is descended from a hairy quadruped, arboreal in its habits." If the Scriptural record is to be believed, man stands at the summit of all created things. He is vicegerent under the universal King; "having," as Emerson says, "in his senses the morning and night and the unfathomable galaxy, and in his brain the geometry of the city of God." But if Darwin is to be believed, Man is the product of insensate laws acting on dead atoms; the last outgrowth of a pedigree of bestial ancestors; the sum total of environment, air, food, water, nurses, physicians, associations and culture. Let Thomas Carlyle speak: "I have known three generations of the Darwins, grandfather, father and son; atheists all. It is related that among the grandfather's effects was found a seal engraven with this legend, *Omnia ex conchis*,—Everything from a clam-shell. A good sort of man is this Darwin and well meaning, but with very little intellect. Ah, it's a sad and terrible thing to see a whole generation of men and women, professing to be cultivated, looking around in a purblind fashion and finding no God in this universe. I suppose it is a reaction from the reign of Kant. And this is what we have got to. All things from frog-spawn! The gospel of dirt the order of the day."

If we must needs choose between the two theories of human origin, let us cling to the traditional self-respect which comes from our belief that we are born of God. Give us to feel ourselves the kings and prophets of this world and the blessed world to come.

The philosophers of the olden time were greatly puzzled to find a definition of man. The best that Plato—who stood head and shoulders above them all—could do, was to say, after long thinking, "Man is a featherless biped." How splendidly in contrast with that sage observation, shines the Scriptural record: "So God created man in his own image; in the image of God, created He him. And He gave him dominion over the fish of the sea, and the fowl of the air and over all the earth and over every creeping thing."

> "O mighty brother soul of man
> Where'er thou art, or low or high,
> Thy skyey arches with exultant span
> O'er-roof infinity."

A triple inheritance comes to us by reason of this divine origin:

(1) Mind. Not simply that faculty of perception and calculation which is seen in many of the lower orders—by which the fox, for example, can measure the brook before he undertakes to leap it—but a faculty by which we are enabled to confront the great verities and problems of the endless life. By this faculty we are enabled, furthermore, to confer with the Infinite, as it is written; "Come now, saith the Lord, let us reason together."

(2) Conscience. By this we are enabled to determine between right and wrong, or as Plato said, "to discern between the worse and better reason." Our moral sense brings us into an apprehension of the word "ought;" by which are resolved all the questions of human responsibility; that is to say, all questions which concern our immediate relations with God.

(3) Will. A sovereign will. It is difficult, if not impossible, to see how God could have created man in his own likeness without endowing him with an independent will. Yet, obviously, that way lies danger. For here is suggested the possibility of going

either right or wrong. It is common in these days to speak of "the reign of law." All things in the universe are indeed under the reign of law. There is no crystal which is not formed according to an invariable rule. The stars of heaven revolve without swerving an inch from their appointed orbit. The flowers of the field are in perfect harmony with the laws of their being. The birds migrate and return when nature strikes the hour. Nowhere will you find disobedience until you come to the province of man. He is distinguished from all existing things, animate or inanimate, in this, that when law says "Thou shalt!" he can answer "I will not!" And in this very freedom of the will, which is perverted into wilfulness, the bitter source of all his miseries, we find the preeminent evidence of his kinship with God.

Second. The Scriptures have a definite message as to the destiny of man. We are reminded at this point that the Scriptures do not assert the immortality of the soul. But why should they? This is the fundamental postulate on which the whole fabric of Scripture rests. If the soul is not immortal, this volume of revelation is as meaningless as a last year's almanac. But in fact while immortality is not stated as a proposition or in syllogistic form, the Book is everywhere full of it.

It says, among other things, that when God created man he breathed into his nostrils the breath of life, and he became a living soul. So then the life of man is the breath of God. A zephyr comes this way laden with the fragrance of an oriental garden or the faint murmur of a distant song and passes by. What has become of it? Has it ceased to be? O no. A mere tyro in science will tell you that even so slender a force as a zephyr can never cease to be. What then becomes of this breath which God has breathed into every man? Can death destroy it? Nay; this is but the passing of the soul. It still lives somewhere and is destined to live forever and ever.

A like suggestion is found in the old problem, "What shall it profit a man, if he gain the whole world and lose his own soul? or what shall a man give in exchange for his soul?" Here is a drunkard in the ditch—red-faced, filthy, ragged, his blood polluted, his flesh sodden, the flies buzzing about him. You can scarcely abide the sight. But look again and deeper, for there is a man within this man, down deeper than clothes and cuticle. A man made in God's image and made to live somewhere forever. You will note the proof of his greatness when he presently rises from his shame and reels along his way muttering his maudlin sorrow. He struggles to his feet. He enters into conflict, ill or well, with his passions. He weeps over his sins. He repents and begins a noble life. Not so do swine return from their wallow or dogs from their vomit. There is all the time something still lingering in this poor wretch far superior to anything which you may find in the lower orders of life. It is his divineness, his manhood, buttressed by a sweet memory and an unspeakably precious hope.

And what mean all these apocalyptic visions; for the Scriptures are a book of visions? Here are doors opening before us, and yonder toward the night behold the smoke of torment ascending and hear cries and curses and sobs of despair. And yonder a city with gates of pearl and pavements of gold; light, beauty and the singing of a multitude like the far-off murmuring of many waters. "Who are these in white robes with palms in their hands and whence came they? These are they which came up out of great tribulation and have washed their robes in the blood of the Lamb. And they shall hunger no more, neither thirst any more; neither shall the sun light on them, nor any heat. For the Lamb which is in the midst of the throne shall feed them, and shall lead them unto living fountains of waters; and God shall wipe away all tears from their eyes."

Third. A clear light is also thrown upon the history of man—the long history that lies between his origin and the ultimate fulfilment of his destiny. It is written in two chapters:

(1) The Fall. The man who was created in God's likeness passes out of the garden, his head fallen upon his breast and his heart bowed under an unspeakable burden of shame. Something has happened. Call it The Fall, or whatever you will. A new and calamitous factor has come into the problem, to-wit,—sin. We follow this man as he turns his back upon the gate of paradise, guarded by its flaming sword. We shall see him tilling the earth, which is accursed for his sake, with groans of weariness. We shall see him bending over his dead with bitter tears. We shall find him mingling in wars and confusions, his garments dipped in blood. Aye, something has happened. It is a long way from Eden to Esdraelon. This man is but a ruin of his former self. The glory is departed. He is, however, a magnificent ruin! As in some old temple we can close our eyes and see the priest disrobed, discrowned, walking amid the crumbling walls and bewailing the glory of the former days, so is it with this fallen child of God.

(2) The Restoration. In the midst of the desolation is raised the cross and the word goes forth; "I will make a man more precious than fine gold; even than the golden wedge of Ophir."

It is plain at the outset that there can be no restoration of this ruin until there has been a clearing away of the débris. The past must, somehow, be gotten out of the way. It is vain to speak of character building so long as our sin abides upon us, But here is our promise; "Come now, saith the Lord. let us reason together, though your sins be as scarlet they shall be as white as snow." "The blood of Jesus Christ cleanseth from all sin."

Then the upbuilding. God who made us, can remake us. The same Spirit that breathed into our nostrils the breath of life can again breathe into us a new and nobler life. The man who, sensible of God's pardoning grace in Jesus Christ, undertakes to perfect himself in manhood, may rest assured of divine reenforcement. He is referred to the precepts of Scripture for his guidance in conduct. He is referred to Jesus Christ, the ideal Man, as his Exemplar, and is instructed to proceed in this holy endeavor looking unto Jesus the Author and Finisher of his faith. And still further, he receives the enabling influence of the Holy Ghost. "Work out your own salvation, for it is God that worketh in you." "Add," "grow," "be strong," "go on unto perfection." Thus the temple rises. The graces are as living stones and life is a long endeavor to attain unto the full stature of a man.

In this connection let us bear with us two practical thoughts: *First*, Know thyself. Know thine origin and destiny as a child of God. The shield of

Luther bore on one side two hammers, the token of his father's handicraft; and on the obverse a winged-heart with this legend, *Astra petimus*. A man may be bound down to the sordid toil of the workshop, but never in such a manner as that he may not realize the responsibility of vaster, nobler tasks.

> " Rise my soul and stretch thy wings,
> Thy better portion trace.
> Rise from transitory things,
> Toward heaven, thy native place."

And *finally*. Know thy neighbor. Know him also as a child of God. As we pass along the crowded thoroughfare, let us realize that every one we jostle is destined to eternity. Let us return to our drunkard fallen by the way and gaze upon him with an infinite sorrow and compassion, nearing meanwhile that divine word: "What shall it profit a man if he gain the whole world and lose his own soul?" By the side of this poor wretch pile up a mountain of gold, private fortunes, national exchequers, crowns, royal jewels, diadems of the Pharaohs and Cæsars, pearls of the ocean, all the gold that lies buried in the bosom of the everlasting hills, and reflect that this Popocatapetl of wealth is nothing, nothing, in comparison with the value of that drunkard's soul. Then let us go our way and remember, that as children of the Kingdom we have no business but to co-operate with Christ in the restoring of all such to their original glory as children of God. The way is clear, the cross has been uplifted, the fountain of blood has been opened for uncleanness, the Spirit of power descends upon us. Let us lend a hand to the glorious work of restoring the race. For this is the true and only "Ascent of Man."

"LOOSE HIM AND LET HIM GO."

"*Loose him and let him go.*"—JOHN xi. 44.

We are introduced in the home at Bethany to the commonplace life of a brother and two dependent sisters. Of the latter we have clear information. Mary was a woman of strong affections, attached to the members of her own household, and devotedly fond of the Nazarene prophet, who was frequently entertained here as a welcome guest. We behold her sitting, in rapt attention and reverent love, at Jesus' feet. Martha was cumbered with much serving; the care of the household fell upon her, and little wonder if she occasionally lost her equanimity amid the fret and worry of her multitudinous tasks. Yet, under the troubled surface of her life ran also a clear stream of affectionate and practical loyalty to Christ. It is a curious fact, however, that we know next to nothing of Lazarus. Was he possessed of brilliant gifts or extraordinary traits of character? What was his handicraft? We have no record of a single word that ever fell from his lips. It is said, however, that "Jesus loved him." And when the end drew near—the dark shadow in the doorway, the breath fluttering and the pulse beating slow—a message was sent to Jesus over at Bethabara: "He whom thou lovest is sick." That was enough. The Master—taking his own time, as if to teach the lesson of patience in faith—answered the summons; and here he is facing the tomb.

It is the crisis of a great battle. The Prince of Life and the King of Terrors are at close quarters. Naught separates them but yonder stone at the mouth of the sepulchre. Christ has no fear of the issue—nay, he is eager to meet his adversary. "Take ye away the stone!" The attendants had already laid their hands upon it when Martha interposed: "Nay, Lord, he hath been dead four days; by this time there is corruption." Death? corruption? dust? What are these to the Sovereign of Life? "Did I not tell thee, Martha, that if thou wouldst believe, thou shouldst see the glory of God?" And then again, "Roll ye away the stone!"

It was done. A moment's prayer. Then the battle was joined. With a loud voice Jesus cried, "Lazarus, come forth!" See yonder in the far recesses of the tomb there are shadows moving. He comes this way, swathed in white, bound about his face with a napkin, moving with tardy, shuffling steps—a blind man groping his way from darkness to light; a dead man feeling his way to newness of life. "Quick; John! Peter! James! Why stand ye trembling and shivering? Unswathe his bandages, unbind the napkin about his face, loose him and let him go!"

So Lazarus returned among men. But of what he did, how he deported himself in the after time, we are as ignorant as of his former life. Did he ever speak, in answer to the eager questioning of his townsmen, of what he had seen and heard during those four days among the shades? Or had God in some manner sealed his lips? It is quite certain that those mysterious days had not been passed in unconsciousness. "Soul sleeping" has no place in reason or in common sense. "To-day shalt thou be with me in paradise" is the Master's word to the soul on the further borders of time. Lazarus had been somewhere mingling with the immortals, and we may venture to assume that the remembrance of that brief sojourn in the spiritual world was not without its influence on his after life.

The word of Jesus, "Come forth," had called him out of the land of shadows into a renewal of the common tasks of life among men. His friends, in response to the injunction, "Loose him and let him go," were given an opportunity of joining hands with Jesus in the induction of this man into newness of life.

I. *He came forth into the glorious liberty of the children of God.* But what does that mean—the glorious liberty of the children of God?

It means, to begin with, the liberty of truth. He is the free man whom the truth makes free. We are mistaken in attributing to the so-called freethinker a freedom which does not belong to those who pursue reverently and with due regard for the laws and limitations of thought, the quest of spiritual and eternal truth. The man who doubts is more or less bewildered, and bewilderment is not freedom, but bondage. The man who yields to prejudice is likewise not his own master. A Brahman, under bonds to observe the sanctity of law, was shown through the microscope a drop of water swarming with animalculae. He could drink no water henceforth without, as he supposed, perpetrating ten thousand murders at a draught. "Is there another microscope in this country?" asked he. On being assured that this was the only one, he broke it in pieces; and so, restoring himself to his former bondage under falsehood, rejoiced to call himself free. Such is human nature. Such is prejudice, but, O for a glimpse into eternity! When Lazarus returned, it was to an untrammelled franchise over all the thoroughfares of truth.

And he entered, also, into the liberty of duty. His conviction as to the great verities must have affected his life. Duty took upon itself a new significance and emphasis. He was henceforth free to do right. He was a citizen of the great Commonwealth which is organized under the Higher Law. Earth seemed small to him and heaven great. Wealth, pleasure, and the emoluments of earthly glory, were as the small dust of the balance in contrast with the great responsibilities which had revealed themselves to him. The tasks of a holy life were no more bondage, but joyous service. The things which had been difficult would now be easy. I have seen a little child lean over the taffrail, and with her slender fingers help the boatswain draw a bucket of water out of the ocean; and she found no difficulty at all until the burden came to the surface; then all her strength could not budge it. So all tasks are easy when we are working "in our element." To do the things of the kingdom is grievous bondage to those outside of the kingdom. But when we have realized the truth and importance of eternal things, then we rejoice in duty as the Master did when he said, "In the volume of the Book it is written of me, I rejoice to do thy will."

II. It may also be safely said that Lazarus in coming out of his old life, through a brief sojourn in eternity into a renewal of his earthly tasks, *entered upon a wise apprehension of the dignity of man.*

He must have regarded himself with an increased respect. If ever he had doubted his immortality, he could doubt no more. He knew whence he came and whither he was bound. He knew his place in the kingdom of truth and righteousness. The Scribes and Pharisees viewed him with suspicion and would have put him to death for his innocent part in this miracle. But what cared he? The Apostle Paul on one occasion was moved to say, with respect to certain criticisms which had been passed upon him, "Let no man trouble me; I bear about in my body the marks of the Lord Jesus." A glorious declaration of independence! He was branded with the stigmata of faithful service. Marks of the scourge, the callous marks of fetters on his wrists, bruises made by the shower of stones. He was entitled to the service-chevron. So Lazarus might say with an added emphasis, "I have been through the valley of the shadow. I have lain in the dungeon of the King of Terrors. I have worn the cerements of night. The pains of death are loosed. Trouble me not! I have looked with open eyes upon my destiny. I know my manhood; and mark me, if henceforth I quit myself not like a man."

And by the same token he was prepared to acknowledge the equal dignity of all his fellow-men. The adventitious circumstances by which men are placed on various levels were as nothing to him. Gold was sordid dust. Crowns were toys for children to play with. Manhood was everything. Here is the glory of the gospel. "The secret of Messiah is the secret of man."

The great manifesto of human equality was that which Paul uttered by divine inspiration on Mars Hill: "God hath made of one blood all nations of men for to dwell upon the face of the earth." The best transcript ever made of that statement is in the preamble of our American Magna Charta: "All men are created free and equal and with certain inalienable rights." This, however, will not bear analysis. In point of fact all men are not created free; multitudes are born into a condition of natural servitude or under horrible bonds of inherited vice and disease and shame. Nor are all men created equal; multitudes are born inferior to their fellows in natural and inherited gifts; born dwarfs, idiots, hopeless paupers. So that if the proposition is to be regarded as true, it must be only as stated in its original form: all are of "one blood," and are therefore entitled to equal rights as children of God.

III. In his return from the grave Lazarus, moreover, *entered into the gospel of reconciliation; he came forth to the service of men.*

In view of his brief experience in the unseen world he must have understood thenceforth that salvation for himself was not a mere process of personal deliverance from death. In recognition of the possibilities of human nature it devolved upon him to bring others to a knowledge of truth. He saw men with his Master's eyes. He saw them as sheep without a shepherd. He could not leave them to their fate without an utmost endeavor to admonish and persuade them respecting the endless life.

You may never have observed the incompleteness of the first part of the "Pilgrim's Progress." In that great allegory the man who flees from the City of Destruction is represented as going alone, leaving his dear ones behind, and crying as he turned his back on the former things, "Life! Life! Eternal life!" Alone he pursues his journey, save as here and there he falls in with fellow-travellers intent like himself on a personal salvation, until he passes through the gate into the City of God. Not so does the Christian life appear to those who have caught its spirit from an intimate acquaintance with the unseen or from the example of the Christ. "They that be wise, shall shine as the brightness of the firmament; and they that turn many to righteousness, as the stars forever and ever." And John Bunyan was not unmindful of this fact, for the sequel tells of the pilgrimage of Christiana and her children.

The reconciliation of the gospel, however, is not merely a restoration of right relations between men and God; it is a gospel of peace on earth and good-will among men. On January 1st, 1863, with a stroke of his pen, President Lincoln liberated four millions of slaves. It was an infinitely grander deed that was accomplished on Calvary when Jesus cried, "It is finished!" There was a rattling of broken chains in that instant over all the earth and down along the ages. Here was the great at-one-ment, not only of man with God, but of man with his fellow-men, in the consummation of which all wrongs shall ultimately be righted. Swords shall be beaten into ploughshares and spears into pruning hooks, and peace shall reign from the river unto the ends of the earth.

As you walk about the streets of Paris you may

see upon the walls of churches, palaces, legislative halls, everywhere, these cabalistic words: *"Liberty, Equality, Fraternity!"* What memories gather about them. They recall the Reign of Terror, the Medicis, the Girondists, the Bastile, the guillotine, mobs, murders and conflagrations, the turnings and overturnings of long despair and a last futile struggle. There is nothing, or next to nothing, to show for it. Yet those words represent the deepest, highest, divinest longings of man in his relations with his fellow-men.

It will be observed that the new world of Lazarus to which he returned from those mysterious days of absence, was represented by these truths: Liberty, Equality, Fraternity; that is to say, the glorious liberty of the children of God, a wise apprehension of the true dignity of man, and the gospel of reconciliation. The world in which we are living, will in the Golden Age be dominated by these truths. And the years of history are hastening on to this consummation.

What the violence of the dreadful period of the French Revolution and of all wars and convulsions have not been able to accomplish, is being brought about by the calm operation of the gospel of peace. If it were proposed to bring down Gibraltar to the level of the sea by the use of gunpowder, it would be regarded as the fancy of an unsettled brain; but the atmosphere and sunlight are doing that very thing. Slowly, silently they are crumbling the mighty rock and sifting it into the sea. So is the gospel doing its work. Wars, tumults, revolutions, play their part in the age-long problem; but it is the power of the sunlight that gathers about the cross and of the atmosphere that emanates from that stupendous manifestation of infinite love, that will ultimately bring about the restitution of all things.

Let us rejoice meanwhile that we are chosen to co-operate in this work. "Roll ye away the stone," said Jesus to his disciples; not because he could not have himself attended to that small task, but he would enlist their service. "Loose him and let him go," he said; he could himself have unwound the bandages, but that is not his way of doing things. He is saving the world through us. There are multitudes of souls awakening to the glory of the better life—moving, like Lazarus, with slow, uncertain, tottering steps from darkness to light. His word to every one of his followers is, "Lend a hand. Loose them and let them go." Why stand we idle at the grave's mouth? We cannot regenerate, we cannot quicken from the dead; but we can suffer the Master to use us. The great Emancipator speaks. Unbind the cerements! This is practical "Altruism." This is the work of all true believers. So may we help our Master in accomplishing the restoration of the race to the glory of God.

THE GENEALOGY OF JESUS.

"The book of the genealogy of Jesus Christ."—MATT. I. 1.

It is a significant fact that the genealogy of Jesus is given twice in the Gospels, to-wit; by St. Matthew and St. Luke. We think it dry reading—this catalogue of names variously spelled and not easy to pronounce; but there is a sufficient reason for it.

"All Scripture given by inspiration is profitable." We readily concede this as applied to certain favorite portions of Holy Writ, such as the twenty-third Psalm, the story of a pilgrim coming out of the wilderness leaning on his beloved; the fifty-third of Isaiah, a splendid foregleam of the coming of Messias; the fourteenth of John, the home-bringing of God's children; the thirteenth of first Corinthians, "Now abide faith, hope and charity, and the greatest of these is charity;" the fifteenth of first Corinthians, life and immortality brought to light. But the statement applies with equal force to all other portions of Scripture; and notably to this genealogical table which is as dry as Homer's catalogue of ships.

I. We may learn from this genealogical table that *the Christian religion centers in a personality*. At this point it is differentiated from all other religions. Observe,

(1) It does not principally consist in a creed; that is to say, a system of formulated truths. It must not be inferred from this, however, that doctrines are unimportant. At this moment the people of America are discussing with great interest and earnestness the Monroe Doctrine; for the defense of which it has appeared possible that we may be plunged into war with our brethren beyond the sea. Let us pray that this may not be the outcome. Indeed war is unlikely for two reasons, namely; England cannot afford it and America cannot afford it. Let this, however, be said, that the so-called Monroe Doctrine—a formulation of the truth that the great powers beyond the Atlantic must not interfere with the integrity of American States and governments—represents a principle which is of vital importance to the welfare and perpetuity of our Republic. Is it not strange, however, that while all our people are practically united in recognition of this political "Doctrine" there should be such a general disposition to deny the importance of "doctrines" in the far higher realm of spiritual things?

(2) Neither does our religion place its fundamental emphasis upon a moral code. It offers indeed the only perfect ethical system in the world; consisting, in brief, of the Decalogue and the Sermon on the Mount; the latter being Christ's exposition of the former. No man can be a true follower of Christ without recognizing the importance of these rules of conduct and adjusting his life and character to them. Nevertheless the heart of Christianity is deeper than this. Buddhism boasts of an elaborate system called "The Noble Eight-fold Path;" touching every possible or conceivable relation of human life. But it

begins and ends in selfishness. There is no spiritual uplift in it.

(3) Nor shall we find the essence of Christianity in ritual. The teaching of our Lord Jesus is very distinct upon this point. He denounced the hypocrisy of the Scribes and Pharisees because, while outwardly blameless and most scrupulous as to the observance of the rites and ceremonies of Israel, they were quite devoid of inward spiritual life. He took occasion to wipe out of existence, with a wave of his hand, the whole ceremonial system of the Old Economy, on the ground that it was fulfilled in the Gospel. In so doing, he preserved the memory of that system, with all that it contained of value, in two simple sacraments, namely; Baptism and the Lord's Supper. And in establishing these sacraments—the former to take the place of all purifications, the latter of all sacrifices—he was careful to prescribe the utmost simplicity in their observance. We, therefore, recognize the importance of these rites, but only in their proper place as incidental to the great underlying and indwelling life of Christianity.

This life of Christianity is in a personal relation of the soul with Jesus Christ. He is Alpha and Omega; the first and last letters of the alphabet of life and character. He is the beginning of all high purpose and splendid hope; the end of all true ambition and holy endeavor. He is first, last, midst, and all in all.

II. We learn again from this genealogical table that *Jesus, as the living centre of Christianity, was "very man of very man."* He was of common blood and lineage with those whom he came to redeem. We shall find his divinity brought out clearly in other portions of Scripture as "very God of very God;" but at this point the distinct emphasis is put upon the fact that he took part of our human nature. And this it would appear was necessary to the accomplishment of his work.

God might have revealed himself indeed in angelic form, as when he stood before Joshua with drawn sword announcing himself as Captain of the host. He might possibly have manifested his divine glory without the intervention of fleshly form. He might have withdrawn the curtains of heaven and appeared in glory, seated upon his throne. But in that event men, corrupted by sin and disabled for such bright visions, would have fled affrighted before him, calling upon the rocks and the hills to cover them. He might possibly have come as the Gnostics and Docetists thought, as the mere inhabitant of a fleshly form without the assumption of human nature—a theophany whose human appearance was a mere phantom. But this is not the doctrine of the incarnation. The fact of the incarnation is that God so assumed a fleshly body as that Godhood and manhood were blended into a single personality, woven in warp and woof of the Theanthropic Christ.

It is not easy to conceive how otherwise he could so have entered into fellowship with humanity as to accomplish its deliverance from sin. It is said of Warren Hastings that he lived only to repair the lost fortunes of his family. He was the son of a village clergyman. As a lad he stood in the doorway of his father's house and looked out on the vast estate as far as his young eyes could see and remembered that these had belonged to his fathers. He resolved then that he would yet be Hastings of Daylesford; and through all his long life he pursued that resolution with dauntless will and courage. Macaulay says: "When under a tropical sun he ruled over fifty millions of Asiatics, his hopes, amid all the cares of war, finance and legislation, still pointed to Daylesford. And when his long public life, so singularly checkered with good and evil, with glory and obloquy, had at length closed forever, it was to Daylesford that he returned to die." So the only begotten Son of God entered into fellowship with us that he might retrieve the fortunes of the family name. He purposed to buy back the heritage which was ours by birth but had been squandered through sin. He took our name, he assumed our blood, in order that he might become our Goël, our Daysman. He became flesh of our flesh, bone of our bone; taking not on him the nature of angels, but of men. He paid the ransomed price on Calvary and restored the glory of man.

III. It is made to appear from this genealogical list that *Jesus was of noble ancestry*. It need scarcely be said that this was not for the mere purpose of blazoning his name. There is no more frivolous business in this world than tuft-hunting.

> "Honor and shame from no condition rise,
> Act well your part, there all the honor lies."

There was, however, a special reason for establishing the legitimacy of Jesus. An inheritance was involved and the succession to a throne. If Jesus is to be recognized as the Messiah, three points must be distinctly shown. First; He must be in the direct line of David. The promise given to David was that the sovereignty should abide in his family until the coming of Emmanuel, in whom the ultimate hope of

Israel should be fulfilled. In this genealogy it is made to appear that Jesus was the son of David. Second; It must be shown that he was descended in an unbroken line from Abraham. For the covenant with Abraham was this, "In thy seed shall all the nations of the earth be blessed." At this point also the messianic claim of Jesus is unimpeached and unimpeachable; he is the son of Abraham. Third; As he is to be an universal Saviour and King of the whole human race, his lineage must be traced to Adam. This also is made clear. He vindicates his title as Son of Man.

IV. *There are some names in this lineage which are obviously no better than they ought to be.* Here is Ruth, a Moabitess; outside of the Commonwealth of Israel and belonging to a tribe forbidden to enter God's house unto the tenth generation. Here is Rahab, the harlot, and of the abominable seed of the Canaanites. Here is Bath-sheba, the wife of Uriah, co-parcener with David in his dreadful sin. Here is Ahaz, a gross idolater who required his own children to pass through the fires. Here is Manasseh, who was transported to Babylon to wear out, in a shameful bondage, the penalty of his misdeeds. Here is Amon, one of the very basest of kings, who was murdered by his servants. Strange links these in the genealogical chain of the Messiah. Why are these incorporated here?

(1) Perhaps to teach that he who would establish his birthright must take the units of succession as they come. Those who are beggars of the past cannot be choosers of their blood. We would probably be slow to utter Burns' words:

> "My ancient but ignoble blood
> Has crept through scoundrels ever since the flood."

Nevertheless it is greatly to be doubted if there is a living man who can trace his lineage backward without discovering any taint of dishonor. And even at this point Jesus, as the Son of Man, became our fellow. The mixed blood of good, bad and indifferent people flows through his veins.

(2) It means moreover that wicked people have a place in the divine economy. They cannot block the divine purpose but are used and overruled so as to accomplish God's glory. Some of our young Endeavorers have recently united in prayer for one of our notorious infidels. The wisdom of so doing is called in question. No promise is given that prayer shall be answered for the gratification of a whim. One soul is of no more value than another soul. Nevertheless all prayer is answered as God deems wisest and best. He forced Sennacherib to serve his own great purpose and said, "I will put my hook in his nose and my bridle in his lips and will lead him back by the way that he came." No doubt some of those who are named in this genealogical table of Jesus would have been glad, if the matter had been submitted to them, to prevent the coming of the Christ. But they were not consulted. God simply used them. They had a place in his general plan. "He maketh the wrath of men to praise him."

(3) The occurrence of these names gives us also to understand that no man is a mere creature of heredity or circumstance. The blood of evil ancestry flowed in the veins of the Nazarene, but he was superior to it. Heredity is indeed a momentous fact, but it is not entitled to a small fraction of the importance

which is assigned to it in moral and material therapeutics. A man is arrested for theft and brought before our civil courts; his attorney searches among his ancestors and discovers that some of them were guilty of theft, and immediately enters this fact as an extenuating plea; and his client is cleared as a kleptomaniac. He is not a kleptomaniac; he is a thief. A man acquires the drinking habit and disgraces himself; a search is made along his pedigree, and it is discovered that he has inherited his taste for liquor; so he is pronounced a dipsomaniac. All rubbish! He is not a dipsomaniac, but a plain drunkard. The fact is that if the taint of ancestral blood could be justly entered as an extenuation for ill-doing, we should all be exculpated. But, blessed be God, we have in the grace of Jesus Christ power over both heredity and environment, and the test of true manhood is to prove one's self superior to them. Every man is, under God, the architect of his own fortune. Every man, be he saint or sinner, is a self-made man.

V. *The length of this genealogical table marks the fulness of time.* There is not a name too few or too many. It was said by Napoleon that the Austrians were defeated at the battle of Rivoli "because they were not on the minute." God is never too early, never too late. He never hurries, yet is he not slack concerning his promise.

The time represented by this succession of names was some thousands of years. Meanwhile the world was waiting for Christ. The hearts of the faithful were agonizing for his advent. Souls were perishing in multitudes, groping after truth and passing out into the endless night. How long, O Lord? how long? But there were reasons for this long delay.

A three-fold preparation was necessary for the coming of the Christ. The Jews, as the chosen people, were entrusted with the work of leavening the nations with monotheism; and they were doing it. The Greeks must perfect themselves in the philosophic method and must formulate a language for the expression of spiritual truths; and they were doing it. The Romans must conquer the earth and cast up an highway for the coming of the King; and they were doing it. The roads which were built to the remotest corners of the earth were supposed to be for the convenience of Cæsar and his armies, but in God's purpose they were for the coming of Messiah and the speeding of his messengers with the tidings of life. As soon as this three-fold preparation had been accomplished, the signal was given and the angels sang their advent song: "Glory to God in the highest, peace on earth, good will toward men."

All history—from chaos to the Christian Era—Eden, the Deluge, the Confusion of Tongues, the Egyptian bondage, the Deliverance, the Conquest of the promised Land; rural life, pastoral life, city life, royalty, yeomanry, handicraft, braincraft, statecraft; Egypt, Assyria, Babylon, Medo-Persia, Rome; legend, tradition, chronicle—all history passes before us, in this genealogical table, on its way toward Bethlehem where it finds in the Christ-child the consummation of all.

The most extensive river course on earth is the Amazon, which rises among the Andes and, flowing along a channel of about four thousand miles, empties itself just under the Equator into the sea. Its current is perceptible two hundred miles out in the ocean and the tides are felt through an upward course of four thousand miles. It waters a valley of not less than two million five hundred thousand square miles. In all that area there is not a river, not a brook, not a fountain gushing from the hills which does not pour itself into the Amazon and flow onward into the sea. In like manner all the history of the early ages, its war and peace, its vicissitudes of men and nations, lead up to the coming of the Christ.

VI. *The name of Jesus marks the end of the family line.* He suffered the greatest sorrow that could befall a son of Israel in that he lived and died a childless man. So it was prophesied; "He shall be taken from prison and from judgment: and who shall declare his generation? For he shall be cut off out of the land of the living." Had he then no posterity? No sons nor daughters?

Read on in the prophecy: "It pleased the Lord to bruise him; he hath put him to grief: when thou shalt make his soul an offering for sin, he shall see his seed, he shall prolong his days, and the pleasure of the Lord shall prosper in his hand. He shall see of the travail of his soul, and shall be satisfied." Children? O yes; an innumerable multitude. The old lineage was indeed cut off; but *Anno Domini* marks the divisional point in the history of the race. A new family line begins. Jesus is the refounder of humanity, the second Adam, the first born among many brethren.

Read again in this prophecy: "For ye shall go out with joy and be led forth with peace. The mountains and the hills shall break forth before you into singing, and all the trees of the field shall clap their hands. Instead of the thorn shall come up the fir tree, and instead of the brier shall come up the myrtle tree; and it shall be to the Lord for *a name, for an everlasting sign that shall not be cut off.*" Aye, an undying name; an endless posterity! Souls like the fluttering leaves of Vallombrosa. Trees clapping their hands; mountains singing; the gladness of a regenerated race. And up in heaven a voice like the sound of many waters. Souls redeemed; ten thousand times ten thousand and thousands of thousands.

> "One family we dwell in him,
> One church above, beneath,
> Though now divided by the stream,
> The narrow stream of death."

It is our privilege—and higher privilege there cannot be—to belong to the new family line which was thus begun in Jesus the Christ. It is recorded that on one occasion, when he was preaching and a great multitude were gathered about him, a message was brought, "Thy mother and thy brethren (that is, kinsmen, probably his cousins) stand without desiring to speak with thee." It was at a critical time in his ministry; these kinsmen loved him; they perceived that he was involving himself in danger and were deeply perplexed and anxious for him. They would save him from impending evil and bring him back, if possible, to the quiet of his Nazareth home. But it was too late. The die was cast; the Rubicon had been crossed. The shadow of Calvary was over him. They had never quite understood his mission; how he must be about his Father's business. He could not, therefore, hearken to them at this juncture. His words were: "Who is my mother and who are my brethren? Whosoever shall do the will of my Father which is in heaven, the same is my mother, my brother, my sister."

What does this mean? Blood is indeed thicker than water; but there is no earthly bond of consanguinity so strong or precious as that which binds together those who believe in the Christ and follow him. This mystic bond is set forth in the parable of the vine and the branches; we dwell in Christ and Christ dwelleth in us. He is not ashamed to call us brethren. We are members of his body, of his flesh and of his bone. In him we are received by adoption into that great household which finds its shibboleth of unity in those sweet words, "Abba Father." "Now are we the Sons of God and it doth not yet appear what we shall be." How all personal kinship dwindles in view of this glorious truth. Far better to be of this lineage than of the line royal. Far better to inherit its wealth than that of all earth's multi-millionaires. Sons of God! "And if sons, then heirs, heirs of God and joint heirs with Jesus Christ to an inheritance incorruptible, undefiled, and that fadeth not away."

ARMAGEDDON.

"And he gathered them together in a place called in the Hebrew tongue Armageddon."—Rev. xvi, 16.

It would be foreign to our purpose to enter into the controversy as to the precise location of Armageddon. Place is neither here nor there. The important point is, that there is to be ultimately somewhere a great decisive conflict between the powers of good and evil; the outcome of which will be the complete overthrow of the Prince of Darkness and the undisputed reign of our Lord and Saviour Jesus Christ.

There is a considerable number of eminently good people who believe that the world is going from bad to worse, that the Church is being more and more honeycombed with worldliness and that the present order of things will end in a shipwreck out of which a few superexcellent saints will escape like the crew at Melita "on boards and broken pieces of the ship." But the great majority of Christians do not share in this melancholy outlook. They are not unmindful of the fact that the Evil One clings with a tenacious grip to his dominion; but they clearly see that there has been a sure, constant, uninterrupted progress in truth and righteousness from the beginning of the

Christian era, and they have faith to believe that the Sun of Righteousness will shine upon this sin-stricken world brighter and brighter until the perfect day.

> For right is right, since God is God;
> And right the day must win;
> To doubt would be disloyalty,
> To falter would be sin.

But why, it is asked, has not God arrested the power of evil? Why did he not long ago put an end to the dominion of the Prince of Darkness? For the same reason that a surgeon allows a felon to come to a head before he lances it. God does nothing except in the fulness of time.

A cursory glance at current events will make it appear that the malignant forces at work on earth are growing more and more desperate, and are displaying themselves in most hateful and abominable forms. It is this very fact which will precipitate the ultimate conflict and put a final end to the power of the Evil One. The Prophet Daniel says that the end of the present æon is to be marked as "a time of trouble." Christ says, "Ye shall hear of wars and rumors of wars; nation shall rise against nation, and kingdom against kingdom; and there shall be earthquakes and famines and troubles; these are the beginnings of sorrows." And again, "There shall be great tribulation, such as was not from the beginning of the world nor ever shall be."

The captains of the contending armies in the great conflict are the beast—a most characteristic term—and the Lamb, that is to say, "the Lamb of God slain from the foundation of the world" who is elsewhere called, Faithful and True, making war in righteousness, clothed with a vesture dipped in blood. The former is followed by a great multitude, bearing on their foreheads "the mark of the beast"; the latter by a greater multitude of such as bear the name of Jesus and have the love of truth and righteousness enshrined in their hearts. The contending armies meet with a shock that staggers the heavens and the earth. When the smoke of the conflict clears away, the armies of Christ are in possession of the field; a cry is heard, "Babylon the great is fallen, is fallen!" and amid a sound of rattling of chains, the beast and his followers are hurled into the pit and "the smoke of their torment ascendeth up."

To this event all history has been tending through the centuries, and the Prince of Darkness is hastening it by his desperate designs. He is fulfilling the prophecy that evil men and seducers shall wax worse and worse, and that wickedness shall abound more and more until the last time. As truth and righteousness increase in potency so much the more does the beast oppose them; he is ever doing his worst and utmost to interrupt the calm progress of Christ. When the tension has reached its last degree, then will come Armageddon. The ultimate demonstration of evil on earth will be like that of the unclean spirit, of which it is written, "He tare the man before he came out of him."

In pursuance of this thought it will be profitable to mark the manifestations of evil in these last days; and then on the other hand to observe some of the sure tokens of the triumph of Christ.

1. Let us note at the outset *the aggravated forms of Avarice which prevail in these days.* This is the Drama of the Street. You may stand upon the corner any-

where and perceive it in the restless eye, the wrinkled brow, the eager step of those who pass by. *Auri sacra fames!* It is not to be observed merely in the increased power of grasping monopolies; it is not the sin of the rich alone; but the humbler people, handicraftsmen, the very beggars with their hands stretched out, are addicted to it. The horse leech's daughters are everywhere crying, "Give! Give!" At this moment seven thousand Jews in this city are suffering from a "lockout." Jews from Bohemia, Servia, Roumania, Russia—thin, haggard, hungry, patient toilers, who beg for the privilege of working ten hours a day, with their needles, for one dollar or less. All that they want, is enough to keep body and soul together. And why not? Because there are middlemen—"sweaters"—of their own kith and kin who, unmindful of their ancestral laws as to oppression, are grinding the life out of these poor men. Here is but a symptom of an awful malady which affects the race. The scramble for wealth is universal, with all its attending selfishness and brutality. There never has been a time in history when it was more malignant or more manifest than just now.

2. Observe also *the defiant front of Intemperance in our time.* It is organized anarchy; an open and flagrant defiance of all law, human and divine. It is the enemy of our home-life, our social life, our political life. It devours the wealth of our republic at the rate of one billion two hundred million dollars per annum. It consumes the wages of a vast multitude of our workingmen, depriving their families of the common means of livelihood and exposing them to unspeakable shame and distress. An employer in this vicinity, in order to test the question as to

what proportion of his workmen's wages was squandered in drink, recently paid his hands on Saturday night in marked bills. The total amount which they received was seven thousand dollars, of which four thousand one hundred dollars was passed into the hands of rum-sellers by those who received it. Who shall portray the want and sorrow involved in that fact! Just now it is stated that the liquor men of the State of New York have contributed a large sum of money wherewith to influence the legislation of the Assembly which is about to convene. They can afford to do it, for this Legislature is arranging to amend our Excise Laws. These are mere intimations of the desperate power of this organized evil. It was never so brazen, never so defiant, since the beginning of time.

3. *As to Sensuality.* We recall with horror how the Virgin Mary was torn from her shrine above the high altar in Notre Dame in the Reign of Terror, to give place to a courtesan to whom were paid divine honors. But was that worse than the movement in behalf of uncleanness which we observe in our social life to-day? Look into the books upon your table written by Hardy, Du Maurier and the like. Run down the amusement column of the newspapers and see how lust, passion, carnality, are holding revel in these days. The bestial man and neurotic woman go reeling and smirking hand in hand along our streets. The mark of the beast is on their foreheads. Poppæa of the Roman court, Aspasia of Athens, Pompadour of the time of Louis XV. are outdone. And, alas! many of the mothers and daughters among us are wittingly or unwittingly surrendering themselves unblushingly to the shame of the carnival. "Public sentiment" favors it.

4. Another of the current forms of malignant evil is *Bibliophobia, or hatred of the Scriptures as the Word of God.* This is the fashionable form of infidelity. God is no longer denied; atheism is out of fashion. Christ is no longer rejected; no, fulsome adulation of Christ is the order of the day. The Church is no longer assailed; the Church is a great institution, a splendid organism for humanitarian effort. But the Scriptures, which are the very citadel of the Christian religion, are assailed with unparalleled fury; and the worst of this movement is that its force comes from within the Church of God. The enemies of the Bible are not avowed atheists and unbelievers; they are Biblical exegetes, whose assaults upon inspiration are met with plaudits from many who profess to be the followers of Christ.

It is said that Agamemnon, king of Greece, besieged Troy for ten weary years without avail; then making a wooden horse, he filled its capacious belly with armed men, and introduced it into the beleagured city; the bolts were drawn and Troy fell. It is by a similar strategem that the enemy assails the stronghold of Christianity to-day. Wheel in the Trojan horse—into the pulpit, into the theological chair, into the Sabbath school, into the Christian home. In this manner the Adversary hopes to destroy the power of the Word of God.

5. *Sabbath Desecration.* Here again the assault upon the power of the Christian religion is in most specious and malignant form; and it comes not from without, but from within the Church. We view with consternation the covert assault made upon the American Sabbath in our legislatures by propositions to legalize various forms of labor and amusement, as well as

the rum traffic, on that day. But the real danger lies in the sentiment of Christian people. There is an outcry against the Puritan Sabbath. There is a disposition to hold that the requirements of the Fourth Commandment are met by a cessation of toil. "Why should we not have the Continental Sabbath, in which men and women lend themselves to the pleasures of the drama and musical entertainment?" It should be remembered, however, that the divine law calls not merely for rest from labor, but also from doing our own pleasure on the Lord's day. Are we to conclude that we have wrought a real deliverance of our laboring classes from the bondage of their secular life, when we have liberated them from the workshop, only to let them loose into the dissipations of the wine-shop and the beer garden, there to squander their earnings which should be given to the replenishing of the oil in the cruise and the meal in the barrel? Nay, it were far better if men were required to toil seven days in every week and three hundred and sixty-five days in every year. Far better never to rest, rather than to rest in pleasures and dissipations which destroy the real sanctions and all the just benefits of the Sabbath. The Fourth Commandment begins with the word, "Remember"; this suggests the danger of forgetting. In this new phase of Christian sentiment, with respect to the Sabbath, we observe again the craft and the desperation of the Power of Evil.

6. *As to Persecution.* We thought that the days of persecution had gone by: but we have lived to see in this Nineteenth Century of boasted Christian civilization, such an outburst of malignant hatred against Christianity as the world never witnessed. It is esti-

mated that one hundred thousand of the Armenians are slain and thousands more reduced to beggary. Nero kindling his living torches, the bones of the Waldenses "scattered on the Alpine mountains cold," the horrors of St. Bartholomew's day, are outdone. And while all this is going on the great Christian powers of Europe stand idly by. Not a hand is uplifted to save the persecuted nation from this fiendish violence.

Let us hear a parable : A certain nation fell among thieves, thugs and murderers, who stripped it of raiment and wounded it and departed leaving it half dead. And by chance the Christian Czar of Russia came down that way and he saw this wounded nation and said, "I would gladly help were it possible, but I cannot risk the possibility of gaining a seaport on the Mediterranean"; and he passed by on the other side. And likewise the Christian war-lord of Germany came that way and he said, "Alas! here is a melancholy sight and I would fain help, but I must needs remember Alsace and Lorraine and the people beyond who await an opportunity of falling upon me"; and he passed by on the other side. And likewise the Christian Queen of England came that way and she said, "Woe is me! Here is a dire calamity for Christian eyes to gaze upon. I would that it were possible for me to help, but I must needs protect my Colonies, collect my opium tax, defend my commerce"; and she passed by on the other side. And the wounded nation lay weltering in blood and crying and wailing, "Is there none among the Christian nations to bind up my wounds, to pour in oil and wine and to bring me to an inn?" And, alas, there was none. There was no eye to pity and no arm to save! And the Power of Evil smiled with satisfaction as he beheld it.

7. *War.* The most horridly repulsive of the dragon's heads is war. We have been saying all along that because of the developments of Christian civilization, war between the great nations of the earth was impossible. Yet how near we have been to it! A war that would have set the two greatest of Christian nations against each other. A war in which probably all the important governments of Europe would have been directly or indirectly involved as well as the lesser governments of America. Has it been averted? Shall it be averted? If so, it will not be by any sentimental consideration of an alleged kinship between the American and English people. William Watson, candidate for the appointment of Poet Laureate, has published the following appeal to the people of the United States:

> " O towering daughter, Titan of the West!
>   Behind a thousand leagues of foam secure;
>   Thou toward whom our inmost heart is pure
> Of ill intent, although thou threatenest
> With most unfilial hand thy mother's breast:
>   Not for one breathing space may earth endure
>   The thought of war's intolerable cure
> For such vague pains as vex to-day thy breast."

But England is not the mother, and America is not the daughter. We are not an English people. The smallest strain of blood that flows in America's veins is English blood. Our laws, our institutions, are not English. The most that can be said is that we speak a kindred dialect of an ancient Germanic tongue.

Nor if this war is to be averted, will it be

by any sentimental appeal to the magnanimity of England. That, by the record of history, is wholly a fabulous factor, or at best an infinitesimal quantity in the problem. When have we had national experience of the magnanimity of England? At the time of the Stamp act? During the War of 1812? During the long and awful period of our Civil War? In our contention respecting the cod fisheries or the seal fisheries? In our contention respecting Alaska or the Nicaragua Canal? In our commercial relations? Never once.

Nor, if this war is to be averted, will it be by a surrender of our just cause. The Monroe Doctrine is the expression of a principle which is bound to be vindicated sooner or later; because it is right, and because it is absolutely necessary to the welfare and perpetuity of our Republic. There is a "balance of power" on the other side of the Atlantic which is accounted necessary to the preservation of peace. The great powers over yonder would not for a moment tolerate an encroachment on one another's rights or possessions. The Monroe Doctrine is simply an expression of the same principle on this side of the water. The balance of power here must be preserved; and certainly the United States, as the overwhelmingly greatest of American governments, can tolerate no encroachment from beyond the sea.

But if this war is to be averted, it will be by virtue of two considerations: *First,* We are afraid. Both parties to the controversy are afraid. So much of blood and treasure is involved! And *second,* The determining factor in the argument will be, must be, a Christian consideration. Both England and America recognize the power of Christian truth, of the spirit of our Lord, of the Golden Rule. This appeals with tremendous power to our sober second thought. It expresses itself specifically in the term "arbitration." It is a noteworthy fact that just when the war excitement was at its warmest, when we were reckoning up our fleets and armies and exchequers with a view to the awful contingency, there came an interruption. The Christmas-tide was here; the song of Bethlehem was heard: "Glory to God in the highest, peace on earth and good will to men."

We have spoken of the forces of evil at work for the disturbance of men and nations. These are foretokens of Armageddon. The tension grows tighter and tighter. The signal may be given at any moment that will plunge the nations into an universal conflict. There is a moment in the history of a snow-drift on the Alps when the mighty mass is poised for its plunge. The bleating of a lost kid, the scream of an eagle, the scurrying of a rodent from its hole may disturb the mass; and then the avalanche.

Let us turn now to the brighter side. If the beast has been manifesting his power in a desperate effort to retain the dominion of the world, the Lamb, the champion of truth and righteousness, has not been inactive. The world has been growing better constantly and Christ has been distancing his foe. It will be sufficient, without entering into detail as to the various manifestations of the power of the gospel, to indicate a few points which mark the certain triumph of Christ.

1. *The Scriptures as divine truth have a deeper hold than ever on the hearts of Christian people.* It has not been for nothing that all the powers of adverse criticism in the Church and outside of it, have been

brought to bear for years upon the Word. The lights have been turned on. The knife of destructive criticism has been ruthlessly applied to the Book. The corrosive acid of irreverence has been poured over its pages. And the Scriptures have come forth out of the fierce ordeal as gold seven times tried. No praise to those who have assailed the oracles; God hath made the wrath of men to praise him.

It is as when the Philistines carried away the Ark of the Covenant from the battle of Ebenezer. They brought it into the house of Dagon, and on the next morning, lo, Dagon had fallen on his face before it. They replaced their idol upon its pedestal; and on the next morning again he had fallen upon his face and his head and the palms of his hands were cut off. In capturing this symbol of the divine presence, the Philistines were now beginning to realize that they had undertaken more than they could manage. In their city of Ashdod the people were afflicted with a painful malady. Their homes were filled with shame and misery, so that the cry of the city went up to heaven. The Ark of the Covenant was too much for them. What should they do with it? They sent it back to Israel.

In like manner God has been pleased to bring to naught the machinations of men who hope to overthrow his Word. The old Book is cherished as it never was cherished before; is studied more earnestly; is believed in more cordially. "The Word of the Lord is tried." It has been vindicated, triumphantly vindicated as a true volume from beginning to end. In this we behold a token of God's special providence; for what can his Church do without the Scriptures? It is vain to contend with the

Adversary unless we can hold in our right hand the Sword of the Spirit which is the Word of God.

2. *Christ is served in his Church more loyally and effectively than ever.* We have a new conception of church membership to-day. The time was when to be a member of the Church meant little more than a name on the roster, an interest in social communion, a sense of salvation from death, and then to sit and sing one's self away to everlasting bliss. But a mighty change has transpired. To-day church membership means, above all, an individual responsibility for service. We are living in an epoch of organizations within the Church; the men, the women, the young people, the children, are banded together in leagues and committees and associations; the object of which is to assign a specific duty to every one.

In the days of Nehemiah the rebuilders of the wall toiled with weapon in one hand and trowel in the other; heeding not the taunts of Sanballat and Tobiah, since all alike were concerned in doing a great work "and could not come down." The secret of the success of those rebuilders is recorded in the words, "*So* built we the wall." In like manner the disciples of Christ are beginning to understand the importance of working each over against his own place.

The various denominations of believers are agreed as to essentials, tolerant as to non-essentials, and cordial in co-operating for the advancement of the kingdom. There is perfect harmony among them. The cry for Church union has given way to a more reasonable insistence on Christian union. There is indeed more of unity among the denominations to-day than there is between the various parties in the Roman Catholic Church or between the divisional sects in the Anglican Church. For this we praise God and take courage. We are approaching a realization of the dream of Wesley, "All at it, always at it, altogether at it."

3. *The personality and power of the Holy Ghost are recognized in the Church as never before.* We have a new conception of the Holy Spirit. It is not many years since the substance of controversy was Christological. To-day we are dwelling on the importance of honoring the Holy Ghost.

It is recorded that on a certain occasion Paul coming to Ephesus found a company of believers to whom he said, "Have ye received the Holy Ghost since ye believed?" They answered, "We have not so much as heard whether there be any Holy Ghost." Whereupon he laid his hands upon them, conferring the unspeakable gift, and straightway they began to speak with tongues and prophesied. It will be a great day for the Christian Church when the truth as to the Holy Spirit shall pervade all hearts.

We are living in the dispensation of the Holy Ghost. We are working under his supervision for the building up of the kingdom of Christ. The Bible is a meaningless book until he illumines its pages and touches our eyes that we may read and understand it. Christ is a mystery until he takes of the things of Jesus and shows them unto us. True service is out of the question until he quickens, enables and directs us. This is pre-eminently the age of the Holy Ghost and by the same token it is the epoch of missionary progress. We are living among the miracles of missions. Under the guidance of the Holy Ghost an army of messengers are going out in all directions to declare the riches of the Gospel and are meeting with unprecedented successes. This means Christ for the world and the world for Christ.

So have the two forces of good and evil been moving onward toward the final struggle and the consummation of all things. The times are ripe for momentous events. As the Nineteenth Century draws towards its close we find that, while wickedness grows worse and worse unto desperation, the Lord's army is more and more mobilized for the last march and the perpetual triumph.

In Mid-Summer Night's Dream the last degree of improbability is suggested when Puck declares

> "I'll put a girdle round the earth."

But the thing which seemed so distant and inconceivable has indeed been done. It is proposed to celebrate the incoming of the Twentieth Century by a circular commemoration of the birth of Jesus Christ; to begin at London and continue successively at Jerusalem, at Hong Kong, at Yokohama, at Honolulu, at San Francisco, eastward to New York and thence across the ocean to London; thus girdling the globe. While the followers of Christ have been lamenting the slow advance of his Gospel, he has been all along the centuries unceasingly accomplishing a splendid progress. The sun never sets on his dominions. The dream of Tennyson is almost realized when the earth shall be every way "bound as with gold chains about the feet of God."

It is not for us to speak definitely as to times and seasons, but when the signal shall be given for the last conflict and all nations shall have done their part at Armageddon, the lifting smoke will disclose a conclusive and perfect victory. Then the tabernacle of God shall come down among men and he will dwell among them and they shall be his people and God himself shall be their God.

THE STORY OF A WAYWARD YOUTH.

Luke 15, 1-24.

It is strange that no playwright has ever dramatized this Pearl of Parables. It contains a "plot" of surpassing interest, and unlikely to become superannuated, inasmuch as it is true to every age, and likely to occur among all sorts and conditions of men.

Scene I.—*The old home.* A farm cottage on the hills of Palestine. The proprietor is a well-to-do farmer with broad acres of pasturage for his abundant flocks and herds, and vineyards on the hill sides sloping toward the south. There are evidences of prosperity on every side. But the shadow of affliction is here; it is a motherless home. Possibly the story might have been different, had the loving, restraining hand of a mother been present. There are two sons, like Jacob and Esau. The elder is a thrifty, industrious, close-handed, narrow-minded youth; the younger is full of generous impulses, fond of companionship and pleasure, a bundle of undeveloped potencies, and is just coming of age.

To this younger son the old-fashioned home was like a cave of gloom. He was restive and discontented. He looked toward the hills and dreamed of the world beyond. He saw the caravans that wound their way along the thoroughfare on the distant heights, as they journeyed from Damascus to Egypt; and the bright apparel of the merchants and the gleaming trappings of the camels gave him a tantalizing glimpse into a larger life. He went up, perhaps, with his father and brother to the annual feasts at Jerusalem, and saw there the thronging multitudes from far distant lands, and sometimes princes and dignitaries; and the sight awoke within him a longing for independence,—a desire to see and touch the wondrous things that lay beyond the horizon of his life.

And he said unto his father, "Father, give me the portion of goods that falleth to me."

"Why so, my son; has anything gone wrong?"

"No, father, but I want to see the world. I cannot be a farmer's boy forever."

"But, my son, you are young still and there is time enough. The years are all before you."

"I know; but I am of age and I am entitled to it. I am not a boy any longer; let me have my way."

And he had his way. What is it the poet says? "A boy's will is the wind's will." The time has come for the youth's departure. I see him at the doorway. His brother has said, "Farewell." His sad-faced father has kissed the lad on either cheek and is giving his blessing in a broken voice: "The Lord bless thee, my son; the God of Israel be with thee!"

Down the road he goes with a long, swinging step, gaily apparelled, his wallet full of coin, humming cheerily to himself. At the turn of the road he looks backward and sees in the doorway a bowed figure which he will remember in the coming days. He waves his hand. Farewell! Free at last! Now for a joyous life; a glorious future. Farewell, old-fashioned home, discipline and bondage. Farewell, loved ones, homely peace and comfort. Farewell, boyhood and innocence. Farewell! Farewell!

Scene II.—*In the far country.* As far as possible from the old life. And here he enters upon his career at a rapid pace.

His first step downward is into bad company. There is no lack of companionship. The wolves are always ready when there is a lamb. But woe to the youth who thus enters upon his city life. "Can one touch pitch and not be defiled by it?" Or, "Can one take fire into his bosom and not be burned?" A man is like a tree-toad which takes its color from its surroundings; gray against the bark of an elm, green on the growing corn. A man is known by his companions. Our youth has chosen the "fast crowd." His friends are hail fellows well met.

The next downward step is into lawless pleasure; revels, carousals. He is sowing his wild oats. Let him take heed: "He that soweth the wind shall reap the whirlwind." Thousands in our city to-day are sowing, thousands are reaping the awful harvest.

In the time of the English Commonwealth it was customary to punish intemperance with "the drunkard's cloak." The culprit was placed in a barrel, with his head protruding from the top and holes for his arms on either side. In such guise he was compelled to walk about the streets. What a cooper's procession there would be on Broadway if that sort of penalty were inflicted now; old drunkards and young drunkards; sots, tipplers and topers; red-eyed and reeling.

It is said that Diogenes once met a young man on his way to a bacchanalian feast and fastening his arms about him, despite all resistance, carried him back to his friends. O would it were possible to carry back these thoughtless youths who are ruining their present and future alike, in drink, sensuality and the "pleasures of the green baize field"; would it were possible to carry them back to friends, to happy homes, to praying parents, to purity and hope!

"And when he had spent all, there arose a mighty famine in that land, and he began to be in want." His wallet was empty, his clothes were thread-bare, his substance was wasted. Wasted! Alas! that's the sorrow of it, the awful waste. His money was gone, but that was least of all. He had squandered his physical strength as well; his eyes were red and watery; his limbs were tremulous; his liver was out of order, his digestion bad; his nerves were unstrung; his breath polluted; his brain confused. He was incapacitated for the common tasks of life.—He had wasted his good name also. In vain did he apply for a situation. In every case he was asked for "credentials"; but who would give him credentials? All knew his record; none had confidence in him. It was hard times; situations were scarce; there were plenty of trustworthy young men.—And he had wasted his self-respect too. He knew himself to be a ne'er do weel. Purity and honesty and character were gone. It began to dawn upon him that he had played the fool.—He had wasted opportunity, also. What a splendid chance he had had of making something of himself, and he had lost it.—Moreover his friends were gone. He felt the pangs of hunger, and, approaching one of his former comrades, asked for the loan of a few farthings. "I am sorry," was the answer, "but I have nothing with me." One by one they shook him off. Friends! Fair-weather friends; they had squeezed him dry, poor fool; and had no further need of him. They no longer recognized him as they passed by. He had reached the end of his tether.

It was under circumstances like these that Lord Chesterfield said: "I have enjoyed all the pleasures of the world. I have been behind the curtain, have seen the dirty ropes and pulleys that work the machinery. I have smelled the guttering candles that furnish the illumination, to the amazement of the juvenile audience. And I am sick and tired of it."

Scene III.—*In the swine field.* "And he went and joined himself to a citizen of that country, who sent him into the fields to feed swine." A swine-herd —and he a Jew! But he had no alternative; beggars must not be choosers. It was that or starve.

So here he is. See him sitting on the trough; pale, haggard, in rags and tatters. Around him are the swine; the unclean things, the rooting, jostling wallowing, gluttonous things. Yet his situation is not so bad as it might be.

> " · · · Sweet are the uses of adversity;
> As night to stars, woe lustre gives to man."

There is something to be said for the swine field. God knows how to deal with the wayward, when to allow them to reach the very depths of shame. Time was when this young man had no taste for solitude; now it is forced upon him. He looks into his own face and sees himself in his proper guise. A fool, if ever there was one! There is nothing here to interrupt the current of his honest thoughts. His conscience is at work. And memory is at work too. He looks over his shoulder at the past. He gazes off toward the hills and recalls the old home life and how gaily he tripped away from it. "In my father's house," he says within himself, "there is bread enough and to spare, and I perish here with hunger." What pleasant days those were by the fireside; under the tree before the door-way; out in the fields harvesting, or among the flocks!

The boys who are away at boarding schools and those who have come to the great city to make their fortunes—who have begun at the foot of the ladder and are working up—get together in their social coteries and sing the old songs. It was so when we sat on the college fence through the evening and into the night. And why do we always drift into songs like this?

> "How dear to my heart are the scenes of my childhood,
>   When fond recollection presents them to view!
> The orchard, the meadow, the deep-tangled wildwood,
>   And every loved spot which my infancy knew."

Or this?

> "Those evening bells! those evening bells!
> How many a tale their music tells
> Of youth, and home, and that sweet time
> When last I heard their soothing chime!"

Or this?

> "'Way down upon the Swanee river,
>   Far, far away;
> There's where my heart is turning ever,
>   There's where the old folks stay."

Or this?

> "Oft in the stilly night,
>   Ere slumber's chain has bound me,
> Fond Memory brings the light
>   Of other days around me:
>   The smiles, the tears
>   Of bygone years,
>   The words of love then spoken;
>   The eyes that shone,
>   Now dimmed and gone,
>   The cheerful hearts now broken."

Or this—always this when the other songs were sung and we were breaking up?

> "'Mid pleasures and palaces though we may roam,
> Be it ever so humble, there's no place like home!
>   Home! home! sweet, sweet home!"

And as this youth in the swine-field thought and remembered there came to his mind the possibility of better things. All was not lost. He was a young man still. "The sun is not down," said Napoleon to his disheartened troops, "the sun is not down, there is time to win this battle yet." The wayward youth is coming to himself; he awakes from his miserable life, as from a bad dream. A resolve is born within him; he says, "I will"—What?

"I will turn over a new leaf. I will be faithful in my position as a swine-herd and work my way upward. I will ask no odds of anybody, but prove myself a man yet." No; this will not answer. He must get out of this country, away from his old associations. He must cut loose from the past.

"I will write home and see if my father still lives; and, if so, whether he would welcome me." No. His extremity is too great; his heart is too sore. His longing is too deep and honest.

"I will arise and go unto my father!" This is as it should be. There is good stuff in this youth; the stuff that men are made of.—And he arose and went.

It was not for nothing that God had suffered this young man to reach the very depths of despair. An English soldier, who had been wounded in one of the battles of Egypt and left behind on the march, lay under the shadow of a rock in the desert. He had given up heart and hope; but as he looked upward he saw a vulture circling about him and waiting, waiting for its prey. The sight drove him to quick resolve. He struggled to his feet and staggered on with a purpose to live. So does the prodigal betake himself from the swine-field with his face toward home.

Scene IV.—*On the journey.* A veritable tramp, ragged and haggard, staff in hand. It is a long journey. Would that he had not gone so far. But he trudges on, making up his speech as he goes: "I will say unto my father, Father, I have sinned against heaven and in thy sight. I am no more worthy to be called thy son; make me as thy hired servant." No place can be too humble for him, he thinks, even that of a door-keeper or a toiler in the fields. Why not? His part of the inheritance is wasted; the right of a son is no longer his.

Had he but known what had been happening meanwhile at the old home! His father had been waiting; not a night when he had not prayed for the return of his wayward son; not a morning when he did not stand in the doorway and look away toward the hills and move his lips until the mist came over his eyes. He had heard rumors of the lad's wild excesses in the far country. His heart was heavy, but he hoped against hope. Ah, if his son had only known!

The heart of the returning wanderer misgave him many a time. Would he receive a welcome? Was the game worth the candle? His father might be dead; his brother's heart might be hardened against him; but the youth trudged on. Aye, there is good stuff in him. It is this sort of experience that tries the soul of a man. So Milton, old and blind, his fondest hopes all blighted, wrote:

> "I argue not
> Against Heaven's hand or will, nor bate a jot
> Of heart or hope; but still bear up, and steer
> Right onward!"

The wanderer climbed a rock beside the highroad and saw in the distance his old home. The trees were there; the fields where he used to play. And then for a little,—weak, despondent, and half-famished,—the heart almost went out of him. But presently he arose, tightened his girdle and trudged on. It was in the after part of the day when he came out upon a slope fronting his home. He drew as near as he dared, trembling now in every limb, and paused. A thousand doubts, misgivings, eager hopes were struggling in his breast. He leaned upon the top of his staff, like Jacob of old, and wept and prayed.

In the door-way of the farm-house stood the old father, shading his eyes and looking off toward the hills. What was yon figure at the spur of the road? It was like his boy; but O so thin, so ragged, so hopeless in his attitude! Nevertheless he knew him. "Bring me my staff!" he cried, and down the path he staggered, his lips moving as he went, his eyes lifted now and then toward the height. The figure was still there, but "a great way off." As he comes near he begins to cry, "My son! my son!" He has fallen upon his neck and kissed him! And the youth is sobbing out—"O my father! I have sinned against heaven and in thy sight, and am no more worthy to be called thy son; make me—make me—"; but he cannot finish that fine speech;— there is that in his father's eyes which makes it impossible to finish it;—a lump comes up in his throat and checks him so that he cannot say, "as one of thy hired servants." Nay, he knows that he shall again be his father's son.

Is there anything like that in the dry disquisitions of the schools on the Divine Attributes? O no; but it is true; this is the loving God, the patient God, the waiting God, the forgiving God. He giveth us the spirit of adoption whereby we cry, Abba Father!

Scene V.—*At home again.* There is a fire in the great fireplace. The returning prodigal has satisfied his hunger and is clothed in comfortable garments. No questions are asked, for everybody knows. No explanations are offered; one word has told it all, "I have sinned." The pride has all gone out of this young man. He watches his father here and there, and notes the love-light in his eyes, and thinks, "How I wronged him!"

As twilight falls, the lights are kindled and the neighbors come in. There is to be a banquet. The fatted calf has been killed. There is music. The table is spread; they are taking their places; the wayward son is moving toward the foot of the table;

but his father leads him to the place of honor. There are shoes on his feet, the token of sonship; the best robe has been put upon him and a ring upon his hand,—the last degree of favor. The father speaks: "Neighbors, rejoice with me; this my son was dead and is alive again, he was lost and is found."

We leave him there. There is an unwritten chapter of life and usefulness; the new life upon which this youth has entered, in which he seeks to expiate the past. But let that go. Amid the lights and music and laughter the curtain falls.

And what does all this mean? You know why Jesus told this parable. It was because the Scribes and Pharisees had murmured, "He receiveth sinners." You know what he meant by the telling of this sweet story of the return from sin to the happiness of a manly life.

> "There's a wideness in God's mercy,
> Like the wideness of the sea;
> There's a kindness in his justice,
> Which is more than liberty."

The new year has begun. Some have already come home and are sitting at the table in the Father's house. Some have set out upon the journey. Others are still in the far country. But there is a light in the window for all wanderers. There is a welcome for all who feel the pangs of famine in their souls. God waits; his hands are stretched out still. Let God be praised for adversity, if it awakens in the breast a longing for better things.

> "Blest be the sorrow, kind the storm,
> That drives us nearer home."

One thing only is necessary, the resolution, "I will arise and go unto my Father."

In one of our Western military posts a volunteer, who had run away from his home and enlisted, was walking up and down on patrol duty. It was Sabbath night and there was divine service in one of the tents. He heard the voice of singing:

> "We're travelling home to heaven above;
> Will you go? Will you go?
> To sing the Saviour's dying love;
> Will you go? Will you go?"

The sentry's memory was busy with former days. He saw the sad mistake of his life, and felt his sin. His heart was tender.

> "We're going to see the bleeding Lamb;
> Will you go? Will you go?
> In rapturous strains to praise his name;
> Will you go? Will you go?"

He was resolved. He looked toward the stars, lifted his hand and solemnly said, "By the grace of God, I will go." So begins the better life. And will you go? All things are ready. The fatlings are killed; the invitations are gone out. And there is no doubt as to the welcome that awaits you. Here is a word that, as an ambassador of Christ, I bring straight from heaven's gate: "Him that cometh unto me, I will in no wise cast out."

THE PART OF THE HAND THAT WROTE.

'In the same hour came forth fingers of a man's hand, and wrote over against the candlestick upon the plaster of the wall of the king's palace; and the king saw the part of the hand that wrote."—DANIEL V. 5.

This Belshazzar was a reckless fool—a weak, sensual, impulsive, arrogant, headstrong fool. He had been admonished again and again in vain. He should have learned wisdom from his father's dreams and the sad afflictions which had befallen him. But all lessons were lost upon him.

At this time his capital city was under siege. Engines of war were planted on the walls round about it; great stones from the catapults went hurtling through the air. Belshazzar ought to have been superintending the defence of the city; but here he sat at a magnificent revel. Imagine him in the midst of his oriental palace with its fountains and hanging gardens; its walls frescoed with pagan parables, winged figures of the national deities and ascriptions of glory to victorious kings. A thousand of his lords are gathered about him, with his wives and concubines. They drink long and deep. The enemy are thundering at the gates; but what matters it? they drink defiance to alien gods and men.

A happy thought! To add to the abandon of the

revels let the golden vessels be brought, which Nebuchadnezzar had taken from the temple at Jerusalem; the cups and chalices are brought and filled to the brim. "Confusion to Jehovah!" is the toast. They drink to Bel and Nebo, to gods of gold and silver and brass and iron and wood and stone. And then, with blasphemous, fevered lips, "Confusion to Jehovah!" He that planted the ear, shall he not hear; he that created the eye, shall he not see?

Look yonder! A spectral hand is moving along the wall. The king is transfixed with terror; his face is ashen, his eyes are starting from their sockets, his knees smite together. Slowly the hand writes; O how slowly! in strange characters: MENE, MENE, TEKEL, UPHARSIN. Come hither, seers, prophets, astrologers, soothsayers, necromancers, let us know the meaning of it!

A hand? No, only the fingers. Why not the whole hand? Why not the clear outline of the mysterious Scribe! Because this is not the order of nature or of grace. We know in part. We see as through a glass darkly. The veil is only slightly withdrawn. Something is left for faith and reason to fill out.

But why this consternation? Why this blanching of the face and trembling of the knees? It is an illustration of a universal fact: we are afraid of the unseen. Children are frightened in the dark. We can remember when the dear mother, having made the good-night prayer and tucked us in, vanished with the light. And then?—then we cowered down and drew the coverlet over our faces. Why? Give a reason if you can. When the mother came back and sat beside us and remonstrated and explained and once more vanished with the light, lo, the room was full of bogies again. There is no reason in it. So we call it an instinct, an intuition. The unseen suggests the supernatural; the fingers imply a hand; the hand a personality. Who or what is it?

First. *In nature.* This is the problem of science. The scientist sees nothing but the fingers of the hand. Here is a maple leaf, bearing the tracery of an exquisite figure; a comparison with ten thousand times ten thousand maple leaves will show an infinite diversity of detail with an absolute uniformity of plan. Here is the veiling of power. One thing is plain, law. A step further will bring us into the presence of a law-giver; but that step must not be taken because it is an inference and unsustained by visible facts; for want of that farther step the scientist becomes an agnostic. What is beyond those fingers? He answers, "I do not know." A child might suggest a solution of the problem, but the undevout scientist will have none of it. He would rather guess than reason by faith. So we have all sorts of conjectures expressed in such terms as law, force, protoplasm, bathybius, universum, the unconscious absolute, elementary life-stuff. But these furnish in fact no solution of the problem. We have made no progress beyond the fingers that write.

Second. *In providence.* We know ourselves to be under the domination of a power not ourselves. We plan, and our plans fall about our ears like card houses. Man proposes, but something else disposes. There is something that "shapes our ends, rough hew them how we will."

We are in the grip of the invisible. Among the last words of David Strauss, the infidel, were these:

"In the enormous machine of the universe, amid the incessant whirl and hiss of its wheels and the pounding of its ponderous stamps and hammers, in all this terrific commotion, I find myself a helpless and defenseless man, not sure for a moment that a wheel may not seize and rend me, or a hammer crush me into powder." This was the language of a man who practically insisted on eliminating the supernatural from the problem of life.

But who or what is this that overrules and thwarts us? Joseph sets out to watch his flocks and finds himself upon the throne of Egypt. Moses sets out to watch his flocks and finds himself in command of an army of fugitive slaves. David sets out to watch his flocks and is turned aside into the forefront of the history of the most important people on earth. Whence is this interference? We are like the patriarch who by the brookside felt himself grappled by unseen hands. All night he wrestled and would fain have known his antagonist; but he vanished with the break of day. Before he went, however, he asked of the patriarch, "What is thy name?" And he said, "Jacob," and added, "Tell me, I pray thee, thy name." And the unseen one said, "Wherefore dost thou ask it?" We must reason out for ourselves the problem of providence. There is something beyond the fingers, which faith alone can fill out.

Third. *In history*. "Go to," they said in the land of Shinar, "let us make brick and burn them thoroughly." "Go to," they said, "let us build a city." "Go to, let us rear a tower which shall stand like a finger of defiance pointed at the unseen and supernatural." But the supernatural said, "Go to, let us go down and confound them;" and the builders were scattered and "left off to build."

It [is] the parable of history. We look back over the story of the past and lo, there are dim shadows; call them Alexander, Cæsar, Charlemagne; they are shadows and nothing more. The thing that hath been, shall be. This is the spirit dance of which Prospero said:

> "Our actors
> Are melted into air, into thin air.
> And, like the baseless fabric of this vision,
> The cloud-capped towers, the gorgeous palaces,
> The solemn temples, the great globe itself,
> Yea, all which it inherit, shall dissolve,
> And, like the insubstantial pageant faded,
> Leave not a [rack] behind. We are such stuff
> As dreams [are ma]de of, and our little life
> Is rounde[d with] a sleep."

If this has a[ny sig]nificance whatever, it means that the Great P[owers] of history have been under the irresistible [con]tr[ol of] a power beyond themselves. There is no [phi]losophy of History which does not reckon [with the] fingers of the hand. Faith, by which alone we [can] grapple with the problem of the invisible, is the necessary part of the equipment of an historian who would get below the [sur]face of things. If we pause here, we are hope[lessl]y bewildered. Nature, Providence, History, are Gordian knots which no ingenuity n[or] [wits], and n[o] [ac]uteness of intellect can s[ev]er. T[he might]y Goeth[e,] whose only deity was hum[an]ity, d[ied excla]iming, "Light! more light!" This [man,] the German philosopher, died mu[ttering,] ["O] truth, where is it?" This [is] why [Ho]bbe[s, the athe]ist, died in an agony of uncertainty, saying, "I am taking a fearful leap into dark!" These men had refused to reason beyond the part of the hand which they saw.

At this point, however, we are not left to conjecture. The spectral fingers write and they write "over against the candlestick," so that he who runs may read. Let us look again at the wall of Belshazzar's palace and read what we may.

First. *God.* An unlettered, unarticulated word. It appears in the blaze of light which furnishes a background for the inscription. The frightened king, when he turned his face that way, had no need to be told there is a God. No need for seer or necromancer to make that announcement. On the instant he perceived it.

This is the great truth back of the fingers. This is the inference to which the naturally springs from the veiling of power. It throws a great light into the problems which vise remain unanswered.

In nature. There is a ... of God in every grass blade. I do not se ... istration of God. There is always room ... and so, *per contra*, always room for unbelief. ... the fingers are there, and the fingers argue a hand, and the hand a personality, and the personality a brain and heart. He who is willing ... son by faith will not need to go to theological schools for the Doctrine of God. He will find it everywhere; in ... air and sky. A Red Republican was saying ... easant of La Vendúe, "We are going to pull ... your shrines, your churches, your monuments ... that can recall to mind the superann ... God."

"Then," said the peasant, "do not forget to pull down stars." He was right; for so long as a twinkling beam is left in heaven, there must be a system of theology on earth. You must take away the fingers if you would prevent us simple folk from going straight on to the hand, the intellect, the heart of God.

In providence. Here again a demonstration is futile. And indeed it is impossible if by "demonstration" you mean a mathematical proof by facts that lie within the reach of one's finger tips. Nevertheless we are conscious of God. You would find it a difficult matter to describe flame to a blind man; or to analyze caloric in such a manner as that he should comprehend it. But when the blind man stands by the hearth, he apprehends the fire and says, I feel it. So are we sensible of God. In him we live and move and have our being. Every breath I draw is an irrefutable argument in theology, though in the province of faith. For what is behind this principle of life? Is life automatic? Nothing is automatic. There are no fingers without a hand; no hand without something behind it. "Whither shall I go to escape from his presence? If I take the wings of the morning and flee unto the uttermost parts of the sea, even there shall his hand lead me and his right hand hold me." Our response to the Doctrine of God in providence is like that of the ocean to the heavenly powers that wield it:

> "And as the waxing moon can take
> The tidal waters in her wake,
> And lead them round and round to break,
> Obedient to her drawings dim,
> So may the movements of His mind,
> The great all-Father of mankind,
> Affect with answering movements mind
> And draw the souls that live by Him."

In history. The philosophy of history now becomes

plain. Politics take definite shape. We hear much at this moment of the Great Powers—the syndicate of Great Powers beyond the sea. Here are armies and imposing fleets; here are captains and commanders with decorations on the lapels of their coats; admirals in flag-ships and secretaries in bureaus of state. But above them all is One, dimly revealed, in whose hand are the issues of life for nations as well as for men. It is a splendid game, this game of politics. Pawns and castles and knights play their part and in turn are tumbled off the board, but the play goes on. Only the King is never taken.

Great Powers! Look down the path of history and see the Great Ruins. This is nothing new. The thing that hath been shall be. Rome, Egypt, Assyria, Babylon, Medo-Persia, gone! Conferences, decrees, protocols, manifestoes, treaties, child's play! There is a Power above and behind them all. God alone is great. The blaze of light on the palace wall of Belshazzar dimmed all the cuneiform inscriptions there; the bulletins of battles; the epitaphs on valiant men, the eulogiums of kings; the processions of victories; commanders with captives at their chariot wheels. The spectral fingers wrote above them all: God alone is great!

Second. *Judgment.* The fingers are writing in that blaze of light: MENE, MENE, TEKEL, UPHARSIN. The part of the divine hand that we see is always writing, always writing the same thing: "Weighed, Wanting, Divided!" The truth was recognized in that palace hall. The king surmised what it meant before it was interpreted to him. Little wonder that he shook and trembled. Conscience makes cowards of us all.

> "That night they slew him on his father's throne,
> The deed unnoticed and the hand unknown;
> Crownless and sceptreless Belshazzar lay,
> A robe of purple round a form of clay."

Was it God's hand that slew him? We are not called upon to relieve God of responsibility. The hand that drove that dagger was divinely allowed to do it. We may make the most of that. What does it mean? Law was allowed to take its course. The Buddhist doctrine of *Karma*—the doctrine of consequences—is tremendously true. "The soul that sinneth, it shall die." "As a man soweth, so also shall he reap." The hand behind these fingers has a sword in it. "When he shall whet his glittering sword, who shall stand before him?"

That phosphorescent inscription in Belshazzar's hall is a foregleam of judgment. Weighed, Wanting, Divided! We must give an account of the deeds done in the body. There is to be a great assize. The account kept here so imperfectly is to be balanced sometime. Things will not be left forever at odds and ends. There is reason in the present disorder of justice. If all sins were punished in this present life, we would think there is to be no judgment because there is no need of it. If no sins were punished in this present life, we would conclude that there is to be no judgment because there is no God. We see the fingers only and are left to infer the right arm. Here is enough to set men thinking. Here is enough to drive men to a conclusion.

It is as Robertson says: "The judgment-coming of Christ is like the springing of a mine. There is a moment of deep suspense after the match has been applied to the fuse; men stand at a distance and hold their breath; there is nothing seen but a thin column of white smoke rising fainter and fainter till it seems to die away. Then men breathe again; and the inexperienced would approach the place thinking that the thing had been a failure; but just when expectation has begun to cease, the low, deep thunder sends up the earth to heaven, and all that was on it comes crushing down again in its far circle, shattered and blackened with the blast." The foolish see a slight token of the doctrine of retribution and give no heed; but the wise are admonished and avoid it.

Third. *Here also is an announcement of God's milder attributes.* God is love. Was that announced in Belshazzar's hall? Aye, it was. Daniel the prophet was sent for to interpret the writing; Daniel the Messianic prophet who could not enter that palace hall without bringing with him the message of pardoning mercy; Daniel the prophet whose whole life and character were bound up in the hope of Messiah—the Christ of God. It was he who called Messiah by name; who prophesied his vicarious death in behalf of the people. He announced His coming in the fulness of time. It was Daniel the prophet who interpreted the vision of the great image and the stone cut out of the mountain without hands. It was he who interpreted the vision of the four beasts, the great world-powers that vanished to give way to the empire of the Son of Man. As Daniel draws near, the Saviour comes upon the scene.

Here is the whole hand. The hand with the nail-prints in it. Here is the hand that explains the fingers of all prophecy. Here is the bleeding hand that interprets the significance of all sacrifice—the Lamb slain from the foundation of the world.

The mysteries are clearing now. *The problem of nature* finds its solution in the word of Christ: "Consider the lilies of the field how they grow; they toil not, they spin not, yet your Father careth for them." *The problem of providence* is solved in him: "Much more shall he care for you." And, "God so loved the world that he gave his only begotten Son, that whosoever believeth on him should not perish, but have everlasting life." We call that "grace"; but indeed it is the very consummation of providence—the one supreme "special providence" in behalf of sinful men. *And the problem of history* is cleared up. Yonder is the effigy of the cross against the sky and over it is the superscription: "I.N.R.I."—Jesus of Nazareth, King of the whole Israel of God. Set that inscription over against the words that were written on Belshazzar's banquet hall. It means that above all kings and potentates, He, whose right it is to reign, shall be supreme over all.

But who hath believed our report? And to whom is the arm of the Lord revealed? The arm of the Lord! When God approached the work of redemption he is represented as rolling back his sleeve like a workman addressing himself to some tremendous task. He made bare his arm on Calvary. The arm of the Lord is made manifest in the redemptive power of his only begotten and well-beloved Son. But to whom is that arm revealed? He shall grow up as a tender plant and as a root out of dry ground, and there is no form nor comeliness that we should desire him. Nevertheless, he is wounded for our transgressions, and by his stripes we are healed. When he shall give his soul an offering for sin, he shall see his seed, he shall prolong his days, and the pleasure of the Lord shall prosper in his hand.

This is the conclusion of the whole matter. This is the *quod erat demonstrandum* at which we arrive when we proceed from the fingers to the hand, from the pierced hand to the strong arm, from the strong arm to the infinite intellect, and from that intellect to the loving, omnipotent heart. Faith can no further go. Here is the end of all problems in nature, providence, history. His kingdom is an everlasting kingdom, and his dominion endureth forever and ever. Amen.

THE CONSPIRACY AGAINST THE LIQUOR TRAFFIC.

A Complaint*

I take pleasure in the opportunity of being heard for my cause. The fraternity which I represent is engaged in a legitimate traffic. The law recognizes and sanctions it. At this juncture, however, owing to a long-continued appeal to prejudice and passion, there is a manifest conspiracy in many quarters against us. We feel that we are wronged, and the class of people represented in this congregation is largely responsible for the wrong which is being inflicted upon us. We are satisfied, nevertheless, that you will be willing to accord us fair treatment when you have listened to our plea. The counts of our complaint are as follows:

I. *The courts are against us.* In nearly all cases, which have recently been submitted to their arbitration, the decisions have been adverse to our interests. The last instance is of a most flagrant character. It has

---

* The preacher in introducing the subject remarked: "It is only just to give the rum-seller a hearing before condemning him. He complains that there is a conspiracy against him. He is entitled to fair play. Let him therefore speak for himself."

been decided that we cannot do business "within two hundred feet of any church or public school." It is conceded that there is an ancient law to that effect on the statute books, but, as everybody is aware, that law has been regarded as a dead letter for many years. It is now proposed to enforce it rigidly.

It is obvious that under this decision a shameful stigma is put upon our business. No other industry is excluded from the immediate vicinity of churches or public schools. Why should a discrimination be made against us? In this manner we are branded like lepers of the olden time who were required to stand afar off, with their fingers upon their lips, crying, "Unclean! unclean!"

We are involved in another hardship by this decision of the court. A considerable number of liquor establishments were set up within the prescribed limit under the old order of things. Of course we knew that the law referred to was in existence, but we had no reason to expect that it would be used against us. In one section of this city there are no less than twenty saloons within two hundred feet of a church. The proprietors of these establishments must, as matters now stand, retire from business. It must be obvious to any fair-minded man that this is not in the nature of fair play.

It is our desire to keep on the best possible terms with all reputable classes of people. We especially desire to cultivate good feeling with the churches. But this unjust provision opens an unnecessary gulf between us. We would be pleased to establish the same terms with the churches which now exist between us and the play-houses and resorts of similar character. The proper relation is that which was to be seen in Bristol, England, where a church stood upon the summit of a hill and at the foot of the stairway a liquor store. A wag wrote this inscription half way up:

> " There's a spirit above and a spirit below,
> A spirit of love and a spirit of woe;
> The spirit above is the Spirit Divine;
> The spirit below is the spirit of wine."

This is as it should be—barring some unfortunate expressions. There is no reason why there should be any ill-feeling between us.

II. *There is a combination of the police against us.* A man named Roosevelt has recently come into power in this city and the dear old times are gone. His preposterous position is this: that he is not appointed to make laws or interpret them, but simply to enforce them. And he is enforcing the laws. And things are getting to be intolerable.

As matters were under the old regime, the proprietor of a saloon, with perhaps a gambling place overhead and a brothel attached, had merely to "see" the police captain of the precinct and possibly the patrolman, and he was never molested. Now, however, the screws are turned on: we are obliged to keep the laws just like grocers, preachers, handicraftsmen, millionaires and other people.

This is in contravention of all precedent. It has never been expected of liquor-dealers that they would keep the laws. Indeed we have been given to understand that the law-makers and the magistrates themselves did not expect that we should observe them. We have no objection to law; our objection is simply to its construction as bearing against us. The fact is that we have never before been included among the law-observing classes. Superintendent Byrnes, before he retired from his place, made the statement that a large majority of the saloon-keepers of New York were openly and avowedly conducting their business in violation of the Excise Law. All this, however, has been changed. We would be glad to "see" the captain of the precinct, the magistrates if necessary, the patrolman, and all who are concerned in these premises, but we are informed that this would merely be a further violation of law.

III. *We are not allowed to do business on Sunday.* The injustice of the situation at this point is evident from the fact that we are not Puritans, do not believe in the Fourth Commandment, take no stock in the Bible or Blue Laws.

If it be said that Sunday is recognized as *dies non* in the constitutional fabric of our republic, we reply that we ought not to be subjected to the imposition of laws which are distinctively American, because our fraternity is almost exclusively made up of foreigners. The population of this country is conglomerate, made up of people from every quarter of the globe. It ought to be clear that, if we are to continue in peace with one another, the laws and customs of the country must be adjusted to the various elements of its population. The Irish will be irritated if they are prevented from raising the green flag upon the City Hall. The Turks—and the Turkish contingent in our city is by no means inconsiderable—ought to be allowed to observe the marital customs of their native land, where every man is permitted to have four wives if he can afford it. And the Germans, who have their beer gardens in the Fatherland, should be allowed to have their beer gardens here. Have Uitlanders no rights? How can Germans live without their beer on Sunday? Let every nationality be permitted to have its own way. This is the proper method of running a free government. The will of the majority has nothing to do with it.

It should be considered also that Sunday is our most profitable day. More than one-third of our entire receipts are from our Sunday sale of liquors. The workingmen get their wages on Saturday night; if in the good old times you had looked into our places of business on Sunday, we could have shown you what became of those wages. In order that our traffic might be as unobtrusive as possible, we have been willing to close our establishments in front and admit patrons through the side-door. But it has been decided that we shall not be permitted to do this. In taking this position you are robbing us and our families of our livelihood. The laboring man's wages, which, if allowed to take their normal course, would come into our tills, are spent for his family's food and clothing, and we get practically none of it.

IV. *We are forbidden to sell liquor to minors.* The law respecting this matter has hitherto been regarded as a dead letter; but we are now admonished that we must observe it.

A considerable part of our income is from this source. There are some of our fraternity who have had special doors for the accommodation of children. You have no idea how many boys and girls have been accustomed to patronize us. If you will consult the records of the Gerry Society, you will observe how important this source of income is to our prosperity. A few days ago a lad of seven years was carried away to one of our police stations and pronounced by physicians to be a confirmed inebriate. That is the work we are doing. That is where our bread and butter largely come from. That is how we are enabled to build our comfortable homes, provide ourselves with diamonds and our wives with jewels, and erect great breweries and distilleries. It must be perceived that the proposition to curtail our income at this point is in the nature of downright robbery.

And further consider the disreputable methods which are being employed to enforce this antique law against us. The man Roosevelt has stooped to the employment of children as spies in order to convict us. The very boys and girls who have been our regular patrons day after day, have been hired to come in with pails and bottles for liquor, and subsequently to testify against us. Think what a debauching of the youthful mind and conscience is involved in such a course as this! How can the children who come under the malign influence of Roosevelt in this manner ever be expected to grow up into good citizens and ornaments of society? The newspapers have duly ventilated the true character of such methods. They have grasped the situation and join us in uttering an indignant protest in the name of violated humanity. Childhood is sacred; let it not be thus wronged and perverted; for it is a true saying, "The child is father of the man." Where are the churches that they do not properly grasp this matter and lift up their voices against it? Have they forgotten what their divine Teacher said: "Whosoever shall offend one of these my little ones, it were better that a millstone were hanged about his neck and that he were drowned in the depths of the sea"?

V. *It is proposed to raise the license.* A bill is now before the Assembly of the State of New York, looking to this end. We have sent, however, an imposing delegation to Albany to checkmate this proposed infringement of our rights.

Why indeed should there be any license upon our traffic at all? Is not ours a legitimate business? Did not God make alcohol? Every creature of God is good. We agree with you that it is to be used as not abusing it. The most of you, however, will concede that it is right to drink. But if it is right to use intoxicating liquor as a beverage, it is obviously right to buy and sell it. That gives the saloon a lawful standing as real as that of the meat-market or the tailor shop.

But if there must be a license, let it be as low as possible so that any honest man, who is disposed to enter upon our business, can do so. The argument that because ninety-five per cent. of the paupers, criminals and insane people are made so by intoxicating liquor, therefore the saloon should be taxed to support the jails, poor houses, and insane asylums, is all rubbish. What is the state for, we enquire, but to take care of its dependent wards? And inasmuch as the people constitute the state, there should manifestly be an equable apportionment of taxes among all.

To increase the license fee at this juncture will freeze out many of the poor but honest rumsellers who find it difficult even under present conditions to make both ends meet. And what will become of them? They cannot dig; to beg they are ashamed. They have never served an apprenticeship in any handicraft. Their skill in mixing drinks, shaking dice and discussing municipal politics, would go for nothing in any other position of life. If you force them out of their present business, you will drive them into some such vulgar industry as hod-carrying or raking the streets. This would be an offense to their manhood and self-respect. Their proud spirits would bow and break, if they were forced to pass from a life of genteel leisure and come under the curse pronounced upon the race, "In the sweat of thy face, shalt thou eat bread."

VI. *The public schools are arrayed against us.* A bill has recently passed the Legislature calling for temperance education. The effect of this will be to cut off our supplies at the very source. Our patrons are dying off at the rate of a million or thereabouts every year. It is estimated that a hundred thousand of these die from drunkenness. But are we to blame for their overdoing the thing? Our whole constituency is practically wiped out every ten years. Where are the further patrons of the liquor traffic to come from, if the rising generation is to receive fanatical instruction as to the influence of alcohol on the human system?

We are aware that for many years there was a law upon the statute books requiring such temperance instruction, but this law was prudently drawn in such a manner as that no penalties were affixed to the violation of it. This left the teachers in our public schools to consult their own pleasure. Many of these teachers —particularly such as were indebted for their appointment to the friends of the liquor traffic in our municipal government and elsewhere—had conscientious scruples against such instruction, and accordingly they forbore to give it.

The new law was passed a year ago in defiance of the

united protest of our friends. As it differs from the former law chiefly in the fact that penalties are affixed to it, the brewers, distillers, wholesale liquor dealers and dramsellers were a unit in opposing it. No attention, however, was paid to this imposing array of respectable influence. The bill was passed in both houses of the Legislature without a single dissenting vote.

In our opposition to this law we were reinforced, also, by "The Church Temperance Society"—which, it may be said in passing, is the only organization of this character which we can endorse. It denounces drunkenness, which we also cordially disapprove. But it favors temperance in the proper and scriptural sense—that is, moderation in the use of intoxicating drinks as in every thing else—and so do we. But despite this combination of forces, the law was enacted, and it is now being carried out with more or less of sympathetic acquiescence by the teachers in our public schools.

We were still further aided in our efforts to prevent the enactment of this law by the State Superintendent of Public Instruction, who addressed to teachers a personal circular, in which they were invited to join with him in a petition to the Governor calling for a veto of this pernicious bill. Many of the teachers who, from conscientious conviction, had previously refused to give temperance instruction to their classes, joined willingly with the State Superintendent in this petition. But it was of no avail; there were other influences at work over which we had no control, and at the eleventh hour the Governor signed the bill. The result is, that at this moment the boys and girls are being taught that alcohol is a poison, that used in excess it defiles the blood, soddens the flesh, injures the digestion, disarranges the nervous system and weakens the functions of the brain. It must be clear to all right-thinking people that this is a blow aimed at our prosperity, and that an unfair advantage is being taken of us.

An effort is being made, however, in the present legislature to so amend this law as to eliminate its objectionable features, and in behalf of justice and humanity it is hoped that no serious opposition may be made to it. If the proposed measure goes through, the form of the temperance education law will remain; but no real or effective penalties will be attached for disobedience. This is as it should be. Laws are unobjectionable—if only they are not enforced. Nobody, for example, would make any objection to the Monroe Doctrine at this present juncture but for the unfortunate disposition in some quarters to enforce it.

VII. *We complain of the attitude of the churches.* What is the church? A religious organization. It is the business of the church to teach free will, fixed fate, foreknowledge absolute. As one of the poets has said:

> "Content you with monopolizing heaven,
> And let this little rolling ball alone."

But what have we? A scandalous exhibition of ecclesiastical degeneration. A general and complete departure from the policy of him who said, "My kingdom is not of this world."

The preachers have taken to preaching politics! What have they to do with politics? That is our affair. From time immemorial we have been permitted to do as we pleased with legislatures and courts. We have been permitted to manage primaries, frame laws, control magistrates, and name, from among our own fraternity, members of the Excise Board. Now everything is at odds and ends. The church has assumed such an attitude that the managers of both political parties are no longer free to consult our wishes. We are frankly admonished that Christian citizens henceforth propose to vote as they pray. If this continues, if the Church so far forgets her high calling as to persist in interfering in the management of sublunary things, what is to become of us?

Nor is this all. Misfortunes never come singly. Until recently we have felt sure of the recognition and the moral support of the Roman Catholic Church. But lo and behold, the papal delegate, Satolli, has recently decided, in the case of an Ohio appeal, that liquor dealers shall not be admitted to the sacrament, and, if they refuse to throw up their business, may be expelled from Catholic Associations. This means that we have no longer an ecclesiastical refuge. It is of momentous significance in view of the fact that a large number, if not a majority, of our fraternity are members of the Catholic communion. "Rum and Romanism" is to be no longer a combination to juggle with. His Holiness Leo XIII. has turned his back upon us; we are delivered over to the uncovenanted mercies of God!

It is manifest, therefore, that there is a conspiracy against us. And under these circumstances we have no alternative but to enter our complaint and to present an earnest plea for fair dealing. The people are probably not informed generally of the dimensions of the liquor traffic. It is an industry of immense importance to the financial well-being of the land.

We have about nine thousand saloons in New York City alone; that is, one for every twenty-five families. If these saloons were drawn up in line, they would make a street thirty miles long; the windows on either side filled with red bottles and nude pictures, and the sidewalks lined with kegs, barrels and loafers. The amount of money which passes through our hands is something immense. It is estimated that last year not less than one thousand millions of dollars was employed in this country in the manufacture and sale of intoxicating liquors. The Chamber of Commerce in this city understands the importance of this traffic; it has accordingly issued its manifesto and appointed its lobbyists to influence legislation in our behalf. Now unless something is done to arrest the present agitation, this great industry must be immensely injured, if not, as some fanatics desire, practically blotted out. We present our complaint, therefore, to you, reasonable people, in the name of justice, of humanity, of pure and undefiled religion, of industrial prosperity, of the proper training of childhood, of the welfare of the working-classes, of personal freedom and of our own prosperity and well-being. Let this conspiracy cease. Leave the rum-seller to the possession of those rights to which he, in common with all other citizens of this free commonwealth, is entitled, to wit, liberty and the pursuit of happiness.*

---

*At the conclusion of this plea, the preacher said, "If I were counsel for the conspirators, I should be willing to submit the case to this jury without argument. As it is, I have but two words to offer, and these are words of the living God. The first is with respect to the rumseller: 'Cursed is every one that putteth the bottle to his neighbor's lips.' The second has to do with his victim: 'No drunkard shall inherit the kingdom of God.'"

THE WHITE SOLAR RAY.

"Because it is written, Be ye holy, for I am holy."—I. Pet. i. 16.

It is safe to say that the average hearer takes no special interest in the doctrine of the divine holiness. Is it because he cannot apprehend it? Yet there is no more of mystery here than with reference to any other of the attributes of God. His love passeth all understanding; his judgments are a mighty deep. Or is it because there is no practical value in a consideration of this theme? But surely we are interested in our own lineage; our father's honesty, our mother's purity are matters of concern to us. The suggestion of a bar sinister on our shield would be instantly resented. Surely then since God is our father, the study of his character should be of deep interest to us. The fact is, however, there is something within us which is antipathetic to the divine holiness—something which is offended by it. This is a serious matter. The eye was made for light and is of no value except as it is properly adjusted to it. If the eye shrinks from the light, or cannot bear it, the time has come for an oculist to exercise his skill upon it.

The importance of this doctrine is indirectly certified by the fact that infidelity has so virulently assailed it. David Strauss argues against the divine holiness because, as he says, "It involves the thought of susceptibility to impressions *ab extra*, which is inconsistent with absolute being." But what of that? God is not "absolute being," if indeed there is any such thing as absolute being; he is a distinct and concrete personality whom we delight to call Our Father. Another objection urged in a similar quarter against the divine holiness is that it implies a vital relation to law; the fact being that Deity is *ex lex;* that is outside of law. But this is not true. So far from being outside of law, God is the very source and centre of it. The laws of the universe, natural and moral, radiate from him as the light of the solar system does from the central sun. Still another objection urged against God's holiness is that it suggests bondage, while Deity must, in the nature of the case, be morally free. This objection, however, rests upon a wrong idea of freedom, namely, an equilibrium between right and wrong. On the other hand freedom is rightly defined to be *felix necessitas boni*, or perfect obedience to perfect law. In this sense holiness is indispensable to it.

In the Scriptures God is more frequently characterized by his holiness than in any other way. His name is the Holy One of Israel. He dwells in a holy hill, sits on a throne of holiness, and his robe is a garment of holiness. He swears by his holiness and those who would worship him must approach in the beauty of holiness. The whole system of rites and ceremonies in the Old Economy had reference to this attribute. This system may be broadly classified under the heads of purifyings and sacrifices. Water and fire are the great purifiers. There were "divers washings;" hands and feet, beds and dishes, the person of the leper,—all were sprinkled with water.

The sacrifices were of similar import; they were intended to set forth that moral purification which is accomplished by the expiatory burning out of guilt. Now turn to the New Economy and we shall find that Christ, in nailing to his cross the handwriting of ordinances which was against us and taking it away, preserved the whole ancient ritual in the two simple sacraments of Baptism and the Lord's Supper. In Baptism is set forth symbolically the washing of the waters of regeneration, and in the Lord's Supper we have a compendium of all burnt offerings in the presentation of the bruised flesh and shed blood of him who was sacrificed once for all. Thus the ceremonial of both the Old and New Dispensations is at all points significant of holiness—God's holiness and the necessity for holiness of all who would approach him.

Once under the Old Economy there was a distinct vision of God. It was at a time when Isaiah was greatly troubled on account of Israel's sin. The national religion was honeycombed with formality and worldliness. "Hear, O heavens," cried the Prophet, "and give ear, O earth: for the Lord hath spoken; I have nourished and brought up children, and they have rebelled against me. The ox knoweth his owner, and the ass his master's crib; but Israel doth not know, my people doth not consider. Ah, sinful nation, ye have provoked the Holy One of Israel unto anger. Why should ye be stricken any more? The whole head is sick, and the whole heart faint. Your hands are full of blood. Wash ye, make you clean; cease to do evil; learn to do well." Then came the prophet's vision; he was transported to a palace of indescribable splendor where he saw the Lord sitting upon a throne high and lifted up. Above it stood the seraphim, each having six wings; with twain he covered his face, and with twain he did cover his feet, and with twain he did fly. And one cried unto another, and said, "Holy, holy, holy, is the Lord of hosts." The prophet was overwhelmed with his vision: "Woe is me! for I am undone; I am a man of unclean lips, and dwell in the midst of a people of unclean lips, and mine eyes have seen the King." Then flew one of the seraphim, having a live coal which he had taken from the altar; and he laid it upon the prophet's lips, saying, "Lo, thine iniquity is taken away." And a voice was heard, saying, "Whom shall we send and who will go for us?" Then the prophet, uplifted and invigorated by his glimpse of the Holy One, answered, "Here am I; send me."

Once at the beginning of the New Economy we come upon a similar vision. John the Evangelist, old and weary, saw from his desert exile the rising smoke of martyr-fires. He knew that his Christian brethren were suffering all manner of persecution for the truth's sake. "How long, O Lord," he cried, "how long?" Then a door was opened into heaven and he saw the great white throne, "and he that sat was to look upon like a jasper and a sardine stone; and there was a rainbow above him in sight like unto an emerald." Then, amid the glory of golden lamps and swinging censers and beauty indescribable, the rush of angel wings and the rapt faces of an innumerable host of worshippers, he heard the *Trisagion:* "They cried one to another, saying, Holy, holy, holy, Lord God Almighty!" And the dreamer fell at his feet as one dead; then a kindly hand was laid upon him, and a voice said, "Fear not, I am he that liveth and was dead and am alive forevermore." And John arose from this vision of the divine holiness and went forth to meet with renewed courage the cares and responsibilities of life.

It is not a vain thing, therefore, to address ourselves to the study of the divine holiness and our personal relation to it. The clearer our view of our Father's majesty, the more distinctly shall we apprehend the possibilities of our own nature as his children; and the more earnestly shall we be moved to keep ourselves unspotted from the world that we may resume our normal relations with him.

But what do we mean by God's holiness? We have spoken of it as an attribute, but in fact it is a bundle of his attributes rolled into one. If a sunbeam be transmitted through a prism, it will resolve itself into the seven primary colors, to wit: violet, indigo, blue, green, yellow, orange and red, and always in that order. It is thus that from the earthward side we perceive the attributes of God. In heaven the angels and archangels know him as the Holy One; but here we emphasize his love, his justice, his truth and all the other qualities that are found in the analysis of holiness. But if we catch the seven primary colors in a concave mirror, we shall find them reunited at its focus, and again we shall have the white solar ray.

The best definition of holiness is to be found in the primitive meaning of the word itself, whole-ness. God's holiness is the symmetry of all divine graces. One of the early fathers said, "The divine holiness is a most perfect pulchritude, which cannot be seen with human eyes nor declared with fleshly lips."

How does this attribute manifest itself before us?

(1) Negatively, in a perfect freedom from sin. It would seem to be a gratuitous thing to speak of the sinlessness of God inasmuch as we are accustomed always to think of him in that way. In fact, however, he is differentiated in this particular from nearly all the pagan conceptions of deity. The best the cultivated Greeks and Romans could do in formulating the divine ideal was to be seen in their Olympic assemblage. And what a gathering of gods! What crimes and revels! what mobs and quarrels! Here is Bacchus, a drunken vagabond. Here is Venus, a drab, whose name is associated with uncleanness in literature and in the drama to this day. Here is Mercury, a thief, the patron god of the banditti who still in our time infest the Italian mountains. And here is Jupiter, the father of the gods, who was defiled with countless vices; who hung up his faithless wife in mid-heaven with anvils tied to her heels. Look on that picture and then on this. What a contrast! God is light; in him is no darkness at all. He is of purer eyes than to behold iniquity. The stars of heaven are not clean in his sight. Angels and archangels veil their faces before him and cry continually, "Holy! Holy!"

This glorious divine attribute is shown positively in God's hatred of everything that savors of sin. Sin is the only thing in all the universe which he hates, and he hates it with loathing unspeakable. Why not? Sin has defiled the world which he created and pronounced very good; has covered it with battlefields and filled it with graves. Sin has ruined his masterpiece, man, whom he created in his own image, but a little lower than the angels, has embittered man's heart in rebellion against his own beneficent authority, and has alienated it from all things pure and lovely and of good report. Nay, beyond all things, sin slew his only begotten and well-beloved Son. It is written that the sons of King Zedekiah were murdered before his eyes. How, think you, did Zedekiah regard the sword that was drawn dripping from their hearts? Was he indifferent to it? That would have been most unnatural. God hates sin with an infinite hatred because it nailed his Beloved One to the accursed tree.

And God must needs punish sin. He is the executive of law throughout the universe. His admonition is as clear in Scripture as articulate speech can make it: "The soul that sinneth, it shall die." Nor are we left to any uncertainty as to the meaning of this death. It is set forth under such figures as these: the fire that is never quenched, the worm that dieth not, outer darkness, weeping and wailing and gnashing of teeth.

> "There is a death whose pangs
> Outlive this fleeting breath.
> Oh, what eternal horrors hang
> Around the second death!"

If it be said that these are mere figures of speech, granted; but this symbolism is quite meaningless and would certainly never have been used unless there were something in fact to correspond with it.

Let us look now at the other and more practical side of this truth: "Be ye holy; for I am holy." There is a world of meaning in that illative conjunction. The ultimate ground of all moral character lies in the fact that as God is our Father, we must evermore strive to be like him.

Let us note the problem. The publican stands

yonder, beating upon his breast—because he knows that the trouble lies there—and crying, "God be merciful to me a sinner!" Off yonder is the sanctuary at a great distance from him. The name of the sanctuary suggests its character; it is the holy place. All things within that enclosure are holy; the posts and curtains, the altar, the candlestick, the lamps and censers, the gifts, the frankincense, every knop and almond blossom and pomegranate, the priest's mitre and breast-plate and gem-clasped girdle, the tinkling bells, wreathen chains and jeweled hangings, are all consecrated to "holiness unto the Lord." At the further extreme of this sacred enclosure is the Holiest of All; within it is the Ark of the Covenant with its cherubim between whose outstretched wings was the token of the peculiar presence of the Holy One. It is meet and proper that the publican should stand "afar off" from that sanctuary, for he is a sinner, and without holiness no man shall see God.

Here is the problem: How to bring that publican, without offense to law or justice, within the precincts of that holy place? It is an iteration of the old question: How can God be just and yet the justifier of the ungodly? or, from man's side, How can a man be just with God?

At the very outset it is obvious, that this sinner must be cleansed from his sin. This will, however, bring him into possession of a merely negative holiness; but he can make no further progress until he has acquired it. The laver stands before the altar of incense. The heathen themselves, with their imperfect conceptions of deity, were sensible of this fact. *Procul! Procul! Abeste profani!* cried the guard before the heathen shrines. When Æneas returned from the wars and was invited to worship, he said to his father, Anchises, "Do you draw nigh and sacrifice; as for me, this is not lawful until I have cleansed myself at the running stream." God has made provision for this cleansing in his gospel. The blood of Jesus Christ his Son cleanseth from all sin. Come now, saith the Lord, let us reason together; though your sins be as scarlet, they shall be as white as snow; though they be red like crimson, they shall be as wool.

But this negative holiness, brought about by the pardon of sin, does not entitle the sinner to enter the presence of the Holy One. He must be born again and he must be built up in character. Provision is made for this also by the influence of the Holy Ghost. The Apostle John says, "Ye have an unction from the Holy One." The reference is to the athletes or agonistai, who were accustomed to prepare themselves for the games by a long course of training, in which they persistently anointed themselves with unguents, to secure grace and suppleness. This was not a mere superficial anointing. The skin indeed shone, but the very flesh of the athlete was pervaded and permeated through and through with the ointment. Such is the influence of the Spirit in sanctification. He is called the Holy Spirit because his special and particular function is to endow the forgiven sinner with those graces which shall qualify him to enter heaven. Here again we come upon the fact that holiness is the sum total of all graces. If the fruits of the Spirit, love, joy, peace, long-suffering, gentleness, goodness, faith, meekness and temperance, be bound together, we shall have the same resultant that we get from uniting the primary colors of the spectrum, namely, the white solar ray.

In the acquiring of these graces we fit ourselves for the duties and responsibilities of common life. It is written that when Alexander and his army laid siege to Jerusalem, the High Priest, Jaddua—all other hope of repelling the enemy having failed—arrayed himself in his white garments and bound on his breast-plate whereon was the inscription, Holiness unto the Lord. At his approach, the legend says, so bright was that whiteness and so dazzling the splendor of the breast-plate, that Alexander and his army were overpowered and fell prostrate before him. So are we qualified by the cultivation of godliness to meet all the trials that await us.

In the same manner are we prepared for death. Could anything be more beautiful than the passing of Chrysostom? He had not time even to lie down on his couch; but as he sat in his chair engaged in devotions, he felt the approach of the death angel. "Bring me," said he to his attendant, "the white garments which I have prepared against this hour." And thus arrayed in "fine linen clean and white" he went over to meet God. The time comes when we also shall be called to pass over. As we approach the gate we shall note this inscription above it, "There shall in no wise enter here anything that defileth, neither anything that worketh an abomination, or maketh a lie; but they which are written in the Lamb's book of life." And as we cross the threshold we shall find ourselves in the presence of a great multitude which no man can number, all of them arrayed in white. Here are men and women who, during their earthly lives, were sinners like ourselves, but they were washed in the blood of Christ and built up in Christian character by the influence of the Spirit of God.

And a voice said, "What are these which are arrayed in white robes and whence came they?" And I said unto him, "Sir, thou knowest." And he answered, "These are they which have washed their robes and made them white in the blood of the Lamb. Therefore are they before the throne of God and serve him day and night in his temple. And he that sitteth on the throne shall dwell among them; they shall hunger no more, neither thirst any more; neither shall the sun light on them nor any heat. For the Lamb which is in the midst of the throne shall feed them, and shall lead them unto living fountains of waters; and God shall wipe away all tears from their eyes."

THE UNIVERSITY OF JERUSALEM.*

"At the feet of Gamaliel.—Acts xxii. 3.

On the bow of a Phœnician grain-ship ploughing her way through the Mediterranean stood a lad of fifteen years or thereabouts, shading his eyes and looking away toward the south. He was "going to college." What a world of dreams and aspirations is in that phrase, "going to college!" Up to this time the lad had pursued his studies at Tarsus; he was now bound for Jerusalem, where greater opportunities were afforded for the obtaining of a liberal education. He was a "Hebrew of the Hebrews," and his heart throbbed fast with all the hopes and prejudices of his race. He could scarcely wait to see Jerusalem that lay yonder in the southern mist. On the left, as they skirted the shore, he saw the snow-crowned heights of Lebanon with the green mantle of cedar along its slopes; and further on, Carmel, fraught with memories of the Lord's controversy, whose cliffs had echoed to the people's cry, "The Lord, he is the God!" It was on the second day out, possibly, that the ship came to anchor in the port of Cæsarea. A brief land-journey brought the youth

---

*This sermon was preached by invitation of the Student's Club of New York.

to an eminence, from which the scene he had so
longed to behold burst suddenly upon his view.
Jerusalem, beautiful for situation, the joy of the
whole earth! Yonder were its homes and palaces;
in the midst of them a roof of gold glittering in the
sun, with marble porticoes around it; this was the
"House Magnifical." A little later, the youth stood
before the city gate, which he did not enter, probably,
without recalling the Psalmist's rhapsody: "Our feet
shall stand within thy gates, O Jerusalem. Peace be
within thy walls and prosperity within thy palaces.
For my brethren and companions' sakes, I will now
say, Peace be within thee. For the sake of the
house of the Lord our God I will seek thy good."

On entering the city he betook himself at once to
the school of Gamaliel. The Jews at this period were
divided into two rival sects, known by the names of
their leaders, Hillel and Shammai; the former the
defender of the traditions of the elders, the latter a
strict constructionist who stood for the exclusive
sanctity of the Mosaic Law. The most eminent parti-
san of Hillel at this time was Gamaliel, whose school
has been called, "The University of Jerusalem."
He was one of the seven theological teachers of Israel
who were entitled to the rank of Rabban. He was
familiarly known as "The Flower of the Law." He
was a Pharisee, but comparatively free from the narrow prejudices of that sect, insomuch that he was
"had in reputation of all the people." He was so
greatly beloved by his pupils that at his death they
raised to his memory such a costly funeral pile "as
had never been known except at the burial of a king."

It is easy to imagine the routine of Saul's life at
this school. The head-master sat upon an elevated

dais with his pupils gathered about him in a semicircle, literally, sitting at Gamaliel's feet. Here they studied the Hebrew Scriptures with the aid of the traditions and all the learned disquisitions and commentaries of the elders. Still further, they addressed themselves to the Greek language and philosophy; this school being distinguished for its liberal policy in that particular. It was here that Saul acquired his knowledge of Stoicism and Epicureanism, and also of classic poetry.

While Saul was thus engaged, another youth, somewhat older than he, was attending the priestly school at Hebron, whose voice would presently be heard as the herald of the King, proclaiming, "Repent ye, for the kingdom of heaven is at hand." A group of fishermen up at Gennesaret were mending their nets and plying their traffic all unconscious of the fact that they were appointed to lead the vanguard in the propaganda of the universal religion. A young man stood in a carpenter shop at Nazareth, chips and shavings about his feet and the implements of his trade upon the bench before him, preparing himself for the announcement of an evangel which should shake the temple of Judaism to its foundation and cause the palaces of the Cæsars to crumble into dust. All this, however, was nothing to Saul the student. His world was hemmed in by the horizons of his ancestral faith. He was busily engaged in the mastery of Jewish dogma, clever feats of logic, the form and significance of rite and ceremony. He was developing an intense zeal, scrupulosity and self-righteousness. His greatest ambition was to become a zealot in defense of Judaism. At length he passed his examinations and, as we have reason to believe, received his diploma *cum laude*. A great future opened before him. In all Jewry there was not a youth of greater promise than he. So under the rainbow of hope he passed into the world of busy life.

We shall find him referring many times, directly or indirectly, to the training which he received at this school; he never forgot its associations. There is something constitutionally wrong with the man who does not gratefully cherish the memories of his college life. Is there in all this land an alumnus of Phillips Academy who does not remember the winds that swept over Andover Hill; the pump at the corner where we paused on our way to the morning prayers; the faces of the boys who sat together in "Number Nine" at the feet of Dr. Taylor?

> "O for the touch of a vanished hand,
> And the sound of a voice that is still."

Is there an alumnus of Yale who does not fondly recall the campus, the over-shadowing elms, the college fence where we were wont to sing our merry songs far into the night? Is there a Union Seminary man who does not look back gratefully to the golden age of that institution of theological learning with its historic triumvirate, Schaff, Hitchcock and Shedd? *Haec olim meminisse juvabit.*

I rejoice in the opportunity of addressing myself to-night to college men and students generally. Let me ask them to consider the Privilege, the Temptations and the Safeguards of their student life.

I. *The Privilege.* They are engaged in the pursuit of knowledge. What is better than this? It was a proud day for Jason and the Argonauts when they sailed forth in search of the golden fleece, hoping to snatch it from beneath the sleepless eyes of the dragon and the bulls breathing flame. A splendid enterprise was that of Launcelot and his fellow knights of the round table who sought the *San Greal*, the Sacramental cup which, tradition said, had touched the Saviour's lips. A noble quest was that of Ponce de Leon after the fountain of perpetual youth. But what were these to the quest of knowledge? Wisdom is the principal thing. It is more precious than rubies, it cannot be valued with the gold of Ophir. Therefore, get wisdom ; and with all thy getting, get understanding.

Truth is to be esteemed for its own sake. All truth is of value. Light ; more light ; sun-light, moon-light, star-light, rush-light, glowworm, firefly. Anything is better than the darkness of ignorance. It was a quaint picture that rare Ben Johnson made of Truth:

" Upon her head she wears a crown of stars,
 Through which her orient hair waves to her waist,
 By which believing mortals hold her fast,
 And in those golden cords are carried, even
 Till with her breath she blows them up to heaven."

But *truth is to be most highly esteemed for its purchasing value.* We are living in a utilitarian age. The only science worth acquiring is "applied science." No man now-a-days will take the trouble to cross the Pons Asinorum unless he wishes to go somewhere. It is a true saying, "Knowledge is power." It is more than power, however ; it is wealth, honor, influence, happiness. These are things which lie within its purchasing value.

It forms a basis of character. What a man knows is the index of what he is. The word "belief" is said to come from the Saxon, "bi-lifian ;" that is, what we live by. "As a man thinketh in his heart, so is he." "I'm a made man!" cried James Marshall when he rode into camp in 1848 with a few shining nuggets which he had gathered from among the pebbles of a brook. There are other discoveries which are of more value than gold. To know that there is a God; that man is immortal; that Jesus is the Christ; that the Bible is true;—is to have a substratum for the building of character. It is such truths as these that formulate life. He who has settled such problems can say with reason, "I am a made man."

But further, knowledge is of value because *it furnishes an equipment for usefulness*. Truth is the stock in trade of the man who wishes to make his life tell. One of Aristotle's wise sayings was this: "How does the educated man differ from the uneducated? As the living from the dead." The acquisitions of our student-life are to be measured by their utility in the broad world of duty and responsibility.

The fact that a flexible thing is contracted by moisture is of little importance in itself. Why should a scholar congratulate himself on knowing it? But the great obelisk, now standing in the square of St. Peter's at Rome, attests the real value of that simple truth. This obelisk was raised to its place by order of Pope Sixtus V. in 1586. Great preparations were made. High Mass was said in the morning. The architect and workmen received the Papal benediction. At the blast of a trumpet a great number of workmen and horses appeared and set to work. Fifty-two vain attempts were made with ropes and pulleys. The great monolith was raised from the earth higher and higher to the very verge of the pedestal, and there it halted. Man-power and horsepower had done their best; the ropes had reached their utmost tension. And yet an inch was lacking. Then a voice was heard from among the crowd, "Wet the ropes." It was done; the needed inch was gained. Knowledge is power. The obelisk was raised to its place, and there it stands to-day.

A scholar's worth in this busy world of ours is measured by his success in using his information for the general weal. Why was Peter Cooper made Doctor of Laws? It was not because he had what is known as a liberal education, for he had attended school only a single year. Whatever of knowledge he acquired was through much difficulty and by persistent application. But the secret of his deserved fame lies in the fact that every atom of his acquisition was used for the good of those about him. In the corner-stone of Cooper Institute there is a scroll which bears this inscription: "The object which I desire to accomplish in raising this fabric, is to open avenues of knowledge to the youth of our country, that they may learn to love Him from whom cometh every good and perfect gift."

II. *The Temptations of Student life.* The most important and alluring of these is one which, by reason of its intangible and specious character, is likely to be unobserved, to wit, *an exaggerated idea of the importance of knowledge as an end and not as a means to an end.* There ought to be some word in the English language with which to label this vice, but there is none. An overweening regard for wealth is called "avarice." And the man who pursues wealth for its own sake, neither giving nor spending, but always loving and hoarding, is a miser. The love of pleasure, mere pleasure for itself alone, is sensuality. And the man who pursues pleasure to the disregard of better and other things is called by many names—a sybarite, a voluptuary, an epicurean, a sensualist. But there is no name by which to characterize this other vice or the man who pursues it. The seeking of knowledge for itself alone is a sordid quest, as really as the pursuit of wealth or pleasure; and he who sets his heart upon knowledge for its own sake is as little worthy of his manhood as the miser or the voluptuary, for he is a thoroughly selfish man. Such an one was Sir Thomas Browne, whose ambition was to know all that could be known about dead men's bones, ashes, cerements, graveyards and epitaphs. He lived in the time of the English Commonwealth and wrote "Hydriotaphia" in his room overlooking the Strand in London. The busy life that surged along the thoroughfare below had no interest for him. Thrones and empires were tottering and falling. Cromwell and the Roundheads were fighting at Marston Moor. The great controversies of the afterglow of the Reformation were being contested in courts and councils. The King's head fell from the block on Tower Hill. The face of the civilized world was being changed. But all this was nothing to Sir Thomas Browne. He knew about bones and cerements, and he cared to know nothing more. He sat in his room on the Strand and wrote "Urn Burial," in sweet forgetfulness of all the duties and obligations of the time which weighed so heavily on the hearts of his countrymen.

Another of the most constant temptations of student-life is in *Cameraderie*. Here a word must be borrowed because there is none in the English language that can describe student comradeship. It is more than friendship. The story of the two friends who came to Vulcan's forge and asked him to lay their hearts upon his anvil and beat them into one, is not a fable; it is the simple tale of what is always transpiring in school life. We read in Scripture of the sanctity of the laying on of hands; but there is an almost equal sanctity in the clasping of hands. Heart thrills against heart; life blends with life. There is a transference of faith and of character. Take heed, therefore, to your boon companionship.

Edgar Allen Poe was an orphan lad, the adopted son of a Baltimore merchant who sent him to London and placed him in a boarding school at the early age of seven years. If at that period he had received a little mothering, poor lad, or if he had fallen in with helpful friends, there is no telling what might have been the subsequent story of that mighty brain and generous heart. But the shadow of evil friendships fell over him. He was led into the downward path, and fell at the very verge of his manhood a victim to the influence of evil associations. He has left on record his own sorrow in these pathetic words:

" And the raven, never flitting, still is sitting, still is sitting,
   On the pallid bust of Pallas, just above my chamber door;
  And his eyes have all the meaning of a demon that is dreaming,
    And the lamplight o'er him streaming throws his shadow on the floor;
    And my soul from out that shadow that lies floating on the floor
        Shall be lifted—*nevermore!*"

It would be impossible to make profitable mention of the temptations of youth at this preparatory period without reference to certain vulgar vices. One of them is named in the ninth chapter of Proverbs: "*A woman sitteth at the door of her house to call passengers who go right on in their ways: 'Whoso is simple, let him turn in hither;' and as for him that wanteth understanding, she saith to him, 'Stolen waters are sweet and bread eaten in secret is pleasant.' But he knoweth not that the dead are there; and that her guests are in the depths of hell."* Another is referred to in the twenty-third chapter of the same book: *"Look not thou upon the wine when it is red, when it giveth its color in the cup, when it moveth itself aright; for at last it biteth like a serpent and stingeth like an adder."* There are still others with which Solomon, with all his sad experience of illicit pleasure, was not familiar; such as the impurity that lurks in current fiction and in the public drama; an impurity that burns its way into heart and conscience and irreparably dulls the fine edge of manhood and womanhood.

The students who are present in this company will remember how Virgil made reference to the consequences of yielding to these forms of temptations:

> " Facilis descensus Averni;
> Sed revocare gradum, superasque evadere ad auras,
> Hic labor, hoc opus est."

It is true indeed, the descent to the realms of darkness is easy, but to retrace one's steps and reascend to truth and purity, this is the task that tries the soul of a man.

It is such resistance, however, that develops the true metal of manhood. Gold is refined in furnace fires. When Prince Hal was surrounded by his foes, a herald sped across the field post-haste and said to the king, "Thy son must have reinforcements, Sire; he is encircled by his foes and his horse is shot from under him." The king answered, "Is he wounded unto death?" "Nay, but he is hard bestead." "Tell Prince Hal," said the king, "that he hath never had so golden an opportunity of winning his spurs."

III. *The Safeguards of Student-life.* It is said that two hundred and seventeen of the three hundred and sixty-nine members of the senior class at Yale are members of the church. This is probably a larger proportion than can be found in any other similar school of learning. And it is of importance in view of recent statements respecting the moral influences at New Haven. It must be granted, however, that Satan is to be found in every school and college in the land and that he is not waiting for youth to pay their addresses to him, but is pressing his attentions upon them, "seeking whom he may devour." Five mischievous or wicked youth in any community of students can create the impression of a Reign of Terror. But if a young man yields to temptation in a voluntary surrender of his manhood, it is absolutely his own fault; for there are many helpful influences to hold him to truth and righteousness.

To begin with, he has *his sense of honor.* And the average youth has a deep sense of honor. When James Harper, the founder of the publishing house, was leaving his home to learn the printer's trade in the great metropolis, his mother, bidding him farewell at the gate, said, "James, remember you have good blood in you." This is an appeal which touches the heart of every true man.

> " Who misses or who wins the prize,
>   Go, lose or conquer as you can!
> Or if you fall or if you rise,
>   Be each, pray God, a gentleman."

A noble ambition is among the most helpful influences of student-life. The higher this ambition is the better. Horace Bushnell said, "Grasp the handle of your being." Ralph Waldo Emerson said something better, "Hitch your wagon to a star." One of the noblest masterpieces of hand-wrought art in iron is the well-curb in the market-place of Antwerp. Thereby hangs a tale. Quentin Matsys, a blacksmith's apprentice, fell in love with an artist's daughter. The girl's father curtly refused him, saying, "Never, until thou hast made a splendid work of art." In no wise abashed, he set himself to the task. The difficulties in his way were as nothing because of the prize before him. With no implements but hammer and file he made the well-curb and won his wife. No man can work well unless he can speak as the great Master did of the "joy set before him."

And this leads me to the greatest of all safeguards and the most encouraging of all stimulating influences to a noble life; that is, *the power of personal religion.* We need something outside of and beyond ourselves. Lead me to the Rock that is higher than I!

I speak to many young men and women who have professed the Gospel of Christ. You can look back to the time when you consecrated yourselves to him. Remember you are not your own, you are bought with a price; not silver and gold, but the precious blood of Jesus as of a lamb without blemish and without spot. Be true to your profession. Be loyal to Christ and to the Christian Church. Be faithful to your moral convictions. Make much of the Bible, which is your only weapon of defense, the sword of the Spirit which is the Word of God. Make much of prayer. You are like couriers bearing a treasure through a wilderness infested by robbers on either side. If you are to uphold yourselves in Christian faithfulness, it will be because God's presence is round about you.

It is related that only two men ever lived who were able to resist the song of the sirens—the temptresses who frequented the rock Peloris off the coast of Sicily and allured passing mariners with songs of gold and glory and pleasure. One who resisted was Ulysses who, as he voyaged homeward after the siege of Troy, hearing the songs afar off, had himself bound to the mast, and so was held despite his own struggles while the ship swept by. So may a man be held by the stern sense of duty, constrained by his obligation to what he believes to be right. But there is still a better way. The other of the two who resisted was Orpheus who, as he heard the alluring songs touched his lyre and sang the praises of heaven so sweetly, so divinely, that the sirens themselves paused to listen as he swept by. It is well to be held as with golden chains to the noblest and best; it is better still to have religion so interwoven with the very fibres of our being as that duty itself shall become pleasure, and life's trials shall turn aside to leave us to the even tenor of our way. This was the mind of Christ Jesus, who was so bound up in his beneficent purpose that earthly and sordid things could take no hold of him; his heart was fixed; the prince of this world came and had nothing in him.

I speak to others who have never professed devotion to Christ. When Saul of Tarsus received his diploma from the hands of Gamaliel, he may have supposed that his education was complete. One thing, however, was lacking. It came to him as he journeyed along the Damascus highway,—an inquisitor breathing out slaughter against the followers of the Nazarene prophet;—a light above the brightness of the sun shone down upon him and he fell to the earth. He was blinded in that instant, but saw such visions as fleshly eyes can never look on. The great truth came to him like a sun-burst, and his whole nature responded in the word, "Lord, what wilt thou have me to do?" This was really the beginning of his life; he laid everything in that moment at Jesus' feet; his birth, learning, Roman citizenship, rhetorical skill, hope, ambition; so that he was able to say thereafter, "I know nothing but Christ and him crucified; the love of Christ constraineth me." Oh, that those before me, who have never known a like experience, might make the same response to God's appeal to-night, so that the new life with all its blessed hopes and possibilities might open before them.

And this last word to all. We are nothing of ourselves save as our all is consecrated to God. Are you an art student? Let your love of the beautiful be devoted to him as really as was the skill of Bezaleel who wrought upon the posts and curtains of the temple. Are you a student of music? Let your skill be devoted to him as was the harp of David, which he made to minister to minds diseased and used continually to magnify the glory of God. Are you a medical student? Follow in the footsteps of that good Physician whose life was spent in allaying pain and soothing sorrow, opening blind eyes, healing diseases, raising the dead, and all subsidiary to the more gracious power of delivering souls from sin. Duty calls you. Be ready to answer, "Here am I."

When Col. Newcome lay dying, he recalled the

days which he had spent at the Charity School. He sat again among the boys and heard the voice of the head-master calling the roll. He rose upon his arm in bed and listened until he seemed to hear his own name called, then answering, *Adsum*, he fell back on the pillow and slept his last sleep. There is nothing better than this, to answer " Present " at the call of the Master, Christ.

The blessing of the Lord be with you all.

AS THE HART PANTETH.

"As the hart panteth after the water-brooks, so panteth my soul after thee, O God. My soul thirsteth for God, for the living God: when shall I come and appear before God?"—PSALM xlii. 1-2.

The love of David for Absalom was the bitter fountain of the most poignant sorrows of his life. Oh, how he loved that wayward boy! And indeed there was much in him to love and admire. He was a handsome youth, with long, flowing hair; vain, ambitious, inordinately fond of display, usually attended by a troop of fifty life-guardsmen. His father could not bear to put a salutary restraint upon him, much less to chastise him. So it happened in the irreversible course of nature that his heart was burdened with ever-increasing sorrows, until at last he staggered up the winding stair-way to his chamber of prayer on the house-top, crying as he went, "O Absalom, my son, my son; would God that I had died for thee"!

Now there were rumors of an insurrection, and with unspeakable grief the king learned that Absalom was chief conspirator. What should he do? He could not take up arms against his favorite son. His love had cut the sinews of his strength. He arose and fled; accompanied by a few faithful friends he crossed the ford of the Kedron, weeping, with his head covered, and went up by the ascent of Mt. Olivet toward the wilderness.

In camp among the trans-Jordanic cliffs, the exiled king was joined by all sorts of adventurers; gathering about him a very Falstaff's army of motley men. Peasants of the surrounding country gave token of their affection by generous gifts of wheat and barley, beans and lentils, butter and provisions of every sort. Nevertheless the king's soul was burdened; not for the loss of his kingdom, for he could endure that. Not supremely for the baseness of Absalom, though indeed he was learning to his great anguish how sharper than a serpent's tooth it is to have a thankless child. But his sins sat heavy on his conscience and God's face was hidden from him. He knew now that he should have thought twice before he married the beautiful Maacah, a pagan princess, the mother of this lad. And there were other sins still more heinous that rose like spectres now to shake their fingers at him.

He stood alone on one of the barren heights, as in a great sanctuary, communing with his own soul and seeking to commune with God. What a sanctuary was this! Its roof was the canopy of heaven. Its aisles were the valleys below where the wild goats were grazing. Its pillars and arches were the rugged cliffs; its tapestries, the verdure of forest and field. As he stood amid the glories of this great cathedral of nature, there was a rustling of boughs near by, and a deer, wounded by the archers, wild with terror, with hot eyeballs, panting sides, distended nostrils, an arrow quivering in its flank, bounded past and onward through the forest glade to quench the fever of its thirst. And David found his prayer at last; "As the hart panteth after the water-brooks, so panteth my soul after thee, O God." It is himself he sees; a troubled, wounded, frightened soul, wounded unto death, hearing God's voice afar off like the murmur of water trickling from the rock. "So panteth my soul after thee, O God."

What have we here for the experience of common life? What are the lessons for us?

I. *A lesson in soul thirst.* It is a false saying, "Man wants but little here below, nor wants that little long." We are born with a cry; "Like our shadows, our wishes lengthen as our sun declines"; we end our lives with a groan, or else a cry of deliverance like the song of a captive bird escaping from its cage into light and sunshine and the freedom of the upper air Ixion bound to the wheel; Sisyphus rolling the stone up hill only to have it rolled back again from the summit and so forever and ever; Tantalus standing up to his lips in a fountain whose waters recede whenever he would drink, stretching his hand toward clusters of fruit that are carried out of reach just as he would pluck them—these are not fables, these are pictures of common life. "Man never is, but always to be, blest."

And the waters of this world can never satisfy our thirst. There is enough and to spare, but it only tantalizes us. It is like the fountain of Marah, bitter and brackish. It is like the taunting miles of sea that lay before the eyes of the ancient mariner:

> "Water, water everywhere,
>   And all the boards did shrink;
> Water, water everywhere,
>   Nor any drop to drink!"

What do these people want, that jostle each other along the streets with restless eyes and furrowed brows and troubled faces? They are not satisfied. What would they have? Gold? They spend their days in grasping—bags, boxes, bonds, and mortgages, houses and lands, thousands, millions, but the wrinkles are still there. One day there is a dimness before their eyes, a sense of cold fingers groping toward the heart, death! The hands unclasp at last; they lie there open and empty. What would these people have? Pleasure? Go to, I will try thee with mirth. Eat, drink and be merry! The glass, the cymbals, the dice. One day a spectre comes, grim and forbidding, and the laughter dies in a long moan like the sighing of a twilight wind. I said of laughter, It is mad; and of mirth, What doeth it? Vanity of vanities, all is vanity and vexation of spirit. What do they want? Honor? Here is the most eager chase of human life. For yonder wreath of laurel they plan and worry and fret and agonize. At last they grasp it; and lo, it drops from the hand a withered thing, dry, valueless; it crumbles into dust. The man whom we Americans have placed upon the highest pedestal of fame was fond of repeating to himself these words:

> "The boast of heraldry, the pomp of power,
>   And all that beauty, all that wealth ere gave,
> Await alike the inevitable hour—
>   The paths of glory lead but to the grave."

II. *The diagnosis of the soul's moral pain.* My soul thirsteth for God.

The wounded deer can interpret its need. Nature has taught it. When lips are dry, when eyes are hot, when throat is parched, water alone can satisfy.

Would that we were as wise as the wounded deer to interpret the longing of our souls. Why did the Greeks rear in the public square at Athens that altar "to the unknown God"? They had Athene, Aphrodite, Poseidon, Father Zeus, a vast Pantheon of helpers, and still they thirsted. This altar is the confession of that thirst. It was from this inscription that Paul found occasion for his sermon on Mars Hill: "God hath made of one blood all nations of men, for to dwell on the face of the earth; and hath determined the times before appointed and the bounds of their habitation; that they should seek the Lord if haply they might feel after him and find him, though he be out far from every one of us; for in him we live and move and have our being; as certain of your own poets also have said, For we are also his offspring." They were seeking the Lord in a poor, helpless way, like blind men groping along the wall.

The plant that struggles into being in the cellar, a poor peasant thing, a child of solitude and prisoner of night, feels with its blanched tendrils, like thin fingers, toward yonder chink in the wall; life groping its way toward light! An apt symbol of the soul panting for God.

Here is the token of our divine birth. They say that when Africanus returned from his campaign the Censors took his father's ring from off his hand because he was unworthy to bear it. But we, degenerate children of a divine Father, have still in this inarticulate cry that throbs forth from our souls the lingering token of our lineage. My soul panteth for God!

Here also is the abiding hope of our immortal destiny. The starling in its cage that cries continually, "I can't get out!" pays tribute to its birth-right and to its franchise for the freedom of the open air. How shall we deal fairly with our poor imprisoned souls? A caravan of famishing men went staggering through a dry and thirsty land. A cry was raised, "Let loose the antelopes!" It was done and the fleet-footed creatures set out all in one direction; for the secret of the fountains was in their breasts. Oh, that we were willing to let loose our love, our reverence, our holy instincts and aspirations! If they had freedom they would soon find God.

III. *Our want can find satisfaction only in Christ.* For Christ alone is God's manifestation of himself among men.

The oldest of the patriarchs expressed his longing in this wise: "Oh, that I knew where I might find God; that I might come even to his seat! I would order my cause before him and fill my mouth with arguments. But, behold, I go forward and he is not there; and backward, but I cannot perceive him; on the left hand, but I cannot behold him; he hideth himself on the right hand that I cannot see him." From that vain quest of the patriarch we pass to the upper chamber where Christ is conversing with his disciples: "And Philip saith unto him, Lord show us the Father and it sufficeth us. Jesus saith unto him, Have I been so long time with you, and yet hast thou not known me, Philip? he that hath seen me hath seen the Father; how sayest thou then, Shew us the Father. Believest thou not that I am in the Father and the Father in me"? Here then is the answer to the old despairing cry, "Canst thou by searching find out God"?

(1) Here is the living God. My soul thirsteth for

the living God; when shall I come and appear before him? It is not enough to bow before a graven image, crying, "O Baal, hear us"! Our souls do not respond to the philosophy that bids us worship law, force, energy. Shall we make our prayers to the star-dust, or pour out our sorrows to the primordial germ? Nor can pantheism meet the desire of our souls. As well try to worship the impalpable ether that fills the interstellar fields of space. No, no; my soul thirsteth for the living God. We are not satisfied even with the word that came to Moses at the burning bush, "I AM THAT I AM." This is but a voice, a definition, a mystery. We must needs find the living God. And here he is coming to us through the tempest in the dark night: "It is I, be not afraid." He comes aboard the little ship; we are fallen at his feet; the storm is hushed; the ship is at the shore.

(2) Here is the incarnate God. Flesh of our flesh and bone of our bone. Nearer to us God cannot come than in Jesus Christ. A letter was taken from one of the postal boxes, written by a poor, friendless child, and addressed to God. It read thus: "Dear God,—We are very poor. We have no bread, no clothes, no fire. Dear God, come and help us." We are taught out of the mouth of babes and sucklings. Here is the God we need, and this the way to approach him. "Except ye become as little children, ye shall in no wise enter the kingdom of God."

(3) Here is the satisfying God. "In hym ye ben fylled." Our thought of deity is not as of one who stands upon the shore looking out over the ocean with shaded eyes, but as one bending over the brook that trickles from the heights. Our Lord stood by the woman of Sychar at the well and said, "Whoso-

ever drinketh of the water that I shall give him shall never thirst; but the water that I shall give him shall be in him a well of water springing up into everlasting life."

In a recent conference of ministers in this city a good deal was said as to the importance of returning to the old method of presenting the sterner attributes of God. "Let us be faithful, however reluctant, in preaching the terrors of the Law," said one; "let us not shrink from preaching hell." No doubt this rests upon us as a stern obligation; to preach hell with bated breath, tenderly, lovingly, faithfully; ever mindful of the fact that while God is love he is also a consuming fire. But what is hell? "It came to pass that the rich man died and was buried; and in hell he lifted up his eyes, being in torments, and cried, saying, Have mercy on me and send Lazarus that he may dip the tip of his finger in water and cool my tongue." The pain of eternal retribution is here represented as a vain regret, despair, unavailing sorrow, an eternal thirst. And the minister must needs present this truth as he would be faithful in declaring the whole counsel of God.

But, behold, I show unto you a better way. Preach Christ! Christ who came into the world to quench the burning thirst of the children of men. As he hung in his last agony on the cross, the night closed about him—that awful darkness at noon-day—and in his solitary anguish he cried, "I thirst"! His lips were dry, his throat was parched, his eyes were hot; "I thirst"! In that moment he, as we are wont to say in our historic creed, "descended into hell" for us. But standing here beneath the cross, in view of that vicarious sacrifice, I hear the patter of rain drops in the grassy fields of Caanan; I hear the ripple of brooks on their way down the mountain slopes of the land that floweth with milk and honey; I hear the roll of the river, the river of life that flows from the cleft rock beneath the throne of God.

Dip down and drink and live. If any man thirst let him come unto me and drink to his fill. O blessed salvation! It is free as the air; the element of life for bird and beast and man. It is free as the sunlight; the king at his window enjoys its warmth and sees the beggar who lies beside his gate basking in it. It is free as the water; there is enough and to spare; the clouds are full of it, the rivers are full of it, the fountains are full of it.

One word from the Old Economy: "Ho, every one that thirsteth, come ye to the waters; and he that hath no money, come ye, buy and eat; yea, come, buy wine and milk without money and without price." And one word from the New: "The Spirit and the bride say, Come. And let him that heareth say, Come. And let him that is athirst come; and whosoever will, let him take the water of life freely." Drink, drink, and thirst no more!

THE CLEANSING OF THE TEMPLE.

"And Jesus went up to Jerusalem, and found in the temple those that sold oxen and sheep and doves, and the changers of money sitting: and when he had made a scourge of small cords, he drove them all out of the temple, and the sheep and the oxen; and poured out the changers' money, and overthrew the tables; amd said unto them that sold doves, Take these things hence; make not my Father's house an house of merchandise. And his disciples remembered that it was written, The zeal of thine house hath eaten me up." JOHN ii. 13-17.

The Jews were expecting the Messiah. The signs of the times all pointed to his near advent. It was written in their oracles, "The Lord whom ye seek shall suddenly come to this temple." What a day that would be when Prince Shiloh, crowned with honor, his face radiant with the glory of heaven, should enter the sacred precincts, lift his hands in blessing and restore to Israel the splendor of former times. This, they thought, would be the manner of his coming. But how strangely was that prophecy fulfilled. A man in the garb of a Galilean peasant, whip in hand, eyes aflame with holy indignation, scourges the traffickers from the temple court and lashes their rulers with reproaches for their defilement of the sacred place. A strange coming of the Christ! Yet so he ever comes; for is it not written, "Judgment must begin at the house of God"?

How are we to interpret this incident? Was it intended to teach that a place dedicated to the worship of Almighty God must not be prostituted to secular uses? Aye, and something more. I was in

St. Paul's in London a few years ago, when a poor fellow, over in one corner of the Cathedral, shot himself through the heart. The sacred edifice was so defiled by his blood spattered upon its wall, that it was presently re-consecrated with solemn rites. It is hard to understand how such a proceeding could be justified except upon the lowest and narrowest view of the sanctity of the place. There are worse things than the blood of a suicide upon the floor and walls of our sanctuaries. And if there must be re-consecration for every defilement, we must needs be intoning our formulæ and swinging our censers all day long. No, this is not the way to keep the house clean. As well undertake to purify a leper by washing his sandals. There is a much current superstition respecting the holiness of a church building. It must indeed be reserved for purposes of worship exclusively, but

> "What's hallowed ground? Has earth a clod
> Its Maker meant not to be trod
> By man the image of his God?"

The house is merely the outward shell of the true temple. It has no sacredness except for the fact that thither the tribes go up to worship God; its pillars and curtains are wood and flax. The Church, *Ecclesia*, exceeds all bounds of roof and walls. No outward garnishing of nave and transept can commend to Heaven a company of worshipers whose hands are unclean and whose hearts are impure. A clean platter may serve to furnish forth a most unwholesome feast.

The Jews were a chosen people—chosen to evangelize the world. Their commission was as wide as that of the Christian Church. For its accomplishment they were entrusted with the oracles and the prophecies of the Christ. The temple was the center of their work of evangelization; its rites and symbols and elaborate ceremonial were all significant of that purpose. To this end there was a Court of the Gentiles; the outer and larger portion of the sacred enclosure, which the heathen of all nations might visit. Its use was precisely that which is served by the so-called "altar" in some of our modern churches, namely, a place of welcome for outsiders who desire to acknowledge the true God. At the time of our text this Court of the Gentiles had passed into disuse. There was no general desire to receive proselytes into the Jewish Church. Why then should not the space allotted to them be devoted to other purposes? It was leased accordingly to those who sold sheep and oxen and turtle doves for sacrifice, and to money-changers who were ready to exchange, for a consideration of five per cent., the coin of other countries for the Jewish half-shekel with which every loyal son of Israel must pay his annual poll-tax.

The cleansing of the temple occurred twice; at the beginning and again at the close of Christ's ministry. On the first occasion he had come down from the north with a caravan of pilgrims to attend the Passover. On a hot April day he reached Jerusalem and betook himself at once to the temple. As he ascended the marble steps, he heard sounds of traffic, the shouts of drovers, the lowing of cattle and bleating of flocks, the clinking of money on the tables of the money-changers. I would give much to have seen the look of righteous indignation on the face of the Nazarene prophet as he stooped to gather from the floor the handful of rushes with which he drave them out. "Take these things hence; make not my Father's house an house of merchandise!" And there was no resistance. Why? Why did not Ahab arrest Elijah at the gate of Naboth's vineyard? Why did not the magistrates of Nineveh lay hands on Jonah as he went up and down the streets crying, "Yet forty days and this city shall be destroyed"? Why did not the people mob Moses when he hurled the golden calf from its pedestal in the midst of the idolatrous multitude? "Conscience makes cowards of us all," and "he is thrice armed who hath his quarrel just." O, there is an unspeakable power in a transport of righteous indignation! Who shall measure the power of that indignation when it flamed forth from the eyes of the incarnate Son of God?

The other occasion of the cleansing of the temple was four days before the crucifixion. Jesus had come down again to attend the Passover. He was accompanied by many pilgrims on their way to the feast. And as he came along the road from Olivet he was met also by a multitude from the city who cast their garments before him and cried, "Hosanna! Hosanna, to the Son of David!" As he entered the gate and passed along the street the people leaned from their lattices and stood in the doorways of the bazaars wondering at this strange procession. Again he entered the temple. Three years had elapsed, but he found the same condition of things. The colonnades had again been invaded by the merchants; here were pens and stalls for sheep and cattle; here were the drovers and the money-changers. Again he drove them out, and again none dared resist his holy zeal. This done, he remained in the Court of the Gentiles; preaching and healing the sick who were brought to him, while from within came the voices of children and the songs of the pilgrims: "Hosanna! Hosanna, to the Son of David! Blessed is he that cometh in the name of the Lord!"

I have never known a time during my ministry of twenty-five years when there seemed to be such a general desire for a revival of true religion in the Churches as just now. The matter is referred to constantly in our preachers' meetings, and the prayers of the people in our devotional services indicate the drift of common desire. O for the coming of the Lord in power to the saving of a multitude of souls! But are we ready? Is the Church prepared for a work of heavenly grace? If the Lord were to come presently, would there be no occasion for his scourge before the lifting of his hands in benediction? Is it not possible that with us also, "judgment must first begin at the house of God"? And if so, what evils would the Lord find to arouse his just and holy wrath?

I. One of the prevailing sins of Christian people is *covetousness;* that is, the turning aside of divine things to personal and selfish uses.

The priests of Israel had appropriated the Court of the Gentiles to the purposes of merchandise, because of the income they derived from it. Why not? What harm was there in leasing this unused space for such trafficking as indirectly ministered to the altar? Thus they justified themselves in turning it to their own account. The canker of gold had infected heart and conscience.

It is stated that the annual gifts of the Christian people of America to the work of missions outside the local parish are about ten cents per capita; that is, one-fiftieth of one per cent. of the average income of a laboring man. And the people who are making such contributions are offering up, day by day, the prayer, "Thy kingdom come." The yearly gifts of all the nations of Christendom for missions would not pay the liquor bill of America for three days. The people of the world—the witnesses who compass us about—when they learn such facts as these, must be led to strange conclusions. For they know that, as Christians, we have consecrated ourselves body and soul, talents and possessions, wholly and absolutely to the service of Christ. And this is the outcome!

We are living in hard times. The long strain is felt in all our Christian beneficences. Our Missionary Boards are all laboring under a heavy burden of debt; our institutions of Christian education are running behind. Whose fault is it? There is money enough in the hands of Christ's disciples in our own country to pay off all the indebtedness of these enterprises without feeling it. I could point my finger at five Christian men in America, multi-millionaires, having in their possession trust-funds belonging to the Lord Jesus Christ, who could place all our missionary boards and charitable institutions on a basis of permanent prosperity by parting with a mere modicum of their wealth. The time has come when God places a clear requisition upon such possessions; he does not call for a tithe of the income; he does not ask the whole of the interest; he demands that those to whom he has entrusted riches shall now cut in upon the principal, for that principal belongs to him. No doubt we have all been impressed by the severity with which our Lord in his preaching spoke of rich men, as where he said, "How hardly shall they that have riches enter into the kingdom of God! It is easier for a camel to pass through a needle's eye than for a rich man to enter into the kingdom of God." It may be that in this passage he desired to teach the impossibility of the salvation of a man whose heart is set upon the acquisition of wealth and upon its selfish use. Or it may be that he referred to that gate of Jerusalem called "The Needle's Eye," which is said to have been large enough to admit a camel, but not with a load upon its back. Unload if you would enter in! The silver and the gold are God's; his people must recognize that fact. Souls cannot be saved while the Court of the Gentiles is perverted to selfish uses.

II. Another of the current sins of the Church in these times is *externalism*. At the very time when the temple court was filled with sounds of chaffering merchants and the bleating of sheep and oxen, the priests within were devoting their utmost attention to the scrupulosity of outward form. Censers were swinging and antiphonal choirs were chanting, "Oh, that men would praise the Lord for his goodness and for his wonderful works to the children of men." This was the golden age of ceremonialism in Israel, and God hated it. "Bring no more vain oblations," he said. "Your incense is an abomination unto me; your new moons and appointed feasts my soul hateth; I am weary to bear them. Wash you, make you clean. Cease to do evil; learn to do well." Jesus in like manner rebuked it. The long prayers, the broad phylacteries, the ringing of the resounding gifts in Corban; how he denounced them! "Ye are as whited sepulchres, fair without, but within full of dead men's bones and all uncleanness."

There is a ritualistic tendency in our time which is greatly to be deplored; a turning away from the simplicity of pure worship to spectacular display. Let it be remembered that our Lord in setting up the religion of the New Economy announced the fulfillment of former rites and ceremonies and the reduction of religion to its very simplest form. The Church at Laodicea incurred his grave displeasure because it was neither cold in abandoning the faith nor hot in zealously defending it; but eminently respectable. The letter which killeth was there, but there was an absence of the Spirit which maketh alive. "So then because thou art lukewarm, and neither cold or hot, I will spue thee out of my mouth. And because thou sayest: 'I am rich, and increased with goods, and have need of nothing'; and knowest not that thou art wretched, and miserable, and poor, and blind, and naked; I counsel thee to buy of me gold tried in the fire, that thou mayest be rich; and white raiment that thou mayest be clothed, and that the shame of thy nakedness do not appear; and anoint thine eyes with eyesalve, that thou mayest see."

There is no more specious temptation to the Church than that of captivating and unwarranted forms in worship. Let it be remembered that whatsoever is not of God is of sin. At the well of Sychar our Lord said to the woman of Samaria, who was much concerned about the rival claims of Moriah and Gerizim with their divers rites and symbols: "Woman, believe me the hour cometh when ye shall neither in this mountain nor yet at Jerusalem worship the Father. The hour cometh and now is when the true worshipers shall worship the Father in spirit and in truth; for he seeketh such to worship him. God is a Spirit; and they that worship him, must worship him in spirit and in truth."

III. Mention must also be made of the prevalent sin of *intolerance*. The priests of the ancient temple were at this time ready to welcome almost any form of heresy; and they had engrafted upon their religion much of pagan philosophy. If liberalism were needed, they had enough of it; but they were intolerant toward truth and impatient of the teachings of their own scriptures. At this hour they were full of hatred toward Christ and his doctrine, and were devising measures to accomplish his death.

There are many of God's people who incline toward liberalism in their treatment of false philosophies; but who cannot abide a reference to the old landmarks, or the "traditional view" of the doctrine of Christ. As ministers and laymen, we stand pledged in solemn covenant to the loyal upholding of Christ and the Scriptures; the Written and the Incarnate Word of God. The bigot of these days is not the man who insists upon loyalty to those fundamental facts, but rather the one who extends the right hand of fellowship to such as reject them, while denouncing the upholders of the faith once delivered to the saints as bigots and fanatics. This is a practical renunciation of loyalty to the gospel of Christ. Let us be liberal toward truth and toward all lovers of truth, and generously disposed toward all who reject the truth in praying that they may be brought to a knowledge of it.

The broadest and most generous of the Apostles was John the Evangelist. He is represented as leaning upon the Master's breast. His constant theme was Love; insomuch that when he was an old man and burdened with his years, he is said to have been carried to the church to deliver his brief sermon, "Little children, love one another." This was the man who, toward the close of his life, writing to the Elect Lady, said, "This is love, that we walk after his commandments. For many deceivers are entered into the world, who confess not that Jesus Christ is come in the flesh. Whosoever transgresseth and abideth not in the doctrine of Christ, hath not God. If there come any unto you and bring not this doctrine, receive him not into your house, neither bid him God-speed: for he that biddeth him God-speed is partaker of his evil deeds." This is the sort of tolerance which prevailed in the Apostolic Church. It is liberalism of another sort that has largely paralyzed the energies of the Church in Holland, in Germany, in Scotland and in England to-day. We cannot afford to compromise with error. To compromise with error is to be intolerant toward truth. We must love those who are without and seek their conversion; but must frankly refuse, in the interest of truth, to hold religious fellowship with them.

IV. Still another of the sins prevalent in the Church to-day is *spiritual conceit*. The Jews were aware of God's plan as to the conversion of the nations. They knew that there would have been no Court of the Gentiles but for his desire that the Gentiles should be brought in. But they did not approve of his plan. They thought of themselves as a select company of people entrusted with the oracles and possessed of certain exclusive privileges. As to outsiders, they were wont to speak of them as "dogs of Gentiles." They had no desire to gather them in.

Our Lord has left us in no doubt as to his purpose respecting the Church. It is the great living organism through which he is working for the bringing of all nations to the knowledge of truth. He came back after his crucifixion and spent forty days with his disciples, apparently for the purpose of marking out the plan of campaign. He said to them repeatedly, from his first meeting of them in the upper room, to his last address on the mount of ascension, " Go ye into all the world and evangelize ; and lo, I am with you alway, even unto the end." His meaning is perfectly clear. And yet it is not an uncommon thing in our time to hear professing Christians say, " I do not believe in Foreign Missions." Was there ever greater arrogance? What right has any believer to set up his own opinion as against the distinct commandment of his Lord? What assumption! what self-opinionated vanity is here! No use for the Court of the Gentiles indeed. What is the Church then? A coterie of saints? A mutual-admiration society? A fellowship of good people who desire to sit and sing their souls away to everlasting bliss? Nay ; Christ settled it. This is his business ; let us allow him to manage it in his own way.

Before we can receive the blessing which the Church needs, the Temple must be purged. The Lord of the Temple already stands in the Court of the Gentiles ; the scourge in his hand falls on the backs of our pleasant and cherished sins. He bids us remove from our hearts and lives the covetousness which has robbed God, the externalism which has mocked God, the intolerance which has rejected truth instead of error, and the spiritual narrowness and self-sufficiency which have dared to limit God's saving grace to us and ours. When the Temple is cleansed, his glory will shine in it like the glory of the sun.

"COME AND SEE."

"Nathanael said unto him, Can there any good thing come out of Nazareth? Philip saith unto him, Come and see." JOHN I, 47.

It would appear that Nathanael had been communing with himself "under the fig-tree." He had perhaps been praying there, and, as an "Israelite indeed," longing for the coming of the Christ. To him came Philip, saying, "We have found the Messiah, the long-looked-for One." Where?—"Jesus of Nazareth."—"Impossible"! At this point Nathanael showed himself to be a prejudiced man. He was familiar with two proverbs of the time, to wit; "Out of Galilee ariseth no prophet," and, "Can any good thing come out of Nazareth"? These proverbs represented tradition and public opinion; the substratum of prejudice. "What the people say" has greater weight in many quarters than, "What is truth"?

In his reply to this rebuff, which spoke with the voice of prejudice, Philip showed great wisdom. He might have railed at Nathanael as a warped, jaundiced, narrow-minded, unreasonable man; but that would have done no good. Vinegar swarms no bees. Or he might have argued with him; but

> "A man convinced against his will
> Is of the same opinion still."

He very properly appealed to the evidence of Nathanael's own senses: "Come and see."

This is the right sort of preaching. As ambassadors of Christ we are appointed, not to display our rhetorical or argumentative skill so much as to stand with pointed finger, saying, "Behold the Lamb of God"! The world cares little for our personal *ipse dixit*: "I am Sir Oracle, and when I open my lips let no dog bark." Men do their own thinking in these days. There is only one man on earth who claims infallibility, and he does not seem to be absolutely sure about it. The best we can do in the pulpit is to present our claim, namely, that Jesus is the Christ; and then appeal to the fair-minded judgment of our congregations, urging them to use their own faculties: "Behold the Lamb of God."

In pursuance of this method I would lead you to-day, as Philip led Nathanael, into the presence of Jesus of Nazareth, saying, "Come and see." See what?

I. *See a Man.* Is there anything remarkable in that? Aye; a man is not easy to find. We have all sorts of lay figures, manikins, leather and prunella imitations; but where will you find a man? Call in Diogenes with his lantern and let him search the world over; then turn your eyes toward this Jesus of Nazareth and behold him. *Ecce Homo!* A man; a veritable man; a man without a fault:

>   —"the elements
> So mixed in him, that nature might stand up
> And say to all the world, 'This is a Man.'"

There are four particulars in which this Jesus of Nazareth differs from all other men:

(1) In respect to his intellect; it was perfectly

clear to discern truth. He saw things in every province of knowledge precisely as they are. An oculist will tell you that there is probably not one pair of absolutely perfect eyes on earth; there is a twist of some sort in everybody's sight. But Jesus saw clearly; saw to the very heart of every mystery; saw the great verities, God and immortality and heaven and hell. He solved the great problems. He untied the knots of philosophy without resorting to any Gordian trick. He touched these things with a fearless hand, and made them so simple in his discourse that it was said, "Never man spake like this man."

(2) As to his heart; it was wholly pure and benevolent. He hated sin only. The wisest detective of whom I have any knowledge, was an old Spartan judge, who, in order to detect the real criminal among a number of suspects, placed his ear to the bosom of each in succession until he came to one of whom he said, "Thou art the man." He knew him by the quick palpitation of his heart. No human heart beats precisely as it should, because no man is wholly free from sin. This Jesus, however, confidently said, "Who layeth anything to my charge"? He taught us to pray, "Forgive us our debts as we forgive our debtors"; but never once did he make such a prayer in his own behalf. He was without sin.

(3) In respect to his conscience; it was clear to discern betwixt the worse and better reason. No ship that sails the sea is without its compass; yet there is no magnetic needle which points with absolute exactness towards the North. It may be diverted from its proper direction by the magnetism in the atmosphere, by something in the ship's cargo, by the very nails that fasten the craft together; so the needle always

vibrates on its pivot and deviates more or less from its true direction. The moral sense of the race is diverted in like manner by sin. The conscience of Jesus, however, pointed ever toward God and right.

(4) As to his will; it led him always to obey the perfect will of God. We complain of a war in our members, so that the good we would, we do not, and the evil that we would not, that we do. But there was no such war in the members of Christ. The source of our trouble is in our perverted wills. When Israel Putnam was leading his Green Mountain boys toward the north in the French War his march was intercepted by a gunboat which had been launched upon the lake. He waited until nightfall and then, providing himself with a beetle and wedge, rowed out under the stern of the boat and drove the wedge behind its rudder. The next morning the gunboat lay there helpless with flapping sails. This is precisely what sin has done for the human will. But the moral sense of Jesus led him into a perfect harmony with the mind of God.

Here then was a quadrilateral man; quite perfect in intellect, heart, conscience and will. For this reason, among others, he was called the Son of Man; that is, the unique, the singular, the incomparable man; the "recapitulation of humanity," the Ideal Man.

II. See, furthermore, *the Son of God*. But what is peculiar in that? I also am a son of God. Was I not created in his likeness and after his image? Have I not, by his infinite grace, been received by the Spirit of adoption so that I have a double right to say, "Abba, Father"? But not in the sense in which this Jesus of Nazareth was called the Son of God.

He is the only-begotten and well-beloved One. Thrice was he so acknowledged from heaven. When he stood in the verge of the Jordan at his baptism, a voice from above was heard to say, "This is my beloved Son, in whom I am well pleased." Again on the Mount of Transfiguration, when the disciples, fearing, entered into the luminous cloud and saw Jesus glorified, his garments white and glistening, a voice was heard, "This is my beloved Son, hear ye him." And once more when he was crucified; the earth rumbling proclaimed it with an inarticulate voice, and the lightnings wrote it against the dark noonday sky in mystic characters, "This is my only-begotten and well-beloved Son."

He is distinguished from all other and lower sons of God in four particulars.

(1) No other can claim pre-existence. He said to the Scribes and Pharisees, who tempted him when he was preaching in the temple porch, "Before Abraham was, I am." Not, "I was," which would be far beyond what any mortal could say, but "I am"; this being an arrogation to himself of the old incommunicable name of Deity, "I AM THAT I AM." He thus claims self-existent being. He is very God of very God, to whom there is neither past, present, nor future; whose life-time is an everlasting now. So it is elsewhere written of him: "In the beginning was the Word, and the Word was with God and the Word was God; the same was in the beginning with God."

(2) No other son of God ever held such a commission as this Jesus of Nazareth. He was the "Sent One." He said of himself: "The Father hath sent me." The persons of the ineffable Godhead are met in council to determine what should be done for the

ruined race; the cry of men's misery has come up to heaven; and the Three are represented as saying, "Whom shall we send and who will go for us?" The Son volunteers to go to the earth as a knight errant for the deliverance of the race, saying, "Here am I, send me." The incarnation was the result. He has come under a three-fold commission: to teach the truth; to illustrate in his own life and character the graces which qualify for kinship with God; and pre-eminently to bear the world's sin in his own body on the tree.

The cross is the consummation of his work. He there uplifts, as a great Atlas, the sin of the world upon his mighty shoulders, even while his heart breaks under the crushing burden. A man went forth into the forest and measured the trees with his eye until he found a suitable one; then he cut it down and had it conveyed to his work shop; there he laid upon it his measuring line and said, "The cross-piece must be twelve spans and the uplift must be ten cubits;" and thus he measured and made the cross whereon this Jesus died. But who shall measure that cross? It is vast as the procession of the ages; it is broad as the world; it is high as heaven; it is deep as hell; and he who hangs upon it—is this Joseph's son? Nay, this is the great living magnet of the universe who said of himself: "I, if I be thus lifted up, will draw all men unto me."

(3) No other son of God ever went to heaven like this one. He gathered his disciples about him and said, "All power is given unto me, in heaven and on earth; go ye therefore into all the world and evangelize, and, lo, I am with you alway, even unto the end." Then he began to ascend out of the midst of them. No

chariot, no horses of flame came to bear him upward ; by his own power, in apparent defiance of nature's laws, he arose with hands outstretched in a last benediction until the opening heavens received him   So he went as he had prophesied, to resume the "glory which he had with the Father before the world was."

(4) And he will come again! "Why stand ye gazing upward"? said the angels to the bewildered disciples. "He shall so come as ye have seen him go." There is one chapter still to be written in the life of this Jesus of Nazareth on earth. He is yet to reign in visible splendor among men.

III. *Behold the Messiah.* The Son of Man and the Son of God are the two distinctive Messianic titles ; the blending of perfect manhood with Godhood constitutes the theanthropic person of the Christ.

Let the conversation of Christ with Nathaniel be observed: "And Jesus saw Nathanael coming to him and said, 'Behold an Israelite indeed in whom there is no guile.'" (By this he meant, not that Nathanael was without sin, but that he, as a true Israelite, was prepared in all frankness to receive the Christ when he should find him. The children of Israel were called a "chosen people"; chosen to possess and transmit the oracles which were in type and symbol and prophecy a declaration of the coming of the Christ. For this reason the expectation of Messiah was called "The Hope of Israel." Jesus saw in Nathanael a genuine and guileless Israelite, who held himself ever in readiness to accept the fulfillment of that hope.)

"And Nathanael said unto him, 'Whence knowest thou me?'

Jesus answered, 'When thou wast under the figtree I saw thee.'" (There is a prudent reserve at this point. Jesus respects the man's secret, even as he declares his acquaintance with it.)

"And Nathanael saith unto him, 'Rabbi, thou art the Son of God; thou art the King of Israel!'" (He knew he was in the presence of one whose eyes pierce with an all-revealing light. This Jesus had perceived the secret imagination of his heart. By such a glimpse of omniscience, he was persuaded that Jesus of Nazareth was none other than the long-expected One.)

"And Jesus answered, 'Because I said, "I saw thee under the fig-tree," believest thou? Thou shalt see greater things than these. Verily, verily, I say unto you, Hereafter ye shall see heaven opened and the angels of God ascending and descending upon the Son of Man.'" (Nathanael had called him Son of God; he calls himself Son of Man. Son of God and Son of Man—the Messiah; the intermediary betwixt heaven and earth, like Jacob's ladder whose foot was on a barren mountain, whose top round was by the throne of God, along which angels ascending bore the prayers of suffering men and returned with blessings from on high.)

In this ladder we have a significant figure of the work of Jesus of Nazareth who, as the great Mediator, is ever present with us. He is present among the children of men. His great work is the conversion of souls; this is his constant miracle. We wonder at the conversion of Saul of Tarsus: at one moment breathing out slaughter against the followers of Jesus, the next moment rolling upward his blinded eyes and crying, "Lord, what wilt thou have me do?" We wonder at the conversion of Luther: one moment a bond slave in the superstitions of a degenerate church, and the next half way up *Sancta Scala*, hearing the voice, "The just shall live by faith," and so entering into newness of life. We wonder at the conversion of John Newton: a pirate swinging in his hammock and seeing a vision of the Christ, and rising to indite his faith in the hymn :—

> " Amazing grace ! how sweet the sound
> That saved a wretch like me ;
> I once was lost, but now am found ;
> Was blind, but now I see."

But there is nothing wonderful here. Such conversions are occurring constantly around us. Regeneration is an "earthly thing." Men and women are being taken out of their misery and set upon their feet ; brought out of chains into freedom, out of darkness into light, out of death into newness of life, every hour of every day. And it is the power of Messiah, an ever-present Christ, that is doing it.

He is at work among the nations in like manner. He converts a nation just as he converts a man. Take a map of the world at the beginning of the Christian era, and beside it spread out a map of the world of to-day ; mark how the Christ has during these eighteen centuries laid his hand on one nation after another, and lifted it out of the darkness of paganism and superstition into the light and glory of Christendom. And to-day he is apparently working in this way. Japan is on her knees under conviction of sin. China is trembling under his glance. Turkey is writhing under his anger as if it were a whip of scorpions. It is doubtful if there was ever a time in history when the nations of the earth were in such commotion as just now. We are looking to diplomacy for a settlement of international affairs :—to the Warlord of Germany, to Salisbury, to our own Secretary of State. Who are these that we should put our confidence in them? The Messiah is walking among the nations; the heart of the king is in his hand as the rivers of water. He is working out his own purposes. He is accomplishing his great work. He is moving on toward the deliverance of the whole world from sin.

Nebuchadnezzar in his dream saw a great image; head of gold, breast of silver, loins of brass, legs of iron, feet of clay. The prophet was called in to interpret the dream. What is this image? It is the Great Powers. And a stone from the mountain side was seen to detach itself and roll downward until it smote the image and ground it to powder; and a mighty wind arose and swept away the dust of the Great Powers as chaff is swept from the threshing floor; and, behold, the stone increased until it became a mountain and filled the earth. This is the parable of Messiah's work. All kings and potentates and statesmen and diplomats are as puppets before him. All powers and principalities are but as card-houses in contrast with the kingdom of Christ. He shall rule when all have vanished. The glory of his kingdom shall cover the earth as the waters cover the sea.

All that is needed in order that men should acknowledge that Jesus of Nazareth is the Messiah, is a frank treatment of his claim. To look calmly into his face is to be convinced. But, alas, men do not stop to think. The average man is too busy with the sordid affairs of this present life to gaze fixedly upon him.

At the beginning of this present century Sir Gilbert West and Lord Lyttleton, who were in profound sympathy with the infidelity which had been developed in the French Encyclopedia, determined on a master stroke for the suppression of the Gospel. It seemed to them that the two great alleged miracles were the Resurrection of Christ and the Conversion of Saul of Tarsus. Gilbert West agreed to write a refutation of the resurrection of Christ, and Lord Lyttleton a refutation of the conversion of Saul. At the conclusion of their work they met by appointment. Lord Lyttleton asked, "What is the result of your work?" The answer was, "I have thoroughly investigated the resurrection of Christ, and have come to the conclusion that he who is said to have come forth from the sepulchre of Joseph's garden, was, as he claimed to be, the veritable Son of God." And Lord Lyttleton said, "I have fully investigated the narrative of the conversion of St. Paul and am satisfied that this man, on his journey along the Damascus highway, really saw Jesus of Nazareth, and that this Jesus was the very Christ of God." The two essays which were written by these men became classics in Christian Apologetics. Would that all men might be persuaded to pursue, as calmly and thoroughly as they did, the study of the great verities of the Gospel. If they are true, they are awfully and eternally true; and they are of stupendous importance to every one of us. Judge ye as wise men. We speak that we do know and testify that we have seen. This Jesus is the Christ. That which our ears have heard, that which our eyes have seen, that which our hands have handled of the word of life, declare we unto you. Behold the Lamb of God!

PROTESTANTISM.

> "And Gamaliel said, Refrain from these men, and let them alone; for if this counsel or this work be of men, it will come to nought; but if it be of God, ye cannot overthrow it; last haply ye be found even to fight against God."—ACTS v. 38, 39.

This was wise counsel. The new religion was making a great stir and the leaders of the Jews were much concerned about it. What should be done? Should they oppose it? Sword and fagot never yet killed a cause. The blood of the martyrs is the seed of the Church. There was nothing to do but to let it alone and trust to the logic of events.

> Truth crushed to the earth will rise again,
> The eternal years of God are hers;
> But error wounded, writhes with pain
> And dies among her worshippers.

In the great square at Wittemberg there stands a monument to the Reformation, on the base of which is this inscription: "Ist's Gottes Werk, so wird's bestehen. Ist's Menschen Werk wird's untergehen." The outcome of these three hundred years of Protestantism proves the wisdom of that apothegm. If this work had been of men, it would long ago have come to naught; but since it is of God, the gates of hell have not been able to prevail against it.

The word Protestant suggests a negative attitude.

This is unfortunate, because Protestantism is distinctly positive and structural. All truths, however are bi-frontal. You must deny before you can affirm. You must fell the forest before you can till the field. You must clear away the debris before you can lay the foundations of your temple. The sun protests before it asserts. It protests against the night, the moon and stars, miasm and disease and death, owls and jackals, ghosts and spectres. But even while protesting it affirms; the birds begin to sing, the heavens are illumined with red and azure glory, the grass blades of the meadow are hung with diamonds, the wheels of commerce revolve, and the roar of industry is heard in the great centres of life.

It is a mistake, however, to suppose that Protestantism began with the Reformation. The Reformation was merely the revival of a dormant principle. In the hand of one of Belzoni's mummies, taken from a crypt by the river side in Egypt a hundred years ago, was found a bulb. It had been within the clasp of that dead hand for three thousand years; but being planted it put forth newness of life. All that the reformers did was to unclasp the stiff fingers of a Church dead in formalism and take therefrom a form of religion, which, though it shared in the darkness of death, had never died; and they planted it, and like the mustard seed it has grown and become a tree, so that the fowls of the air lodge in the branches of it.

But what is Protestantism? What is its doctrinal fabric? Wherein does it differ from the Greek religion and from Roman Catholicism? There is a difference between apologetics and polemics. It is not at all necessary that in vindicating our position as Protestants, we should make war upon those who differ with us; they are entitled to respectful treatment. At the same time it is becoming that all who are in the Protestant communion should be able to give, to every one that asketh, a reason for their faith. The fundamental facts on which Protestantism rests are three, to-wit: *Christ, Scripture* and *Freedom*. Let us address ourselves to these.

(I) *Christ*. At the outset Protestantism protests against the relegation of Christ to a subordinate place in Christian doctrine and life. In making this protest, it formulates a great truth in most positive terms.

(1) *Christ is the foundation of the Church.* Protestants believe that when Christ said, "Thou art *Petros*, and on this rock I will build my church, and the gates of hell shall not prevail against it," he meant not that Peter was to be the foundation of the Church, but rather the great truth to which Peter had just given utterance: "Thou art the Christ the Son of the living God." To say that Peter is the Rock is bad philology, bad philosophy, bad history, bad religion and bad common sense. The Apostle was called *Petros*, a stone, because, on account of his brave statement of the great fundamental truth, he was as a stone hewn out of the rock; just as Scipio was called Africanus because he had traversed Africa, and just as Balboa was called Pacificus because, from the crags of Panama, he first had seen the great western sea. This view is consistent with Scripture; for "other foundation can no man lay than hath been laid, which is Jesus Christ." It is also consistent with history; for in point of fact Christ, and not Peter, has been and is the foundation of the Christian Church. Had it been otherwise, the story

of the Church would in all probability have been written in these words: "The rains descended and the floods came and the winds blew and beat upon it, and it fell." As it is, however, the history stands thus: "The rains descended and the floods came and the winds blew and beat upon it, and it fell not, because it was founded upon a rock." Thus the promise is fulfilled, "The gates of hell shall not prevail against it."

(2) *Christ stands alone in his relation to the Church.* Indeed he is alone everywhere; in his incarnation, in his unique life and character, in his passion, in his triumph over the grave, and in his intercession at the throne of the heavenly grace. That was a significant event which occurred on the Mount of Transfiguration where five of the most distinguished believers who ever lived were met in conference with Christ as to the decease which he was presently to accomplish for sinful men. The two sons of thunder were there and Peter himself; Moses the representative of the Law, and Elijah, who stood for the historic line of Prophets. And when the luminous cloud enclosed them and Jesus had appeared to them in garments white and glistering, it was Peter who said, "Lord, let us make here three tabernacles; one for thee and one for Moses and one for Elias." But he wist not what he said. The cloud vanished; Moses and Elijah went their way; "and they saw no man, but Jesus only." Jesus only! He is first, last, midst, and all in all. The saints in glory are at an infinite remove from Him. Mary, the virgin mother, was blessed among women, but she was a mere woman, after all. It was a grave rebuke that was administered to John in Patmos when he fell at the

feet of the angel to worship him. If ever a being, other than God himself, was worthy of adoration, it was surely that strong angel who, with glowing face, had drawn the veil to reveal to the exiled evangelist his visions of the endless life. But when John would have accorded to him this honor, he recoiled with horror from it, saying, "See thou do it not; for I am thy fellow-servant, and of thy brethren the prophets; worship God." This is why we Protestants have no saints in our calendar. This is why we have no *Ave Marias* in our liturgy. We believe that the word is imperative and final: "Worship God!"

(3) *Christ is accessible to all.* We deny the need of any intermediaries between the soul and him. His word is, "Come unto me." The rending of the veil from the top to the bottom in the very hour when Jesus dying, cried, upon the cross, "It is finished!" meant that a new and living way was now opened into the holiest of all. Let priests and pontiffs and ecclesiastical principalities and powers of every sort now stand aside! Out of the way! The function of the Church and her ministers is not to guard the mercy-seat against the approach of the sinner, but simply to announce that Jesus waits to hear and comfort and strengthen and pardon and save him. Mediators? Oh no. Intercessors? Oh no. Confessors? Oh no. This is child's play, but with serious consequences. Out upon all such interference with the sovereignty of Christ in holy things. In the new dispensation of the Spirit every man is made a king and priest unto God.

II. *The Bible.* Here also we begin with a protest; a protest against the co-ordination of the Scriptures with any other writings on earth. The positive statement of our belief is this: "The Scriptures are the only infallible rule of faith and practice."

(1) *We believe in the inspiration of the Scriptures as the veritable Word of God.* It is not for us to closely define inspiration or declare the method of it. The Mohammedans can tell you precisely how the Koran was delivered to them. It had been recorded from all eternity on the tables beside the throne of God. In fulness of time it was transcribed by the angel Gabriel who caused it to be written on palm leaves, the shoulder blades of camels and the breasts of men, and so placed before Mohammed's eyes and made current among men. But we cannot speak so clearly as to the manner in which our Scriptures came from God. It is quite enough for us to know that holy men wrote as they were moved by the Holy Ghost. We are satisfied with the assurance that all Scripture given by inspiration is profitable for us. The word is, *Theopneustos;* that is, God-breathed. God breathed it.

(2) *The Scriptures thus delivered stand alone as our infallible rule of life.* They are separated by their absolute truth and trustworthiness from all other books. We sometimes speak of the inspiration of Homer and Dante and Virgil and Shakespeare; it is hardly necessary to say, however, that their inspiration is of a totally different sort and implies no gift of infallibility. The holy men who were chosen to write Scripture were endued with power to declare without error the whole counsel of God. The touchstone of Scripture is inerrancy. There is a vast accumulation of apocryphal writings, traditions and pseudo-gospels which are not without historical value, but not to be mentioned in the same breath with

the inspired Word. The man who denies the truthfulness of Scripture sets himself against the consensus of the Protestant Churches and is, so far forth, a rationalist. The Protestant Church asserts its faith in Scripture as a true declaration of the divine will.

(3) *The Scriptures are free and open to every man.* The Reformation began when Luther, rummaging through the library of the University at Erfurt, came upon a dusty copy of the Scriptures and opened it. He read there, "The just shall live by faith"; a truth which came to be known historically as the doctrine of a standing or a falling Church. And still further he read, "Search the Scriptures; for in them ye think ye have eternal life, and these are they which testify of me." Here was the search-warrant placed by the Master in the hand of every believer, entitling him to read for himself and interpret for himself this revealed Word. In pursuance of that truth the Protestant Churches have multiplied the Scriptures in the vernacular until they are now circulated in more than three hundred various tongues and scattered over the world like leaves of the tree of life. We hold that all power is in this Word; the power of conversion, as it is written, "The Word of God is quick and powerful and sharper than any two-edged sword, piercing even to the dividing asunder of the soul and spirit"; the power of sanctification, as implied in our Master's pontifical prayer, "Sanctify them by thy truth, thy Word is truth"; the power of the world's ultimate deliverance, as it is written, "Go ye, evangelize," and again, "Preach the Word," and again, "As the rain cometh down and the snow from heaven and returneth not hither, but watereth the earth, and maketh it to bring forth and bud, that it may give seed to the

sower, and bread to the eater : so shall my Word be that goeth forth out of my mouth; it shall not return unto me void, but it shall accomplish that which I please, and prosper in the thing whereto I sent it."

The last three hundred years are the glory of all history. At the beginning of the 16th century the world was in darkness. The Scriptures were laid away in monasteries, where the monks were engaged in illuminating missals, chanting prayers and swinging censers. The people without, the unshod people under the shadow of the monasteries, were in midnight darkness. The truth in the open Scriptures flew abroad like Milton's angel with the flaming torch. Schools, hospitals and institutions of mercy were multiplied along the way. The people became a power. The world began to recognize the dignity of man. Light came not in a sun-burst, but, as it pierced the primeval shadows of chaos, glimmering and trembling, brighter and brighter unto the perfect day. So the world moves on, under the illuminating power of the Scriptures, toward the restitution of all things.

III. *Freedom.* Here again, we begin by protesting against the subjugation of the individual mind and conscience to any other than God. Then we affirm the freedom of mind, conscience and heart; the voluntary principle in religion, the enfranchisement of the nations, and the deliverance of the race from spiritual bondage into the glorious liberty of the children of God.

(1) *The underlying principle is that of personal responsibility.* Every man must answer for himself at the judgment bar. It is said that when our forefathers came together in the Continental Congress to

consider the Declaration of Independence, there was a long silence. Why? They had before them a manifesto to which it was proposed to mutually pledge their lives, their fortunes and their sacred honor, and for which they would be called to account, not *en masse*, but personally. It was not the Continental Congress, but John Adams, Roger Sherman, John Hancock, Charles Carroll of Carrolton and the other members of that Congress who, one by one, must answer for the decision of that day. Well might they be silent. In like manner we face all the great duties of life. The thought of a personal judgment is thrown backward over all that we do.

(2) It follows, therefore, that as we are personally accountable, *we can take orders only from God.* In vindication of this principle the great battles of Protestantism have been fought. The glory of the recent history of civilization gathers about the Protestant Quadrilateral; the four peoples who have stood as in a solid square confronting the aggressions of ecclesiastical tyranny. The Waldenses, whose bones lie scattered on the Alpine mountains cold; the Beggars of Holland, at cost of home, treasure and life, facing the Spanish Fury; the Covenanters of Scotland, exiled from their churches, worshipping in conventicles among the hills and uplifting the banner "For Christ's Crown and Covenant;" and the Huguenots reddening the pavements of Paris and the soil of all France with their consecrated blood. These constitute the great battalion who, devoting themselves to death for the truth's sake, have liberated the nations of Christendom in refusing to receive orders from priest, presbytery, œcumenical council or ecclesiastical judicatory; from anywhere save the throne of God.

(3) *And this accounts for modern progress.* Lay down the map of Christendom and see how that progress has been limited by the boundaries of Protestant nations. The motto of the Protestant Church is not "*Semper idem,*" but "*Nunquam idem.*" There are only two great facts that abide ever the same. Jesus is the same yesterday, to-day and forever; yet all the world is ever catching new glimpses of the beauty of his face. The Scriptures, also, abide unaltered, because God sealed the Book with seven seals and marked it, "Finis." There is no appendix, no addendum. The revelation was adjusted to the progress of all time. Nevertheless, as John Robinson said, there are new truths ever bursting forth from the Word. But between these two abiding facts, Christ and the Bible, the Church moves onward in new enterprises to ever greater conquests of faith. It is from the bell towers of the Protestant Churches that the announcement of progress is heard.

> Ring out, wild bells, to the wild sky!
> Ring out the old, ring in the new,
> Ring out the false, ring in the true,
> Ring out old shapes of foul disease,
> Ring in the thousand years of peace.
> Ring in the valiant man and free,
> The larger heart, the kindlier hand,
> Ring out the darkness of the land,
> Ring in the Christ that is to be!

We say in the historic creed of the centuries, "I believe in the Holy Catholic Church." Holy, because it magnifies the perfection of the life and character of the only begotten Son of God. Catholic, because its only rule of faith and practice is the Scripture which is adjusted to the needs of every soul of man,

Indestructible, because it rests upon the eternal Rock and the gates of hell shall not prevail against it.

This is Protestanism. Its only pontiff is Christ, whose name is above every other which is named in heaven or on earth. Its only hierarchy is the procession of torch bearers, who go forth to illuminate the dark places of cruelty and the habitations of death, and of reapers who come from harvest fields bringing their sheaves with them. Its only Book is that which was written by holy men who were moved by the Holy Ghost; and its only creed is that which is framed from the Scriptures by men sitting at the feet of Christ. Its grandest cathedrals are the lives of holy men who realize their holy birth and destiny and who "know their rights and knowing dare maintain." Its most fervent litany is this, From all tyranny of mind and conscience and heart, good Lord deliver us. Its grandest music is the breaking of chains; and its magnificent gloria is—*Ave Maria*, Hail Mary, mother of God, pray for us? No! No! No! But this,

> "All hail the power of Jesus' name!
> Let angels prostrate fall,
> Bring forth the royal diadem,
> And crown Him Lord of all."

KING SAUL AT THE WITCH'S CAVE.

"Then said Saul unto his servants, Seek me a woman that hath a familiar spirit, that I may go to her, and inquire of her. And his servants said to him, Behold, there is a woman that hath a familiar spirit at En-dor."
1 SAMUEL xxviii. 7.

It is said, "There is no character in a photograph, because it is a portrait taken at a single sitting." The "composite photograph" gives the best impression of the real man. We want therefore to view Saul at different periods of his life.

Our first glimpse of him is out upon the mountains where he seeks his father's asses. He is "a choice young man and a goodly, and among the children of Israel there is not a goodlier person than he." His stature and sturdy bearing remind us instantly of John Ridd in "Lorna Doone." In the course of his quest he comes upon the home of the prophet Samuel, of whom he inquires the whereabouts of the lost asses. The prophet replied, "Set not thy mind on them, for they are found. And on whom is all the desire of Israel? Is it not upon thee?"

He is next seen at the school of the prophets. Here he is getting rid of some of his roughness, the odor of the soil, and preparing in a measure, unawares, for the high office that awaits him. His character is changed; as it is written, "God gave him another heart, and the Spirit of God came upon him."

He is moved by new hopes and purposes. His remarkable presence in this company "coming down from the high place with a psaltery, and a tabret and a pipe and a harp before them," is remarked upon in a phrase which afterwards becomes a proverb—" Is Saul also among the prophets"?

Next at Mizpeh. The people have been called together in solemn assemblage for the formal choice of a king. The lot is taken, and it falls upon the tribe of Benjamin; of the tribe of Benjamin the family of Matri is chosen; and in the family of Matri, the lot falls upon Saul, the son of Kish. He is sought for and cannot be found, for "behold, he hath hid himself among the stuff"; that is, the baggage which surrounds the camp. He is brought forth into the midst of the assembly, and his presence inspires the greatest enthusiasm, for when he stands among the people he is higher than any of them from his shoulder and upwards. And all the people shout, " God save the King"!

But Saul himself seems to have been indifferent to his high calling. There were some among the people who looked upon him as a mere yeoman, and said, "How shall this man save us"? The king-elect returned to his farm. He gloried in the open air and the sunlight. He loved to throw back his shoulders and rejoice in the freedom of the fields. He was following the plow when messengers came to announce an incursion of the Ammonites. The town of Jabesh-gilead was besieged, and the cry of the terror-stricken people rang in his ears. He hewed in pieces a yoke of oxen, after the rude custom of that time, and sent them throughont the borders of Israel to enkindle their patriotic zeal, as the Scots were aroused in later times by the flaming cross upon their hills. He found himself at the head of a considerable army of volunteers; the martial spirit was aroused within him; he marched to the relief of the besieged city, and accomplished a great deliverance; as it is written, "He slew the Ammonites until the heat of the day."

Then Saul assumed his proper place in the palace. He was every inch a king, just and resolute, ruling in equity. A cabinet of remarkable counselors was gathered about him. Samuel was his court chaplain Abner was his secretary of war, Abiathar was the high priest; David soon became his lieutenant and confidential friend. The king now showed himself a man of magnetic control, and entered upon a remarkable career. Victory succeeded victory in the field. Those of the people who had formerly distrusted Saul now gathered loyally about him.

But as time passed a strange malady falls upon him. We find him giving way to his passions and eccentric impulses. He is filled with envy and jealousy. He shows himself cruel and vindictive towards those who oppose him. At Michmash, in the absence of Samuel, desiring to offer sacrifice before the battle, he profanely takes matters into his own hands. He hurls his javelin at David, who seeks to comfort his melancholy. He massacres the priests at Nob. Is it the intoxication of power that has seized him? Is he realizing, in moral bondage, the result of his self-indulgence; as it is written, "He that doeth sin is the servant of it"? Or is he indeed possessed of an evil spirit? He rejects all divine counsels and admonitions, and seems determined to run upon the bosses of the shield of God. There is scarcely a more lamentable picture of the decay of character than this:

> So fallen! so lost! the light withdrawn
>   Which once he wore!
> The glory from his gray hairs gone
>   Forevermore!
>
> Of all we loved and honored, naught
>   Save power remains—
> A fallen angel's pride of thought,
>   Still strong in chains.
>
> All else is gone; from those great eyes
>   The soul has fled.
> When faith is lost, when honor dies,
>   The man is dead!
>
> Then pay the reverence of old days
>   To his dead fame;
> Walk backward, with averted gaze,
>   And hide the shame!*

The affairs of the kingdom have now reached a crisis. The Philistines have crowded their way through the borders of Israel and massed themselves at the old battle-field of Esdraelon like a Tartar horde. The desperate and remorseful king knows not where to turn. His old adviser, Samuel, is dead. Abiathar, the priest, has gone and taken the Urim and Thummim with him. The priests, outraged by the massacre of their brethren, have forsaken him. He is no more counseled in dreams and visions of the night. The chill shadow of approaching disaster has fallen over him. He cannot go into this battle without some supernatural support. He is at his wits'

---

*These words were written by Whittier on the political recreancy of Daniel Webster in 1850.

end. At this point he learns of a female necromancer who plies her lawless trade among the hills. He disguises himself, and with two faithful friends makes his way to the witch's cave at En dor. It is night.

And the king said, "I pray thee, divine unto me by the familiar spirit and bring me him up whom I shall name unto thee."

Then said the woman, "Whom shall I bring up unto thee?"

And he said, "Bring me up Samuel"—Samuel of all men—whom he had loved and hated, grieved and persecuted, and ultimately driven to his death!

The witch waved her wand, mumbled her cabalistic charms and suddenly uttered a shriek of surprise. And the king said, "Be not afraid. What seest thou?"

The woman said, "I see a god rising from the earth"; and then, "An old man cometh up; he is covered with a mantle." The king bowed himself to the earth and received the intimation of his approaching defeat and death.

It is an open question whether or no it was the real Samuel who appeared on this occasion. Not that the spirits of the dead may not return on occasion to this world; for did not Moses and Elijah commune with the Christ on the Mount of Transfiguration? But there are two suspicious facts in the present case; one is that Saul did not see Samuel. He took the witch's word for it, and he was in the very mood to believe that it was he. The other is that the message delivered by the spectre was nothing new. The king had previously been warned again and again of the calamity which was to overtake him. But I am not disposed to turn aside here into irrelevant or collateral questions, for there are certain practical truths and lessons which demand our attention.

I. *As to the probationary character of life.* Saul had all along been on trial. In his call to the throne he had been required to meet certain tasks and responsibilities and was endowed with peculiar gifts and faculties for the discharge of them. If ever God was patient, it was with this man. He surrounded him with faithful counsellors who warned, exhorted and entreated him. He had a fair chance to make a success of character and life. So have we all—" a fighting chance"; no more, no less. In many ways our circumstances are against us; but the "mark of true greatness is for a man to prove himself superior to his environment." It is for us to say whether we will fight down our lower nature and be true to our best impulses and to the God who is ever stimulating and remonstrating with us, or give way to our besetting sins and temptations. To triumph means character and usefulness; to yield means an utter loss of manhood and ultimate exile from God.

II. *The touch-stone of spiritual success is obedience.* There is no room for wilfulness in the better life. Saul was determined to have his own way and he had it. The turning point in his life was in his famous campaign against the Amalekites. The Lord had said, "Go and smite Amalek, and utterly destroy all that they have, and spare them not." The result was an utter rout of the enemy; "Saul smote the Amalekites from Havilah until thou comest to Shur; and he took Agag, the king, alive; and spared also the best of the sheep and the oxen and the fatlings, and would not utterly destroy them." On his return from battle he met Samuel and said, "Blessed be thou of the Lord; I have performed the commandment of the Lord." And Samuel said, "What meaneth then this bleating of sheep and lowing of oxen which I hear?" The truth was, Saul had spared Agag to grace his own triumph; but he was probably right when he excused himself further by saying, "I have spared the sheep and oxen to sacrifice unto the Lord thy God." And the prophet said, "Why didst not thou obey the voice of the Lord? To obey is better than sacrifice, and to hearken than the fat of rams." And rending his mantle, he said, "The Lord hath rent the kingdom of Israel from thee this day."

The beginning of the higher life is in a covenant of absolute subjection to the divine will. There must be no reservation. There can be no wilfulness. "Ye are my friends, if ye do whatsoever I command you." No half-hearted service will answer. "My son give me thy heart." All or nothing! We cannot serve God and have our own way. "Whatsoever he saith unto you, do it."

III. *There is such a thing as "grieving the Spirit";* this is for those who profess to be the people of God. For the impenitent there is another phrase, "quenching the Spirit"; this is done in rejecting the overtures of mercy which are extended from time to time, as one puts out a kindling flame by repeatedly throwing water upon it. But we "grieve" those whom we profess to love, our friends, our mothers, our counselors; we grieve them by repeated slights and affronts and inattentions. Our best friend is the Holy Spirit; he is constantly urging us to larger measures of grace and virtue and fruitfulness. He is grieved when we refuse his invitations and admonitions. He is grieved by habitual disobedience, by worldliness, by neglect of known duty, by persistence in sin. And with what result? Coldness of heart, discomfort, self-accusation, departure farther and farther from God. Then misery and hopelessness; no more Urim and Thummim; no more blessed visions in the night watches; no more walking with God in the cool of the day. We feel ourselves to be as Saul was,— alone, forsaken. The awful consummation of such a course is seen in the bitterness of Christ's anguish on the cross, when, not for himself, but in behalf of those who have exposed themselves to this grievous pain of abandonment, he cried, "My God! My God! Why hast thou forsaken me?"

IV. *But we must have some sort of religion.* I call you to witness that no matter how far we may have wandered from our original devotion to Christ, we cannot live without some form of devotion. The soul craves it. If we cannot find God, we shall seek the witch of En-dor. We know that we belong to two worlds. We must keep up our communication with the invisible and supernatural. The soul's thirst must be slaked at wayside pools if not at the river of life.

Whither shall we go in our wandering? Into atheism? That is most unnatural; the evidence of "a power not ourselves making for righteousness" is so interwoven with the fibres of our being that denying God is like wrenching off an arm or plucking out an eye. It is the fool, and the fool only, who hath said in his heart, "There is no God."

If not into atheism, where then? Into rationalism? To reject the revelation from above in order that we may follow the dictates of unaided reason is pure wilfulness; it leads us into all manner of error and unbelief. We wander about like a man lost on the prairie, with no landmarks anywhere. A level stretch of boundless, monotonous prospect on every side; no path except that made by our own foot-prints, to which we ever return. We refuse to get our bearings from the only hopeful quarter, the stars that shine in heaven above us. This is to be lost indeed.

Or if not into rationalism, perhaps into agnosticism? This is the logical outcome of the habit of rejecting truths which are constantly set before us. We begin by doubting and end by saying, "I know not. There may be a God; but I cannot see him. It is possible that there is a future life; but no one has returned to speak definitely about it. The Scriptures may be true; but there is a difference of opinion, and I am not wise enough to solve it." So we find ourselves at the last like those eyeless fish in the waters of the Mammoth Cave, who have nothing but scars to show that once they could see.

Or it may be that we find ourselves joined to some form of base superstition. Saul was a spiritualist. I do not say that there is no truth underlying this most specious form of falsehood. But for the so-called "spiritualism" of these times I have no feeling but of contempt and abhorrence. The idea that our dear ones who have gone to glory, to sit at the feet of Jesus in the heavenly splendors, should return to earth to tap tables and hide in cabinets and submit to materialization in darkened rooms, to drivel sentimental nothings and meaningless trivialities at the call of male and female transcendentalists of generally doubtful character, is too puerile and contemptible for a moment's thought. And experience proves that danger lies that way.

I had a schoolmate once, the son of a clergyman,

taught by a Christian mother to receive the simple truths of the Gospel, who as time passed, following his own inclinations, forsook the covenant with its moral precepts and yielded himself a willing attendant at the witch's cave. He deemed himself a profound thinker, and asserted that he had found a system of philosophy far better than the Gospel of Christ. He finished his course in the murder of President Garfield; and he excused himself for that dreadful crime by saying that he was under the control of a supernatural influence.

The danger point is at the divergence of the paths. The star that swings out of its orbit by a single inch, is lost forever in infinite space. God, the Bible, the influence of the Spirit, these mark the appointed route of the Christian life. The moment we depart from them we are on dangerous ground. The Christian system is like a chain whose strength is lost if but a single link be broken. To say that we believe with a reservation, is to say that we do not believe at all. And this is the tendency of our time,—to place one's own heart and reason over against the divine authority. "For I bear them record that they have a zeal of God; but not according to knowledge; for they being ignorant of God's righteousness, and going about to establish their own righteousness, have not submitted themselves unto the righteousness of God." If we persist in such a course, wilful and unrestrained, it is certain that we shall ultimately be "given over to believe a lie."

The last chapter in the history of Saul remains to be told. On the heights of Gilboa he met the Philistines. The figure of the stalwart king was to be seen amid a shower of arrows, desperation in his face, despair in his heart. A troop of the enemy had driven him up a steep hill, and there he stood at bay. His three sons had been slain; his armor-bearer lay dead beside him; his shield, stained with blood, had been cast away, and he leaned heavily upon his spear, weak from a self-inflicted wound. The dizziness and darkness of death were before him; he reeled and fell. The next morning his armor was fastened above the altar of the Ashtaroth and his headless body was impaled on the wall of Beth-shan like a captured bird of prey.

Let us hear the conclusion of the whole matter. Back to thy first love, O believer in Christ! Back to thy covenant and thy vows of espousal! Back to the old-fashioned Book which is thy only infallible rule of faith and practice! Back to the mercy seat where once thy communion was so sweet with God! It is not too late; the hands of mercy are stretched out still.

In the recent exhibit at the Luxembourg there was one picture by an American artist which attracted great attention. It was called "The Return." A wandering son in rags and tatters has come home; he kneels in an attitude of hopeless anguish by the side of the high bed whereon his father lies dead with the candles about him. Too late! too late!

This is not true. The Father never dies; the prodigal may. The Father waits with outstretched hands. Here is the divine record, "And he arose and came to his father. But when he was a great way off his father saw him and had compassion, and ran and fell on his neck and kissed him."

HOW JERICHO FELL.

"By faith the walls of Jericho fell down, after they were compassed about seven days. HEB. XI, 30.

The children of Israel were at the borders of the promised land. They had crossed the river and were encamped at Gilgal in the edge of a magnificent grove of palm trees. Two miles away they could see Jericho, a strong city with "walls up to heaven," encircled by an amphitheatre of hills; and beyond that was the land flowing with milk and honey, the land which had been promised to Abraham four hundred and thirty years before. The key of the situation was Jericho. It stood like a sentinel guarding the way.

At night Joshua went out to reconnoitre. He passed through the palm-grove and surveyed the barred gates and towering walls, searching for some point of attack. On a sudden there stood over against him a man with a drawn sword in his hand. "Who goes there?" He instantly stood on guard and uttered the challenge, thinking the intruder to be one of the enemy. The answer was, "Nay, but as captain of the Lord's host am I come." It was the Angel of the Covenant. Then ensued a conference respecting the siege of Jericho.

The plan traversed in that conference was carried out in due time. It was a singular performance, the like of which has never been seen in military tactics. This was the arrangement of the army that was to compass the city: a band of armed men led the way; then came seven priests with rams' horns; after them the Levites bearing the Ark of the Covenant; then again the armed men. There was to be perfect silence in the ranks, except for the blowing of the rams' horns.

On the first day the guards, who stood upon the walls of Jericho, saw this strange procession come down the road from Gilgal and begin its march around the city. On the second day they probably remarked upon the singularity of the proceeding. On the third day they looked into each other's faces and smiled. On the fourth everybody in Jericho probably turned out to see it. There they come! the same priests, the same order, the same wooden chest, the same rams' horns, the same solemn silence. It is safe to say that on the fifth day and the sixth there was much derision and laughter;

> "The King of France, with twice ten thousand men,
> Marched up the hill, and then marched down again."

On the seventh day the procession having completed its living circumvallation, did not turn out into the Gilgal road, but proceeded to compass the city again, and so on until seven times. Then, on reaching the gate, they paused; the priests lifted the twisted horns to their lips and sounded a blast; whereat the armed men began to shout with one accord, perhaps, Jehovah Nissi! "The Lord our banner!" The people of Jericho, watching with smiling interest, felt the stone fabric under their feet begin to shake and tremble as if ten thousand giants were tugging and straining at the parapet; their laughter ceased; their faces blanched, and in another moment the great bulwarks tottered and fell asunder! Then amid the cries of the wounded and dying, over the ruined heaps the army of Israel rushed in to possess the city.

How shall we explain this? The secret, if known to the Great Powers of Europe, would save them an expenditure of millions of money for arms and armaments. It would be of incalculable value to the Church also; for an important part of her work is the casting down of the strongholds of evil. There is Islam, a frowning Jericho, standing in the way of Christian progress. There is Judaism, founded deep in divine tradition and with walls towering to heaven. There is infidelity entrenched in bulwarks that have resisted the assaults of ages. There are the dram shop, licentiousness, Sabbath desecration—Jerichos all. How shall the church reduce them? Here is the secret: "By faith the walls of Jericho fell down." By faith! Let us see how Faith proceeded to the task.

I. It *began by throwing up its hands*. It confessed an utter inability. When Joshua on that moonlight night saw the barred gates and towering walls, he knew that the task was hopeless. But just here is the beginning of strength. "I will glory in my infirmities," says Paul, "that the power of Christ may rest upon me. I take pleasure in my infirmities for Christ sake; for when I am weak then am I strong. I can do all things through him who strengtheneth me."

II. Faith *fell on its knees and called on God*. At this time the children of Israel kept the Passover. It involved them in a delay of an entire week and gave the enemy an opportunity of strengthening his defences. But no matter; the Passover must be kept. The lamb was slain, the altar blazed, the prayers were made, and Israel was set right before God.

The Duke of Alva, engaged in a campaign, was asked if he had observed the eclipse. "No," he replied, "I am quite too busy to look toward the sky." This is a common fault. But he makes a grievous mistake who enters upon a day of solemn tasks and duties without the morning prayer; and you will be a foolish man if you to-night shall go into the unknown country of darkness and danger without, at the least, folding your hands as the dear mother taught you long ago, and saying,

>"Now I lay me down to sleep,
> I pray the Lord my soul to keep."

III. Next, Faith *got hold of a promise.* The captain of the Lord's host said, "I deliver Jericho into thy hand." That was enough; Joshua believed it.

It is a great thing to have a promise at the outset. A young man from a western town wrote me recently, "I am ambitious to come to New York and make my way. Can you give me a word of encouragement? I must have something to bank on." O, what enheartenment there is in a word from heaven! And the Book is full of promises. Here is one of boundless possibilities: "Ask and it shall be given you, seek and ye shall find, knock and it shall be opened unto you." Here is another that rings like a trumpet: "They that wait upon the Lord shall renew their strength; they shall mount up with wings as eagles; they shall run and not be weary, and they shall walk and not faint." Here is another as a strong staff to lean on : "Lo, I am with you alway even unto the end of the world." Get hold of a promise, my friend. It will be a starting point for your journey ; a postulate for the great argument of life. Get hold of a promise ; spread it out ; meditate upon it night and day ; grasp it tighter ; stretch it wider, wider ; lie down upon it ; rest in it. The great bridge over the Niagara began with a kite string, then a whip-cord, then a rope, then a larger rope, then a wire, then a strand of wire, a cable, a larger cable, a foot bridge, and finally a magnificent fabric over which the loaded trains are passing to-day.

IV. Faith *found out a divine plan and fell in with it.* If you or I had been in Joshua's place, it is probable that we would have called a council of war. One would have said the way to reduce Jericho is by sapping and mining ; another would have suggested that catapults should be put on the hills round about to batter down the gates ; and still another might have insisted that the only hope lay in a protracted siege and the slow processes of famine. But Joshua did the better thing ; he hearkened to what the captain of the Lord's host had to say.

God's plan for our daily life is all marked out in Scripture. The plan of salvation is here : repent, believe and be baptized ; that is to say, turn your back on sin, accept the Lord Jesus Christ and confess him before men. The plan of sanctification also is here, to-wit : a creed, an ethical code and a rule of service. Our creed is whatever God says as to spiritual truth. Our code of morals is the Decalogue plus all the other precepts of the divine law. And our rule of service is, Go evangelize ; do good as you have opportunity unto all men.

There are other plans of salvation besides that of Scripture, but this is the only one that saves; as it is written, "There is none other name under heaven given among men, whereby we must be saved, than that of Jesus Christ."

Other methods of sanctification are proposed also, but the Scripture plan which brings us under the influence of the Holy Spirit is the only one that brings us into Christ-likeness and up to the full stature of a man.

V. Faith then *proceeded to business.* Joshua and the children of Israel did precisely as the Angel of the Covenant had commanded them to do. They formed in line, took the Ark along with them, kept perfect silence in the ranks, marched round and round once every day, seven times on the Sabbath, and then shouted. Here was exact obedience. This is the secret of success in serving God.

A passive faith is no faith at all. Faith without works is dead. People do not reach heaven by sitting in their pews and singing hymns. Off yonder is a vessel on the sea; let us hail it.

"Ship ahoy!"
"Ay! ay!"
"Whither are you bound?"
"To Canaan's happy shore."
"Where's your skipper?"
"Down below."
"Where's your helmsman?"
"Down below."
"Where are your crew?"
"Down below."
"What are you doing?"
"Drifting."

"You'll never get there!"

And they never will. People do not reach Canaan that way.

It took courage for the children of Israel to carry out the divine plan. No doubt while they were marching around the city, many an arrow came from the walls, and, worse than that, laughter and derision; but they kept right on.

It took patience also. *Patientia omnia vincit!* A little fellow in kilts with a fire shovel in hand was engaged in carrying a ton of coal from the sidewalk to the shute. A gentleman passing by said, "Do you expect to shovel that all in?" "Yes, sir,' said the little fellow, "if I keep at it." There was a world of philosophy in that reply. He that believeth shall not make haste. All things are accomplished by bravely, patiently keeping at it.

VI. But after all, *Faith did nothing*; nothing at all. The rams' horns did not blow down those walls. There was no virtue in that weary tramp, tramp, of the queer procession. The final shout had surely nothing to do with it. Who then or what overthrew those walls? God did it. And God has everything to do with the triumphs of our spiritual life, that all the glory may be his.

It is so in the matter of our salvation: repent, believe, be baptized; these are conditions precedent, but the one thing needful is regeneration, and that is wholly the work of God. "Not by might nor by power; but by my spirit, saith the Lord." "Except a man be born again he cannot see the kingdom of God."

It is so in our sanctification. "Work out your own salvation with fear and trembling." Work it out—

that is, to its glorious fullness and consummation in Christ-like character; "for it is God that worketh in you both to will and do of his own good pleasure." If we breathe spiritually, it is because God furnishes the air. If we eat, it is God's bread. If we drink, it is water out of the King's well. All glory to him!

It is so also in service. Paul may plant and Apollos water, but God giveth the increase. In all things faith is a conditional but not an efficient cause. No matter what we do, we come up ultimately against the absolute need of a miracle. The children of Israel went out of Egypt and down the road toward Canaan until they reached the border of the sea. They could go no farther; on either side were the mountains and behind them they heard the rumbling of Pharaoh's chariots; they were wholly in the power of the foe, as far from deliverance as ever. All their doing thus far was as naught. In their impotency they fell upon their knees and cried to heaven. Then came the word, "Stand still and see the salvation of your God." The waters of the sea were piled up in crystal walls on either side; they passed through dry shod; and on the further shore they sang, not of what they themselves had done, but of what the Almighty God had wrought in their behalf; "Who is like unto thee, O God, glorious in holiness, fearful in praises, doing wonders? The horse and his rider hast thou cast into the sea."

Here is the secret of self-conquest. All earnest men and women are engaged in a stern conflict with the pride and passion of unregenerate nature. We wrestle not against flesh and blood, but against principalities and powers. Let us begin aright by kneeling at Calvary and invoking the help of him who said, "No man shall pluck you out of my hand." It is a serious warfare and there is no discharge in this war.

> O watch and fight and pray,
> The battle never give o'er;
> Renew it boldly every day,
> And help divine implore.

And here is the secret of the conquest of the world. Out of the upper chamber went a little company of humble folk to be the vanguard of a great procession, who have ever since been compassing the world. Their only weapon is the sword of the Spirit, which is the Word of God. The "foolishness of preaching" by force of example as well as in pulpit ministration is destined to overthrow all the strongholds of evil. The very essence of preaching is foolishness; as it is written, "We preach Christ crucified; to the Jews a stumbling block; to the Greeks foolishness; but to them which are saved the wisdom and the power of God."

Marching, rams' horns, silence, shouting; O this seems a hopeless task! But we are going to win the world yet. This is the victory which overcometh the world, even your faith. We follow the divine plan; and just in the measure of our obedience we are winning the world for God. It is a glorious work. Lend a hand, good friend! To hold aloof would be the mistake of your life. The unspeakable joy of heaven will be that you had some part in it.

"TOM BROWN OF RUGBY;" OR, MANLY CHRISTIANITY.*

"Till we all come in the knowledge of the Son of God unto a perfect man unto the measure of the stature of the fulness of Christ."—EPH. iv. 13.

Tom Brown is dead. A week ago he crossed the tropics. Had I said Judge Hughes of Chester you might not have understood, but everybody knows Tom Brown of Rugby and Oxford. His age was above three score and ten, but he kept his boyhood to the end. The width of the Atlantic was between us, yet he was dear to all Americans; for during our Civil War he stood beside John Bright in his defense of freedom and the Union. Was his life a success? Not as a lawyer; for he dwelt a briefless barrister at Lincoln's Inn. Not as a business man; he was the founder of Rugby Colony in Tennessee in 1880; made up of young Englishmen familiar with lawn tennis and fox-hunting, it soon dwindled out. Not as a statesman; for, though he was a member of Parliament in his time, he was rarely heard of. But he did one thing well; he painted the portrait of a manly youth. He did it in such a manner as to captivate

---

*This discourse was preached on the Sabbath following the death of Thomas Hughes, the author of "Tom Brown's Schooldays," "The Manliness of Christ," and other works.

and stimulate the nobler impulses of youth throughout the world. And throughout his life he sought to exemplify this: a frank, kindly, broad-hearted, generous, earnest Christian man.

He had his faults; that goes without saying. But he stood for manliness in Christian living; and for this the world will always revere him. The children of the market-place may not judge wisely as to Christianity, and often they do not; but the world knows a thorough Christian when it sees him. It has no patience with sentimentalism on the one hand or with worldly Christianity on the other. It detests the holy whine, the melancholy accent, and the mere outward garb. It equally detests that profession of Christianity which is ever compromising with the world's fashion. "Ye are the salt of the earth: but if the salt have lost his savour, wherewith shall it be salted? it is thenceforth good for nothing, but to be cast out, and to be trodden under the foot of men. Ye are the light of the world. A city that is set on a hill cannot be hid. Neither do men light a candle and put it under a bushel, but on a candlestick; and it giveth light unto all that are in the house. Let your light so shine before men, that they may see your good works, and glorify your Father which is in heaven."

In thinking over the life of Thomas Hughes I have constantly associated him with the familiar phrase, *Sana mens in sano corpore:* "A sound mind in a healthy body."

I. *The healthy body to begin with.* Tom Brown was the champion of college athletics. The boat-race between Oxford and Cambridge took place yesterday on the Isis. Had he been living, he would in all probability have been there and "running with the crews." Our American colleges are indebted to him for the introduction of the Rugby game of foot-ball.

I confess to a sincere sympathy with the college athletics of our time. In the entire calendar there is no better exhibition of the manliness of American student-life than in the annual Yale-Princeton football game. No doubt there are many excesses and extravagances. Nevertheless, the present order of things is much better than that of former days. You may take your choice; a slender youth, narrow-chested, stoop-shouldered, with watery eyes, a hacking cough and a profoundly laborious devotion to his books, on the one hand; on the other, the stroke oar, the first base, or the quarter-back—broad-chested, robust, brown as an Indian, and with no reason in the world why he should not be equally devoted to his books. As a rule, the modern system of athletics is conducive to health. We have sixty thousand physicians in America, all good men; but God is better than all, and the air and the sunlight are his Materia Medica.

And athletics practiced within the bounds of reason are also conducive to moral health. There is a sense in which the proverb, "Boys will be boys," holds true; and that other proverb also, "You cannot put an old head on young shoulders." There must be some vent for the exuberant spirits of youth. A great change has come over college life since the days of the "Thanksgiving powwows" and the "Freshman rush," hazing, society dinners and carousing of various sorts. It is far better that a boy should break a finger or lame himself than spend his days and nights sowing wild oats. Better water on the knee than water on the brain.

II. *But the sana mens is of high importance.* A healthy body is of little use unless it be occupied by a healthy mind. The word *sana* here is suggestive. The beginning of true manhood is in coming to one's self. "The mind" in this connection must be taken as a comprehensive term, meaning the whole spiritual nature. A sane mind is simply a soul at complete peace with itself and God.

I am like one awaking from a bewildered dream and finding myself in a prison cell. I cannot remember how I came here; but I want to escape. I begin to investigate; I climb up to the windows, they are securely barred; I inspect the lock, it is fast; I examine the floor to see if the slabs can be lifted; I cry aloud in my despair, and my cry echoes back to mock me. I hear the grating of the hinges and turn to see; the door is open and one stands there with hands outstretched, pierced hands, saying, "Come with me and I will liberate you." To answer that call is faith; to follow him is to come forth into the glorious liberty of the children of God. So I find my manhood. So I come to myself again. Henceforth my mind is a right mind; a sane mind reconciled to itself and God.

And this was the sum and substance of the teaching of Thomas Hughes; a Christian resolution dominating the whole habit of life. It was natural that in pursuance of this thought, he should make much of the three manly graces; Courage, Courtesy, and Cheerfulness.

1. *Courage.* If you have formed a conviction as to truth and duty, be ready on occasion to stand for it. Let no man take thy crown; let no man despise thee.

There is one episode in Tom Brown's school-days at Rugby which is calculated to stimulate all that is noble in a youthful heart. The new boy Arthur from Devonshire had just entered school; a pale lad, with a delicate hand, large blue eyes and fair hair. He had a rough reception from the boys and was almost scared out of his wits. On the first night, at the retiring hour, he was shown to "Number Four" where there were twelve beds. The other boys were laughing and chatting, but poor Arthur was overwhelmed with the strangeness of it. How could he ever sleep in a room with twelve other boys? At length, however, he summoned resolution and managed to get into his night-gown. Then came the tug of war! He had promised his mother to kneel down and say his prayer. (Now, boy, to thine own self be true!) Some of the lads were already in bed with their chins on their knees. It was a trying moment for lonely Arthur. But he dropped on his knees by his bedside just as he had done ever since he could remember. There was a momentary lull in conversation; then somebody laughed, and the fun began. Tom Brown was sitting on the foot of his bed unlacing his boots and failed to see what was going on. A brute of a fellow, standing in the middle of the room, picked up a slipper and shied it at the kneeling boy. Tom turned and saw; and the next moment the boot he had pulled off flew straight at the bully's head.

"Confound you, Brown," he roared. "What's that for?"

"Never mind," said Tom. "If any fellow wants the other boot he knows how to get it."

That ended the matter just then; but Tom couldn't

sleep; his head throbbed, his conscience troubled him. He too had promised his mother years ago. When he awoke, his trouble was still with him. At length he determined to quit himself like a man. He leaped from his bed and knelt down, but he could not pray; the bell as it rang seemed to mock him; he listened to every whisper in the room. What were they thinking of him? He was ashamed to remain upon his knees and ashamed to rise. He could only repeat to himself over and over, "God be merciful to me a sinner." But the battle had been fought and won. Rise up, Tom Brown, Knight of the Cross of Jesus Christ! He arose to face his schoolmates; two of them had followed his example and were kneeling beside their beds.

2. *Courtesy.* Tom Brown was as gentle as he was brave. So it always is; "the bravest are the tenderest, the loving are the daring." A gentleman is simply a gentle man.

It is a difficult thing for a man of noble birth and breeding, or of wealth or education, to be courteous. A plain man on a humbler level finds it easy; but for those of higher station the temptation to be arrogant or else patronizing in their manner is almost irresistible.

> Oh it is excellent
> To have a giant's strength; but is tyrannous
> To use it like a giant.

A lady hurrying along the street in London turned a corner and ran against a grimy newsboy. With the instinct of a lady she said, "I beg your pardon, my boy. Did I hurt you?" He looked at her in a dazed sort of way and then whipped off his cap like a gentleman of the old school, and said, "You have my parding, Miss, and welcome; and the next time you run ag'in me, you kin knock me clean off my feet and I'll never say a word." He followed her out of sight and turning to a fellow Arab, said, "I say, Jim, its the first time I ever had anybody ax my parding, and it knocked me all in a heap." There is an incalculable power in such courtesy as that; kings and potentates, as well as beggar boys, have been conquered by it.

We speak of chivalry; it is not necessary to go to courts or tilting grounds to find it; an opportunity awaits you in a Broadway car. This young man is so industriously engaged in reading his newspaper that he does not heed the old lady who, with her arms full of bundles, is holding to a strap near by. A woman opposite, whose neighbor has just vacated a seat, thinks nothing of the weary waiters, but shakes out her skirts and occupies twice her former space. A youth rises to offer his seat to a pretty girl, not realizing that the colored maid or seamstress yonder, being much more weary, has a tenfold claim upon it. And she who draws her dainty skirts aside, because a laboring man with soiled and callous hands, has taken his place beside her, no doubt thinks herself a gentlewoman. There is much of this sort of behavior, and much of the other also. True religion projects itself into the smallest things of life. You may show yourself a Christian in a cable car.

3. *Cheerfulness.* Why not? This is a good world and there is a gracious God above it.

There are some people who are always gruff and in a captious mood. Nothing agrees with them; nothing suits them. The weather is never right. The country is going to the dogs. And, except themselves, the people generally are no better than they ought to be. Then there are others like Mark Tapley, cheerful under all circumstances; or like Sidney Smith, who said, "I have gout, asthma, and seven other maladies, but otherwise, thank the Lord, I am very well."

It is cheerfulness that makes the wheels of this old world go merrily round. A few years ago a fire occurred in Minneapolis which destroyed one of the large business houses and wiped out its owner's wealth. He was in the far west at the time, and when the disaster was telegraphed to him fell into a deep melancholy from which nothing could arouse him. He took the train for home. At Omaha he received a bundle of letters which he listlessly read one by one. At length the passengers saw him open a letter which made him smile and presently he laughed audibly. The tide was turned, and this was what did it: "My dear Papa, I went down to see your store that was burned and you can't think how pretty it looked all covered with ice. Love and kisses from your little Lilian." He saw the vision which his little daughter had conjured up; icicles hanging in crystal beauty over the ruin of his fortunes. There was something to live for yet. God be praised for the bright sunny people who make the best of life for themselves and for others around them!

But after all in this matter of right Christian living, all depends upon the way we begin. What is our purpose? Have we "grasped the handle of our being"? Do we propose to spend and be spent in our own interest alone? Or, do we mean to live for others and the glory of God? The aim is everything.

And the true inspiration of life is caught only by fixing our eyes upon the Ideal Man.

The Ideal Man was never seen on earth but once. Thomas Hughes saw him in Christ, and his thought of Christian manliness was borrowed directly from him. All youth are familiar with "Tom Brown at Rugby" and "Tom Brown at Oxford;" but Thomas Hughes wrote one thing which is more universally known and read than these, a pamphlet on "The Manliness of Christ." In his early life he saw Christ, loved and revered him, and resolved to be like him.

The Man of Nazareth was a man of the people: brave, gentle, generous, true to his convictions, faithful unto death. In his carpenter-shop he did honest work, and vindicated the dignity of labor for all time. In his ministry he "went about doing good." His ear was open to every cry of distress; his hand was ever stretched forth to help. How brave he was in denouncing all shams and hypocrisies: "Woe unto you, Scribes and Pharisees! How shall ye escape the damnation of hell?" How gentle he was to the weak and erring and penitent: "Go and sin no more." How eager to relieve pain and weariness: "Come unto me all ye that labor and are heavy laden and I will give you rest." And how gladsome withal. The sun shone through his eyes. He scrupled not to attend the marriage in Cana and make himself at home among the guests. And his life was crowned with one deed of self-sacrifice the like of which the world had never seen and never will see again, by which our human nature is exalted and glorified forever. He died for sinners. They had wronged him and had no claim upon him. They scourged him, mocked him, nailed him to the accursed tree. And while he hung there in mortal anguish, and those for whom he had died passed by wagging their heads at him, he prayed, "Father, forgive them; they know not what they do!" Never a Cœur de Leon or Sir Philip Sidney wrought like that. We stand under the cross in the presence of such magnanimity and say as Thomas Hughes was fond of saying of him,

> "The best of men that e'er wore earth about him
> Was a sufferer, a calm, meek, patient, loving spirit,
> The first true Gentleman that ever lived."

This then at the outset; to come into the fellowship of Christ. How? By a frank acceptance of the proffer of his grace. The manliest deed that earth ever saw was Christ's bearing of his cross; the manliest deed possible to our human nature is the acceptance of it. "If any man will come after me, let him deny himself, and take up his cross and follow me." So by the imitation of Christ; that is, in the knowledge of the Son of God, shall we come at length to a perfect man, to the measure of the stature of the fulness of Christ.

THE PROPHECY OF PALM-SUNDAY.

"All this was done, that it might be fulfilled which was spoken by the prophet, saying, . . ."—MATT. xxi. 4.

There is nothing more remarkable in the ministry of Jesus than the reticence which he frequently observed and enjoined on his disciples with respect to his own character and redemptive work. He opened the eyes of a blind man and forthwith said to him, "See thou tell it not." He wiped away the leper's spots and commanded him, "Tell no man concerning this matter." On the Mount of Transfiguration he appeared to the chosen three in garments white and glistening, revealing to them a momentary glimpse of his heavenly glory; but, as they were coming down from the mountain, he enjoined them to tell no man what they had seen until after he had risen from the dead. At the very close of his ministry, when at his own solicitation and to his own great satisfaction Peter had witnessed the good confession, "Thou art the Christ, the Son of the living God"! he still insisted that no man should be told of it. The purpose of this injunction was no doubt to prevent the precipitation of the last sad, yet glorious, chapter of his life. But now the hour has come! He is on his way to Jerusalem, his face set steadfastly toward the cross. This thing must not be done in a corner; he must be lifted up before the eyes of all the people, so that the ends of the earth may look unto him and be saved. With this intent he allows himself to be escorted to Jerusalem by a multitude of Passover pilgrims. It is, however, a strange publicity. Never was such a triumphal advent as this. There are no heralds going on before him to trumpet his coming; no retinue of slaves following after, or captives at his chariot wheels. He would enter the city as a man of the people; a wayfaring man with the dust of travel on his homespun garb. Men on their way to worship, and women and little children, shall be his attendants. Why so? All this was done that it might be fulfilled which was spoken by the prophet. And here we come upon our first helpful truth, to-wit:

I. *The unity of Scripture.* The Bible is called *Ta Biblia;* it is however one Book; it is not a mere aggregation of truths and moral precepts like the Analects of Confucius, but rather a living movement of truths advancing to a final consummation in the restitution of all things.

In the margin of our narrative we are referred to Zech. ix. 9. Let us accordingly go back five hundred years and we shall find ourselves in Jerusalem during the rebuilding of the Temple. A caravan made up of five thousand of the flower of Israel had been permitted to return from Babylon. At once they set to work, animated by the most patriotic and religious motives, to rebuild the Temple. They had received contributions of about half a million of dollars in free-will offerings for this purpose. In Ziph, the blossom month, the work began in earnest; and it was continued for a period of some years despite many discouragements and the opposition of the surrounding tribes. Then their enthusiasm ceased; the fires upon the altar died out; the workmen longed to return to agricultural pursuits; the fields lay fallow in their sight; one by one they laid by the hammer and trowel and went forth to attend to their own affairs. The sanctuary was deserted; its bare walls were open to the skies; the winds from the heights of Moab swept through its unlinteled doors; owls made their nests in its nooks and crannies; foxes from the ravine of Hinnom crept in and out its Holy Place; the outer precincts were filled with heaps of uncut stone and lumber. This was the condition of affairs when Zechariah came. He exhorted the men of Israel to return to their sacred task; he sought to rekindle their ardor by reciting a series of glowing visions through which walked in divine majesty their Messianic King. The climax of his exhortation was reached in this prophecy; "Rejoice greatly, O daughter of Zion; shout, O daughter of Jerusalem; behold, thy king cometh unto thee; he is just and having salvation; lowly, and riding upon an ass; and his dominion shall be from sea to sea, and from the river to the ends of the earth."

Now link that event with this triumphal entry which occurred A. D. 30. It is the darkest hour in the history of Israel. The religion of the chosen people is much like the unfinished Temple, and their government is trodden down by alien feet. The Man of Nazareth is on his way to Jerusalem. He has passed the night in Bethany, and at daybreak resumes his journey, staff in hand. His disciples are with him, and a company of pilgrims to the great annual feast. Not far from Bethphage he rests for a season, and sends two of his disciples for the beast of burden which is to carry him into the city. In the meantime it is known in Jerusalem that Jesus of Nazareth is drawing near. The story of his preaching and miracles is on every lip. The people, encamped in leafy booths on the hill sides, see the caravan approaching on the heights overlooking the Kedron. They hear the shouting and commotion; they know what it means. They stream up the road, tearing off branches of the palm-trees; so the two companies meet; those going before joining with those that follow after in the cry, "Hosanna! Hosanna to the Son of David"! They wave the palm branches, they cast their garments in the road before him, and so escort him over the ford of the Kedron and on through the city gates. The people on the roofs and in their doorways see the procession passing by; traders and camel-drivers, and rabbis in robes embroidered with gold, all gaze with interest. Who is this? It is the carpenter of Nazareth, who claims to be the Messiah of God. On toward the Temple moves the strange procession, crying, "Hosanna! Hosanna! Blessed is he that cometh in the name of the Lord"!

Now link that event with still another which is as yet behind the veil. It was seen by John the Evangelist before the Book was sealed; for the triumphal advent was itself a mere prophecy of John's vision. In his vision the moon was covered with a bloody veil; the stars fell as when a fig-tree is shaken of its untimely figs; the heavens were rolled up like a scroll; the earth was on fire; the hour struck; the spirits of the dead came forth; angels and archangels crowded the expanse above. Armies! Armies! Armies! Palms in their hands and shouts of victory!

Far as the eye can reach, angels and archangels and saints triumphant. Now the trumpet blast! The heavens are opened and the Son of Man appears, robed in light and glory, and crowned with a diadem of stars; he lifts his hands in benediction, intercessory hands, marked with the scars of his mediatorial anguish, "Hosanna! Hosanna! to the Son of David! Worthy art thou to receive honor and glory and dominion and power for ever and ever"! The end has come; the tabernacle of God is among men. The prophecies are ended. Close the book and seal it. Jesus of Nazareth is universal king; his dominion is from sea to sea and from the river unto the ends of the earth.

II. Here is also a suggestion as to *the philosophy of history;* for history is not a mere record of events and happenings thrown together and tied up by old Father Time like a bundle of fagots, but rather a living tree; one event growing out of another, as boughs from the trunk and twigs from the bough and blossoms from the twig and fruit from the blossom; its roots deep down in the divine purpose and its life borrowed from the very throbbing of the heart of God.

There is no chance; there are no accidents. We cannot say it happened that Zechariah had a vision, or that it happened that Jesus came riding into the holy city, or that it will happen some day that he will come through the open heavens to rule on earth in the Golden Age. Nothing happens. It is said that William the Conqueror slipped and fell as he landed from his little boat. There was a loud cry from his followers, who knew that this was the worst of evil omens. He recovered himself cleverly, however, and said, "See, my lords, by the grace of heaven I have taken possession of England with both hands," as if he had intended it. But God indeed intends all things. The vision of Zechariah, though it wait five hundred years, will find its sequel; and the triumphal advent of Jesus, which has already waited nigh two thousand years, will find its complement yet.

And there is no confusion. The builders on the unfinished Temple said, "Cyrus is dead and his son Cambyses, and Darius knoweth us not; Tyre and Sidon are breathing out slaughter against us, and the Philistines are rattling their chariots down yonder in the maritime plain." But God said to Zechariah, "Speak unto the children of Israel. The king's heart is in my hand as the rivers of water. As for Tyre and Sidon, behold their villages are all aflame. Syria shall be made a gazingstock. The bleeding carcass shall be torn from Philistia and the cup of trembling placed to her lips. For behold, the king cometh." And indeed there is never a moment in history when there is aught but confusion to human eyes; wars and rumors of wars, entanglements among the nations and distresses among the children of men. But if we could take our position beside the throne of heaven and look down, we should see the procession of the King marching through all events toward the throne. God's ways are not as our ways, nor his thoughts as our thoughts. We shall go out with joy and be led forth with peace, for the mouth of the Lord hath spoken it; the mountains and the hills shall break forth before us into singing and all the trees of the field shall clap their hands. Instead of the thorn shall come up the fir-tree, and instead of the briar shall come up the myrtle-tree; and it shall be to the Lord for a name, for an everlasting sign that shall not be cut off.

And in all this vast proceeding of history there is no haste. The life-time of God is from everlasting to everlasting, and with him a thousand years are as one day. Haste is the infirmity of finite beings, of business men whose obligations fall due to-morrow, of lawyers whose briefs must be ready for the assembling of court, of preachers who must be in their pulpits at the ringing of the bell. But God never hurries to meet his appointments. The world is under condemnation; men are dying; saints cry, "How long, O Lord, how long?" and still he awaits the fulness of time. Time is not a reaper with sickle in hand; but a weaver sitting at the loom, throwing his shuttle to and fro, weaving in the bright with the sombre— each cast of his shuttle, a year, a generation, an æon —but when he cuts the thread, the pattern is perfect, the fabric is complete and the King shall array himself in it. So let us rest in the old truth:

> "Right forever on the scaffold,
>   Wrong forever on the throne;
> Yet that scaffold sways the future,
>   And behind the dim unknown
> Standeth God, within the shadow,
>   Keeping watch above His own."

III. Still another truth suggested here is *the continuity of life.* No man liveth unto himself. History is genealogy; dynasties are generations only; fate is heredity. If eighty men of three-score years and ten, succeeding one another, were to be placed in line they would cover all history back to Adam.

But each must stand in his allotted place; in right relation to those going before and coming after. I am a part of God's definite plan, so are you, and so is every other. A man in Bethphage tethered his ass in the early morning before his home; two men came and led it away; a fourth man held it while Jesus mounted; a man cried "Hosanna"! another and another and another joined in. All these are nameless, but each had his part in the proceeding. The whole world knows how Sir Walter Raleigh threw down his cloak at the crossing for Queen Elizabeth to tread on; but no one knows aught of those men who cast their garments in the way before the Man of Nazareth. However, God remembers; some of those names are doubtless written on the palms of his hands.

It is for us to stand in our places and do the work divinely appointed for us. One day last summer a rivet in the engine of the steamship St. Paul said, "If I were a walking-beam or a piston-rod, I should be of some importance; but I am only a rivet and of no use." And it shook itself loose and fell into a crevice of the cylinder. There it stopped the rod and arrested one of the propellers, so that the ship came like a poor cripple hobbling across the sea. My place is planned; if I refuse to fill it, I may hinder the progress of the King. God waits for all his people to do their part. The work will doubtless go on without us, but we shall lose our opportunity and fall short of the possibilities of life. And every act, every word, every thought tells. A child throws a pebble into the sea and creates a ripple that, however infinitesimal, goes to and fro forever. It was Anna Boleyn's charming smile that sundered the Church of Rome and changed the current of subsequent history. She did not know and did not intend such a change.

So comes responsibility. We must answer not only for the things done, but for the things undone.

Sin is by default as well as by transgression. They erred who refused to cry, "Hosanna"! as well as those who subsequently shouted "Crucify him"! The words of the verdict are, "Inasmuch as ye did it not." Let us address ourselves, therefore, to all duties, however humble, which the spirit is ever suggesting to us. For all things are written down in a Book of Remembrance. God knows; we forget, but he, never. And the glory of our life is in being laborers together with God.

It is recorded that Christ, as he approached Jerusalem, paused on the slopes of Olivet and wept over the city; "O Jerusalem," he said, "if thou hadst known in this thy day—but now thy house is left desolate." "If thou hadst known"! Oh the sorrow of lost opportunity! The procession passes by; let us have eyes to see and ears to hear and hands to wave the palm branches. Hearken to the sound of tramping feet; now is our salvation nearer than we thought; "Hosanna! Hosanna to the Son of David! The kingdom of heaven is at hand! Blessed is he that cometh in the name of the Lord!"

To-day is Palm-Sunday the world over. In St. Peter's at Rome the Supreme Pontiff, golden crucifix in hand, followed by his cardinals and priests, approaches a chamber which is closed throughout the entire year; he knocks on the closed door thrice with the crucifix in the name of the Father and the Son and the Holy Ghost; and the door swings open and the company enter, singing, "Hosanna to the Son of David"! It is an apologue of the work of the universal church. We march toward the open heavens with the uplifted cross before us. The cross is the key of the apocalypse. When we shall stand and knock with sufficient earnestness, and unitedly cry, with all our hearts, " Open, open unto us " ! the clouds will roll back like mighty gates and the King of Glory will appear. Then the cry, " Maranatha " ! the Lord cometh. The Scripture will have met its fulfillment; all history will reach its consummation; and the long procession of life will enter into the enjoyments of a Palm-Sunday whose sun shall never set— the ultimate and endless triumph of the King ; the eternal rest which is prepared for the people of God.

HOW TO READ HISTORY.

"And Jesus said, I beheld Satan as lightning fall from Heaven."—LUKE x. 18.

Jesus had been a wanderer for eighteen months, an exile, to all intents from the Holy City. "He came unto his own, and his own received him not." On being driven out of Jerusalem, he had gone to his own townsmen at Nazareth, and they refused to entertain him. He had gone out for a while, and tarried at Capernaum, and there wrought many wonderful works, and preached the unsearchable riches of the Gospel to people with hard hearts and dull ears. At last he was moved to cry, "O Capernaum, thou hast been exalted unto heaven; thou shalt be cast down unto hell." He had gone out among the villages of Galilee, and they had refused, also, to receive him, insomuch that his apostles would for their ingratitude have called down fire from heaven upon them. Now the end of his ministry was drawing near, and Christ was on his last journey to the Holy City. As he went, he appointed seventy to go to and fro as evangelists among the villages, and to preach the gospel of repentance to them. The function of the seventy was not that of the twelve apostles; the twelve corresponded to the heads of the twelve **tribes** of Israel, but the seventy corresponded to the seventy elders of Israel, and they were to serve as lay workers. But in sending them out the Lord endowed them with great spiritual gifts—charismata; the power not only to speak the truth with flaming lips, but also to work miracles of healing and blessing. As he journeyed on, the seventy came in from time to time, until they were all back again. Then they made their report. Their hearts were beating fast with the enthusiasm of a magnificent triumph. They had expected great things, but had accomplished a thousand-fold more than they had ever dared to hope. One of them said, "I saw the lame man leap as an hart when I touched him." Another, "I saw the blind man open his eyes and go seeing when I touched them." Another, "I saw the white spots of leprosy fall from the leper when I touched him." Another, "I saw a raving maniac who was possessed of demons, sit, clothed in his right mind, tractable and docile as a little child, when I spoke to him." So they all reported marvellous success. Jesus stood by; and at length, with a far-away look in his eyes, he said, "I beheld Satan fall as lightning out of Heaven"—as a meteor; light for a moment, and then vanishing in the night; as a meteor, illuminating the skies from horizon to horizon, and then gone out forever!

It may be that Jesus alluded to the traditional mutiny which had occurred away back in the remote ages of which Jude tells in his word touching the angels that lost their first estate, and fell, and are reserved in chains unto the last day. The Apostle Peter also speaks of it; Milton sings of that great defection in Heaven; and Shakespeare says: "Cromwell, I charge thee, fling away ambition; by that sin fell the angels." But I believe that the immediate reference of Jesus was not to any event whatsoever. He stood there in the midst of all history, and in this glowing account of the triumph of his disciples he perceived the splendid consummation of all. The events of all the centuries passed before him in an instantaneous panorama. His own life-time was central to all human history. Past and future were alike to him. From everlasting to everlasting he was God. With those glowing eyes of his he saw all in a moment. They had observed a merciful miracle here and there. He saw everything in an instant of time. And thus he spoke of the great ultimate victory: "I beheld Satan fall as lightning out of Heaven."

The Lord here teaches us how to read history. O for those illuminated eyes of Jesus! O for that far-seeing vision of Jesus! O for that world-consciousness of Christ, that was able to open the pages of earthly chronicles, and see what he saw that day!

He teaches us here, to begin with, that *history is an argument*. It is not a mere bundle of assorted facts, but it is an argument by the process known as progressive approach to an ultimate conclusion. We speak of the logic of events. He knew the meaning of that significant phrase, the logic of events.

Here is his first premise,—GOD. He always began with God. Kant says that there is no need of God in philosophy, and La Place said the same thing—"I have no need of God in my system of philosophy." But there is no philosophy of history without God, who is Alpha and Omega, the beginning and the end of all. We borrow all our confidence from the fact that God is in the midst of history, and that he reigns among the children of men. The mother of Sisera looked out of her window, and cried, "Why do the wheels of his chariot tarry so long?" We also mourn because of the long delay of the coming of Jesus Christ to reign from the river unto the ends of the earth. The mother of Sisera did not know that her son was lying in the tent with a nail through his temple, and that the bodies of the men of Harosheth were being swept down the river Kishon to the sea. But our God is a living God, who manifests his love and power continually among us.

And his second premise is *Redemption.* The word has in it an immense power. Redemption—the buying back. Of what? Of this old, sin-stricken world of ours, that was sold and forfeited under sin, and passed under the reign of Satan, who thenceforth called himself "The Prince of this World." Redemption is the buying back. At what cost? On the cross is the ransom price: the Lamb; the Lamb of God, slain! Slain when? We date historical events from the building of Rome or from the birth of Christ at Bethlehem. But redemption, to those clear eyes of Jesus, was an event that stretched from the very beginning to the end of the ages. The Lamb was "slain from the foundation of the world"; from the beginning of sin to the bowing of the knee of the last stubborn sinner who will confess that Jesus is the Christ of God.

The conclusion of the argument from those two premises is *the triumph of Christ.* We stand here under the cross, where he was standing, and where the seventy also were standing, though they knew it not, and under that shadow we may see for ourselves.

I see the stars of Heaven, and hear God promising to the Messiah, "So shall thy seed be." I see the ocean stretching afar, and I hear God saying that his glory and kingdom shall cover the earth as those waters cover the deep. I see the forest, and I hear God say, "The trees of the field shall clap their hands before him." I see the first budding of the vegetation of spring by the brookside, and I hear God saying to him, in a universal promise, that his followers shall "spring up like willows by the water courses." I hear the sound of the rustling of wings, as doves that fly to their windows; the sound of the footfall of a caravan of camels coming this way, the dromedaries of Midian, the rams of Nabaioth; the patter of raindrops, the murmur of brooks down the mountain side, the roll of rivers on toward the sea. What is this? The coming of souls to Jesus Christ; the flowing of the Gentiles, the nations, as a mighty torrent to the feet of this Only Begotten Son of God. This is the argument of history as Jesus shows it: God, Redemption, and the ultimate and eternal Triumph of goodness and truth.

As we stand here with Jesus, while his bright eyes are cast over all the ages and generations marching before him, we may learn to read history not only as an argument, but *as a problem also*—a problem full of confusion to us, unless we can approach it in the power of a clear-seeing faith.

I remember well that there was one place in arithmetic that I never could get over. It was Partial Payments. And to this day, if I were to take up arithmetic again, I should be puzzled with Partial Payments. It was all confusion. So is history to a man who looks at it with the stolid eyes of mere fleshly sight.

There are some things that cannot be solved by the lower mathematics, that will not yield to the Rule of Three. It is a hundred years since the beginning of the missionary epoch of the church. A glorious century! But how long will it be, at this rate, before Jesus Christ comes to reign? We have had a hundred years since William Carey sat at his lapstone studying the map of India there on the wall before him, and to-day the doors of the whole world, and of all nations, except Thibet alone, are open to the messengers of the Cross. To-day there are two hundred missionary societies organized for the evangelization of the nations that lie in darkness and the shadow of death. To-day, after the lapse of this single missionary century, the Bible is printed in three hundred tongues and dialects of the earth. To-day there are thirty thousand laborers at work in the foreign field, their feet beautiful upon the mountains as they carry the glad tidings of salvation; climbing the Andes; climbing the Himalayas; climbing the mountains of Africa; their feet beautiful upon the mountains because they say, "Thy God reigneth." To-day there are a million and a half of converts to show for this century of work among the benighted nations of the pagan world. Since we gathered here on the last Sabbath, two thousand souls, at the lowest estimate, have been brought from darkness into light, and that among the pagan nations only. Oh, if they could file before us here! Two thousand men and women with dusky faces, born out of darkness, out of ignorance, out of superstition! If they could come filing in here before us to-day, how it would thrill our hearts! Born into the Kingdom since a week ago! And at an outlay of fifteen dollars for every soul! I blush for the mere mention of it, because, I say again, there are some great moral facts to which the rules of arithmetic cannot be made to apply.

There is an energy at work in the missionary Church to-day which will not yield to any mathematical rule. What is the power of a tear? Ask a scientist, and he will tell you exactly how many pounds it will lift, if it be transformed into steam. But who can estimate the love, the sympathy, the mother's prayer, the heart-break, that is in that tear? The night before he set out from Atlanta on his famous march to the sea, Sherman sat down and made an estimate. "We shall need certain things. We must needs have certain power to work with. How many miles is it from Atlanta to the sea? How much ammunition must we have? How many mules and wagons? How many troops?" There was his mathematical problem. But if that had been all, would he ever have reached the sea? There was one thing that he could not put down on paper: the blood that was throbbing fast and hot with patriotic fervor in the hearts of his brave men; the fire that flashed for the Republic from the eyes of the soldiers who were going to march with him.

We cannot estimate the progress of the Church in figures such as I have given here to-day. It is folly to undertake it. Can a man measure the stature of God Almighty with a yard-stick? Can a man measure the progress of God Almighty with a surveyor's chain? Or can you test the stability of

His throne by shaking it? We must come up into higher mathematics; up out of arithmetic into algebra; up where we shall find an unknown quantity, and make allowance for it; and when we find X, we must bring faith to bear upon it. Here is the unknown quantity — God walking in the midst of the Church; dwelling in the hearts of his people; going with their feet; working with their hands; seeing with their eyes; loving with their hearts; the King, hand in hand with his bride, who looketh forth as the morning, fair as the moon, clear as the sun, and terrible as an army with banners.

The disciples on the Day of Pentecost, made their prayer, and Peter rose and preached his sermon. Off yonder in the corner of the open court two rabbis were standing, and one of them said: "This is the new movement. How long at this rate will it take these followers of the Nazarene to organize their Church? See them standing here, and hear yon fishermen muttering their prayers and preaching about Jesus. How long will it take to bring a thousand men into the following of the Nazarene Prophet at this rate"? And while they looked and pointed their fingers, the strange thing transpired—the X in the problem, the unknown and constantly working factor that men never, never can estimate: the wind began to blow, and the fire came down, and the disciples stood upon their feet; and those that were round about began to cry out under a power that was invisible, imponderable, and undebatable, "Men and brethren, what shall we do"? and about three thousand were brought into the Church that day.

You cannot calculate by the lower mathematics the power that is working in the Church of Jesus

Go forth in obedience to our Lord's great injunction and when we have done our part, and reached the end of the problem, it will all be as clear as any solved problem in algebra ever was; for God will come.

And then, if we go and stand again beside Jesus, as he looks with those clear eyes, we shall read history as he reads it now, *as a volume of Christian economics.* For here is a field to which all the followers of Jesus Christ are called. Lift up your eyes and see. This is husbandry. Lift up your eyes and see. "Say not. It is yet four months, and then cometh the harvest; behold the fields that they are already white unto the harvest."

Where is thy sickle? Go, thrust in thy sickle and reap. That is thy glorious privilege. Blessed be God for that word privilege which applies to all Christian service. Privilege is *privus lex*—a private law. That is to say, a law which has a peculiar application to some particular individual or class; as the king's privilege, the privilege of the hierarchy. There were laws for the people, but there was a special law, a private law, a *privilegium*, for kings, for nobles, for hierarchy. There is a special law for me. My privilege is to stand, sickle in hand, touching hands with the Only Begotten Son of God, in the great harvest field of the kingdom. To that I am called, and all my glory in Christian living is in these two words —"Go" and "Give."

Go! The Church believed during the first two centuries that Jesus meant it, and to this belief her tremendous success in the apostolic era was due. Then came fifteen centuries when the Church cared nothing about missions. Those were fifteen hundred years of lost time in history. If I see a boy without any spirit, a languid lad, whose arms hang down, whose eyes lack lustre, and who moves with a slow step, I say, "The boy has no 'go' in him." That was precisely the trouble with the Church for fifteen centuries. It went nowhere, but worked with centripetal force until the beginning of this last era, the hundred years of the miracles of missions; of Carey and Hans Egede, and David Livingstone, and all the glorious ambassadors of the cross who have gone out to preach, to suffer, to die, and to live forever in the progress of the ages.

Go ye! The Master meant *you* when he said it. In our Civil War the loyal people were all at the front. The boys in blue marched through our streets, and we gave them Godspeed as they kept step to the battle hymn, and passed out of sight. But we lads sent out our hearts after them. Good women went by proxy, sending their husbands and their sweethearts, the very light of their life, out into the high places of the field. And poor cripples, who could not march in the rank and file, went when they staid by the stuff. And the grandmother in the chimney-corner went with the soldiers for the defense of the Republic when she did nothing but knit stockings, while they won fights. Go ye! If not by following the fight, go ye in prayer, in sympathy. Never, never murmur against the Master's plan of the propaganda. And if you have ever said never say it again—that you do not believe in the evangelization of the heathen nations of the earth.

Go, and give! The secret of all giving is in giving your own self, first of all. So Paul wrote to the Churches of Macedonia. He said that out of their extreme poverty they had abounded in their liberality, first of all in this: that they gave their own selves unto the Lord. Body, soul, spirit, heart, conscience, hands, feet, substance, all we have, let us give. "Ye are not your own; ye are bought with a price—not silver and gold—but the precious blood of Jesus, as of a Lamb without blemish, and without spot." If a man has once given himself, the giving of all that he has will be as nothing to him. The old Kaiser Wilhelm, grandfather of the present war-lord of Germany, was driven out to war with an empty treasury. He made an affectionate appeal to his people to sustain him. The one stimulus to their generosity was the iron cross, which is the proudest decoration of the German people to-day. They brought in that exigency their jewels of gold, their rings, their bracelets, and gave them up; and to every donor was given an iron cross, upon which was this legend: "I gave gold for iron." One of these days, when we are in the Kingdom of Heaven, we who calculated upon our gifts, and gave so little in consequence, will be glad that we gave at all; and our proudest boast yonder will be that we gave iron for gold, and in our giving made ourselves forever rich unto God.

In the Reformed Church of America we are talking of retrenchment,—of closing the doors of some scores of high caste Hindoo schools. We have been twenty years opening those doors, and preparing the way for the most excellent missionary record among the denominations of Christians to-day; and we are talking of retrenchment now! O, God forbid that one of the shaggy locks of this Sampson of ours should ever be shorn!

I know it is hard times, but what of that? Do you remember Lord Nelson in the battle of Copenhagen?

It was a stern fight. The Admiral, Nelson's ranking officer, an old man whose heart misgave him, put up at the masthead of the flagship signal 39—to retreat. Nelson, pacing the deck of his ship, looked askance and saw it, but fought on. His lieutenant said to him, "My Lord Admiral, see the signal 39 yonder on the flagship"? Nelson raised his glass to his one blind eye and said, "No, I see it not. Nail to our mast signal 27—for close quarters." Nelson won the day. That is the sort of courage, that is needed in the universal Church of Christ in these hard times. We have not strained a muscle or a sinew yet. We have not put one drop of our Christian blood to its last crucial test. O for the clear eyes of Jesus Christ! O for the brave heart of Jesus Christ! O for the strong faith of our Master! that we may stand where he stands now, and see what he sees,—all the dominions of this world, sin, shame, the strongholds of iniquity cast down; Satan fallen like a meteor out of the sky; the great triumph assured, and the throne of Messiah set up! O that we might hear his word that was uttered on Ascension Mount, "All authority is given unto me, in heaven and on earth. Go ye, therefore, into all the world, and preach the gospel unto every creature." There is the commission of the Church to the end of the ages. "Lo, I am with you." There is the promise. Let your heart never tremble. Let your faith never fail. "Lo, I am with you alway, even unto the end of the world."

THE BOUNDLESS PRAYER OF FAITH.

"If ye abide in me, and my words abide in you, ye shall ask what ye will, and it shall be done unto you"—JOHN xv. 7.

At one of our military posts on the frontier, an old Indian was often found, hungry and in rags and tatters, begging of the soldiers a little to keep soul and body together. And they were used to his approaches, for he had come year after year in that misery. At length one felt moved to inquire what it was that hung from an old ribbon about the Indian's neck. A locket was suspended there; and when he opened the locket, there fell out a bit of parchment; that parchment was a Revolutionary pension bearing the signature of George Washington, the Commander-in-chief of the American Army, which entitled him to a comfortable competence during all the remainder of his days. And he had not known it!

Here is a promise for Christian people to-day: if ye abide in him, and his words abide in you, ye shall ask what ye will, and it shall be done unto you. It is a draft on the Bank of the Kingdom, signed by the King himself, with the amount left in blank for us to fill out, and absolutely no limitations or conditions affixed to it. And we never have begun to use it! If we had, we should not be going about mourning, "Oh, my leanness! my leanness"! God intends us to be strong and enriched by his grace, with enough of everything that is needful in order to the satisfaction of our souls to the very uttermost. "Ye shall ask what ye will, and it shall be done unto you."

But, mark you, that promise was given only to such as believed in Christ. It was addressed to them in that marvellous discourse in the upper room. Not that an unbeliever cannot pray. He cannot say, "My Father," for "He that hath not the Son hath not the Father"; he cannot say, "For Jesus' sake," for he has never accepted him of whom it is written, "He ever liveth to make intercession for us." But there is one prayer that every man may make—and for his life let him make it!—the prayer of the publican, who beat upon his breast as he stood afar off, with fallen eyes, crying, "O God, be merciful unto me, the sinner"; and God, out of his infinite grace, will hear him.

This promise was uttered in connection with the Parable of the Vine and the Branches; "If a man abide in me, and I in him, he shall bring forth much fruit: for without me ye can do nothing"; and, "If ye abide in me, and my words abide in you, ye shall ask what ye will, and it shall be done unto you." "If ye abide in me"—that is the inner life; "If my words abide in you"—that is the outer life. The world cannot see whether Christ is abiding in you or not, but the world can see by your walk and conversation whether or no his words are abiding in you. Under this twofold condition, "ye may ask what ye will, and it shall be done unto you,"—all things, anything, everything! Whatsoever! That is the term of the promise. Ask, and it shall be given unto you. There is no such thing as a Divine failure to answer. All prayer is answered; all prayer, mind you, offered in the filial spirit—for nothing else is prayer. The only true prayer is that which goes up from the heart of God's child to the throne of the Heavenly Grace; which begins with "Our Father," and ends with "For Jesus' sake." And that gets hold upon the strength of God, and nothing is impossible to it. So our proposition is, the boundless prayer of faith; absolutely, literally, the boundless prayer of faith. It rests upon three boundless facts. Here they are:

The first is *the boundless power of God*. He has infinite resources at his command. Why should not he give us whatsoever we ask? Do you feel the hand of death gripping at your heart-strings? Has some mortal malady taken hold upon you? And has the physician said, "Nothing can be done"? I believe in the faith cure: not in the professional charlatanry using that phrase; but in the power of the prayer of faith to do precisely what it did when Jesus went along the highways in the Holy Land. "If I may but touch the hem of his garment, I shall be made whole." It was the touch of absolute faith that got hold of the hem of his garment, when virtue went out of him.

Are you in distress respecting your temporal estate? Oh, the cattle on a thousand hills are his, and all the gold and silver that lie buried in the deep bosom of the everlasting mountains,—they are all his. What a little matter it is for God to relieve you!

Do you want to grow in grace toward the full stature of the manhood of Christ? He loves that desire, and is ready at the first impulse of your heart to grant it unto you.

Are you praying for a friend? Pray on. God loves an unselfish prayer. God can reach out anywhere to save a soul. How easy it is for him! If one of my dear ones was over yonder struggling in the water for life, and you were nearby, and could reach out a hand, and I should call to you, "Oh, save him!" would you hesitate? Why shall God hesitate when I plead for the deliverance of my beloved from spiritual and eternal death?

Do you say, "True, but his laws stand in the way"? Can a watchmaker adjust the machinery of a chronometer and turn the hands backward, if he will? And shall God not be able to manage the machinery of the universe as he will? The laws of the universe are God's laws. The universe is his chronometer. "Sun, stand thou still upon Gibeon! and thou, Moon, in the valley of Ajalon"! There was a man named Joshua praying down yonder, and God moved the laws of the universe, and answered him.

Let us believe in his inexhaustible resources. Nothing is too hard for him. When Scipio was over in Egypt, he said to the inhabitants, desiring to conciliate them after their subjugation, "Now, draw upon me, as you do upon your generous Nile, and see how magnanimous I can be." It was a splendid hyperbole. He could not do it, even if he had the heart for it. But if you and I were to sit upon the banks of the Nile until the almond-tree of old age blossomed and watch its current rolling along to refresh the earth, and satisfy the thirst of successive generations, and if that current were all of molten gold, flowing out of the Divine exchequer, yet would it not diminish God's treasury so much as one drop of water exhaling from the boundless deep exhausts the immeasurable supply of it.

And then, this boundless prayer of faith rests on a second fact: *the boundless goodness of God.* He is able; is he willing? His *name* is Love. Oh, the length, and the breadth, and the depth, and the height of it!

> "There's a wideness in God's mercy
> Like the wideness of the sea."

His *promise*, also, is given to us. "Ask and it shall be given you; seek, and ye shall find; knock, and it shall be opened to you." There is not an "if" there; not a "perhaps"; nor "it may be so": "it *shall* be opened unto you." And as if he thought some of us might question his sincerity in making so vast a promise, he immediately repeats it in this wise: "For *every one* that asketh, receiveth; and *every one* that seeketh, findeth; and to *every one* that knocketh, it shall be opened."

Besides, we have an *argument* back of that promise —a great argument, a fortiori, from the less to the greater—so that we may not misunderstand or question it. "For which of you, if his son shall ask bread, will he give him a stone? or if he ask a fish, will he give him a serpent? or if he ask an egg, will he offer him a scorpion? If ye then, being evil, know how to give good things to your children, how much more shall your Father which is in Heaven give good things to them that ask him."

And then, in addition to all that, his name, his promise, his argument, he adds the tremendous *earnest* which we have in Jesus Christ, when he says, "He that spared not his own Son, but delivered him up for us all, how shall he not with him also freely give us all things?" He bared his heart, took the very heart of his love out of his bosom, and cast it down upon this guilty world to save it. Now, "shall he not with him also freely give us all things"?

It is nothing for him to give. He delights to give. It is the joy of the Divine life to be giving all the time. The most delightsome day in the life of the Empress Josephine, she said in one of her letters, was when coming through the walks with her husband, she was left for a little while to rest in a humble cottage. She saw that the eyes of the lone woman there were stained with tears, and she asked her trouble. The woman said it was poverty. "How much," said Josephine, "would relieve it?" "Oh," she said, "there is no relieving it; it would require four hundred francs to help us out, to save our little vineyard and our goats." Josephine counted out of her purse the four hundred francs into the woman's lap, and she gathered them together, and fell down before her, and kissed her feet. And that was the happiest day in that poor Empress's life. But all God's life is filled with days like that. His name is Love. He delights to hear our prayer, to answer it, to relieve and to enrich us.

This boundless prayer of faith rests upon yet a third fact, to-wit: *God's boundless wisdom.* He knows precisely what I need, and for that reason I am emboldened to ask. I would not dare to ask if God were no wiser than myself. I would not dare to kneel down and ask him for a temporal gift that might be to my moral and eternal ruin, for all I know. I cannot see beyond my finger tips, but I can trust him. My Father knows; knows what is best for me. "But if he knows before the asking what I need, why should I make a prayer at all"? That is the word of an objector who never knew God's love in Jesus Christ. It is enough for you that he bids you keep up the constant current of communication between your heart and him. "Ask, and it shall be given you."

Ask largely. The prayer of faith knows no limit. Be not afraid. Your large request honors every attribute of God. In one of the Psalms it is written "Open thy mouth wide and I will fill it." I wonder if the figure came from David's life among the hills, where, watching from yonder cliff, he saw the fledglings in the eagle's nest, saw them as the mother bird came back with with some rich morsel, open their bills and wait? I wonder if that suggested to him our helplessness, and God's desire to honor our requests? Open your mouth wide and he will fill it.

Ask confidently. Be assured that he will answer you. You are a child of God. The filial spirit is the only condition that is presupposed as to prayer. It is the only prerequisite, and includes all other conditions that affect our approach to the mercy seat. Pray as a son or daughter of the loving God, that is, being mindful of his superior wisdom. You may ask a stone; he will not give it, but he will give you bread; and will you say, "He did not answer me"? You may, out of the shortness of your wisdom, ask a scorpion; He will not give you that, but he will honor your prayer, and give you a fish; and will you say, "He did not answer me"? The Lord Jesus once, in the weakest hour of all his earthly life, when all his flesh was crying out against the approaching anguish of a bitter death, made the prayer of a real man. (And God wants us to pour out our whole soul before him. Better make a wrong prayer than no prayer at all.) In that awful hour in Gethsemane, the Lord implored, "My Father, if it be possible, let this cup pass from me." But, after all, as the light of the great redemption work dawned upon his soul, he went on to say, "Oh, my Father, Thy will be done"; and so his prayer was answered that day.

The widow of a minister, long, long ago, came to the prophet's house, and wept out her sorrow, saying "My creditors have come, and they require my two sons as a pledge, and they are all that I have. The good man is dead. You knew him—how he worked for God; and I am left alone with my two lads." And the prophet said, "Go back to thy home. What hast thou?" "Nothing." "Nothing?" "No; only a pot of oil; that is all that is left." "Go back to thy house, and take thy two lads, and make ready the pot of oil; then go borrow vessels. Borrow of all thy neighbors round about. Now, borrow vessels not a few, remember; and then enter into a room with thy lads, and the pot of oil, and the vessels, and shut to the door, and pour out." And she did so, and she filled the first vessel with oil, and the supply was not gone. "Bring me another vessel," said she to the lads; and they brought her another, and she filled it; and the oil was not stayed, yet. Another, and another, vessels not a few; all the vessels that were there. "Bring me yet another." And one of the lads said, "Mother, there is not another vessel here"; and the oil stayed.

There is supply under God's bounty forever, if we will. What limits the supply? Faith. God's resources are infinite. The oil flows on forever, but the vessels give out. O for faith! O for a larger faith! —a faith that shall approach the infinite love of the infinite God!—a faith that shall rest absolutely on his unbounded power, his unbounded goodness, his unbounded wisdom, and shall believe his Word: "If ye abide in me, and my words abide in you, ye shall ask what ye will, and it shall be done unto you"!

THE EPWORTH SINGER.

"And his songs were a thousand and five."—I. KINGS iv. 32.

We hear a great deal from our elders about the good old times. If you question your grandfather, he will tell you that we have fallen on evil days; that the world is not what it used to be when he was young; that the Church is not what it once was, and that politics is not what it used to be. "We had Clay and Webster in those days"! If you question your grandmother, she will tell you that the prints are not what they were when she was young and that the carpets will not turn any more, and that the workingmen these days do not put their consciences into their work as they did in the good old days.

> "Should auld acquaintance be forgot,
> And never brought to mind?
> Should auld acquaintance be forgot,
> And days of auld lang syne"?

But then, we know we are living in vastly better times. There is a living God, and every time the world rolls around His face shines a little more brightly upon it. There never was a century like the one we are passing through just now. All things are better than they used to be. God is " the same, yesterday, to-day, forever"; but everything else in the universe is better than of old. The Church is better, politics is better, and light is better; we have better food than they used to have, and better sanitary arrangements; and the fashions are better than they used to be. It is a better world to live in. Praise God for it!

We are going back to-night into the seventeenth century and the early half of the eighteenth. That was a period of great spiritual declension. The Church had just got through fighting for the Reformation, and was resting for a while. It was a time of great spiritual weakness. The ministers of those days gave themselves over to the finest points of casuistry; they discussed sublapsarianism and supralapsarianism, and they were extremely scrupulous about nice distinctions in doctrine. But there was a deplorable condition of immorality among them; gambling was very common, profanity not infrequent. Clerical dishonesty—the dishonesty of the pulpit—was not at all unusual; and it was condoned, as, blessed be God! it is not condoned in these days. The Archbishop of London gave such balls and festivities in Lambeth Palace that the king had to interfere, as he said it was a scandal to his reign.

But the people? Were they better than the ministry? Do not flatter yourselves—"like priests, like people," always. The Bible was a closed book. The mind of the people dwelt upon outward circumstance, and rite, and ceremony. And they were spiritually ignorant. It is a matter of historic fact that a man in one of the London churches brought his minister to task, and had him before one of the ecclesiastical courts for profanity, because he said in one of his sermons, "He that believeth not shall be damned." It was a time of great moral declension, and God must interpose somehow.

In 1708 there was born in Epworth parsonage, a mud cottage with a thatched roof, a child who was destined to have a great influence upon his time,— a weak little one, the son of a minister of the Church of England who was content on fifty pounds a year. This was the tenth child of the household. For several weeks the infant did not open its eyes, and had scarcely a perceptible pulse; but the fond mother held him in her arms, and at last was gratified to see him look up into her face with a glance of such gentleness and appeal that she at once opened her great heart and took him in. A wonderful woman was this mother of the Wesleys, who said, "O God, I shall be forever happy if with my ten children I can come up to heaven's gate at last, and say, 'Here am I, and the children whom thou hast given me.'"

The boy Charles grew up a long-limbed, awkward, homely lad, and went trudging afoot to Oxford. As yet he had made no profession of faith in the Lord Jesus Christ. His brother John was concerned for him, and often importuned him; and Charles would say, "I have no feeling about it, and you surely would not have me be a Christian all at once." But while he was in the University, he went up to London and visited for a time in the family of a Mrs. Turner. Her name is seldom spoken, and what I am about to relate is all that is known about her; but the dear face of Mrs. Turner shines all through the inspired hymns of Charles Wesley as we sing them to-day; for that night as he slept in her upper room she heard him groaning under conviction of sin. The sword of the spirit was dividing asunder the very joints and marrow of the man, and he cried out in his anguish, "God be merciful to me, a sinner." Mrs. Turner at last plucked up courage, went up the stairs, and spoke to him from outside the door: "In the name of Jesus Christ of Nazareth rise up, and thou shalt be whole." It was a word in due season, and has been bearing fruit ever since; for the next morning he arose with the light of God's countenance shining in his heart. And he sat down then, before he brake his fast, and wrote:

> "Oh, for a thousand tongues to sing
>   My dear Redeemer's praise;
> The glories of my God and King,
>   The triumphs of His grace.
>
> "He breaks the power of reigning sin,
>   He sets the prisoners free;
> His blood can make the foulest clean,
>   His blood availed for me."

So he went back to the University. He called in his brother John, and another of the Oxford boys, whose name passed into the history of England, and of our American nation as well—George Whitefield—and seven others; and they formed themselves into a Christian fraternity. It was a time when the finger of derision was pointed at an earnest Christian man. That little coterie in Oxford was dubbed "The Holy Club," and its members were called "Bible Moths," bigots, fanatics, and all that. But they had the courage of their convictions; and those ten Oxford students, standing up before the pointed finger and the laughter of their fellows, went out to shake that irreligious century with extraordinary power.

When his University course was over, Charles, who had made up his mind to enter upon the service of the Gospel, found himself settled in a colliery town. His heart went out to the sorrows of those who were in darkness and the shadow of death. Just as he entered upon his first settlement, he went up to London to be married. Here is the record as he left it: "It was a cloudless day. I rose at five in the morning, and spent three hours in prayer and singing praises to God. At nine o'clock I led my Sallie to church, and my brother John there put our hands together, and prayed God to come as he came to the marriage supper at Cana, when he turned the water into wine. And then we went to our temporary home, and knelt down together, and gave ourselves anew to the service of Christ. We spent the day cheerful without mirth, and serious with sadness."

And then away to their country parsonage. Under that doorway there passed many a time the shadow of sorrow and of death, but never was there an hour when the singer of Epworth could not praise God, making melody in his heart.

He was out preaching among the colliers once, and because he declared the whole counsel of God, they received his sermon with an ill grace. After a while they gathered up stones and drove him away, and followed him up, until, poor man! he found shelter in a cottage by the roadside. There, with the blood streaming from his wounds, he wrote:

> "Worship and thanks and blessing
> And strength be unto Jesus;
> For He alone defends His own,
> When earth and hell oppress us.

> Accepting our deliverance,
>   We triumph in His favor;
> And for His love, which here we prove,
>   We give Him thanks forever."

On another occasion he was preaching to a great multitude of the common people out in the open fields, as his custom was, when the earth began to tremble and shake. It was the Lisbon earthquake; but these humble, ignorant and superstitious people supposed it was the end of the world. Wesley at once changed his theme, and preached on this text: "God is our refuge and strength, a very present help in trouble. Therefore will not we fear, though the earth be removed, and though the mountains be carried into the midst of the sea." It was down on the seashore; the hills were vibrating all around him, and out yonder a tidal wave was coming in, rolling and tossing its masses of foam. In the midst of his sermon he exclaimed:

> " Earth unhinged, as from her basis,
>   Owns her Great Restorer nigh.
> Plunged in complicate distresses,
>   Poor distracted sinners lie.
> Men, their instant doom deploring,
>   Faint beneath their fearful load.
> Ocean working, rising, roaring,
>   Claps his hands to meet his God!"

That is the way Charles Wesley was accustomed to break out into sacred song. He was preaching in a stone quarry, and all around him the men were using their hammers upon the cliff. Now and then they paused and looked over to him. O, if they would only listen to him as he spoke to them about our

Lord and Saviour, Jesus Christ! But he met no response, and at last cried out:

> "Come, O Thou all victorious Lord,
> Thy power to us make known:
> Strike with the hammer of Thy Word,
> And break these hearts of stone!"

Once he was at Land's End, away out at the further edge of the British Island, with Bristol Channel on one hand, and the Atlantic Ocean stretching before him. He seemed to be standing between two eternities, and there, all alone, he sang to himself:

> "Lo, on a narrow neck of land,
> 'Twixt two unbounded seas I stand,
> Yet how insensible!
> A point of time—a moment's space—
> Removes me to yon heavenly place,
> Or shuts me up in hell!
>
> "O God, my inmost soul convert;
> And deeply on my thoughtless heart
> Eternal truth impress.
> Teach me to know its awful weight,
> And feel its import ere too late;
> Wake me to righteousness."

I suppose the romance of his life attaches more to the hymn known as "Wrestling Jacob" than to any other. He was at Kingswood when he wrote it. All night he had wrestled alone in prayer, for he knew what it is to be trusting and importunate both. Then he wrote that strange hymn:

> "Come, O Thou Traveller unknown,
> Whom still I hold, but cannot see;
> My company before is gone,
> And I am left alone with Thee;
> With Thee all night I mean to stay,
> And wrestle till the break of day."

But, after all, the hymn that has come to the very center of the Christian heart of the world is one that he wrote when a bird came fluttering into his window one day, pursued by a hawk :

> "Jesus, lover of my soul,
>   Let me to Thy bosom fly,
> While the nearer waters roll,
>   While the tempest still is high:
> Hide me, O my Saviour, hide,
>   Till the storm of life be past;
> Safe into the haven guide;
>   O receive my soul at last."

Henry Ward Beecher said, "I would rather have written that hymn than to have all the crowns of all the sovereigns that have reigned upon the earth, and all the wealth of all the millionaires that ever were rich among us."

Thus he lived, preaching among the humble people and writing his hymns, till he was burdened with his years—for his life-time covered almost a century—and in 1788 he lay down to die. But even in death, the ruling passion still strong, he murmured at the last :

> "O, could I catch one smile from Thee,
>   And sink into eternity."

That is the way he died. They held the service in the village church, and John Wesley, his elder brother who was now very decrepit with age, came to take part in the funeral service. The Scripture was read, the funeral discourse was preached, and John rose to give out "Wrestling Jacob." All went well until he came to the place where it is written,

"My company before is gone,
 And I am left alone with Thee";

and thereat he fell to sobbing, and sat down, and all the congregation was given to tears and silence. After a while they arose, and began to sing, and the chronicler says he never heard such singing as he heard that day:

"I know Thee, Saviour, who Thou art—
 Jesus, the sinner's only friend;
Nor wilt Thou with the night depart,
 But stay and help me to the end.
Thy mercies never shall remove;
 Thy nature and Thy name is Love."

They laid him away in old Marylebone churchyard, and there you may see his gravestone now, and read upon it the epitaph which he himself wrote:

"A sinner saved, by grace forgiven,
 Redeemed on earth, to reign in heaven."

Is it not worth while to spend a little season on a Sabbath evening in thinking upon the work of a sweet singer like Charles Wesley? Is there anything for us to take away with us? Yes, the lesson of the one talent. He could not preach like John Wesley. It was his older brother who laid the foundations of the great Methodist Church, God bless it! And Charles was never such a preacher as he; but O, he could sing!

"Take my voice and let it be
 Consecrated, Lord, to Thee."

There is some one here who has only one talent; who can preach, who can sing. It may be some dear old father or mother in Israel whom age has almost blinded; you may be shut in from the world, and seemingly laid aside from usefulness; but there is one talent left to be used for God. O, do not wrap it in a napkin, and bury it in the earth! Use it! Sing for God! Pray for God! Toil for God! "What hast thou in thy hand, Shamgar"? "An ox-goad." "Go, scourge the Canaanites with it"! "What hast thou in thy hand, David"? "A harp." "Go, sing and play upon it to the glory of God"! "What hast thou in thy hand"? A needle? A broom?

> "Who sweeps a room as to God's laws,
> Makes that and th' action fine."

Anything else for us? Yes, a lesson in enthusiasm. that is the secret of the magnificent success which has attended the hundred year history of the Methodist Church. That is the secret of the power of the Salvation Army. And God grant that it may be the secret of the future power of the Volunteers! Blood and fire! The blood of Jesus Christ! The fire of the Holy Ghost! The blood bathing the heart, and the fire quickening and energizing it! We can be enthusiastic for anything else but our religion. O that there were more Holy Clubs in our colleges! O that there were more of us ministers who dared, like Charles Wesley and his brother John, to stand up and declare the whole counsel of God! O for more of holy enthusiasm to set our lives on fire for the glory of God!

Anything else for us? Yes, a lesson on the power of sacred song. Let us sing and make melody in our hearts, in these sweet hymns that Wesley and the other singers have left us. Ours is the religion of song. There is no place on earth for a melancholy Christian. I know your sorrow. I know there is disappointment in your heart. But then, "all things work together for good to them that love God." You are redeemed. "There is no condemnation to them that are in Christ Jesus." You have the privilege of service. Can you not go singing with your sickle in hand? All heaven is opened before you, and the angels are singing there, and you are presently to join them. Is there a man here, is there a woman here, who does not know what the gladness of Christian living is? Come and fall in with us as we go singing on our journey towards heaven's gate. "He giveth songs in the night"; songs in the night of sorrow, of pain, of ignorance, and of forgiven sin. "He giveth songs in the night," like those with which Paul and Silas shook the arches of the Philippian prison, when, it is said, the prisoners heard them. Blessed be God for a religion of song! Come with us! Believe in the Lord Jesus Christ! Take at his hands the glory of redemption! Receive at his hands the commission for service! Take from his lips the hope of the everlasting life! And go on singing with us toward heaven's gate. All these dark days will presently be over: the days of pain, of sorrow, of weeping, for "he shall wipe away the tears from off all faces"; the days of faith, for faith shall be lost in sight, and hope in fruition; the days of prayer, for in him we shall be filled there. But, as has been written,

> "Our days of praise shall ne'er be past,
> While life, or thought, or being last,
> Or immortality endures."

Come, with us, as we journey singing with the

multitude of the redeemed, who shall, after a while, "come to Zion with songs and everlasting joy upon their heads"; to fall in with that other multitude, who are singing now:

"Worthy is the Lamb who was slain to receive honor, and glory, and power, and dominion, forever and ever, Amen."

THE SUNDAY NEWSPAPER.

"Take us the foxes, the little foxes, that spoil the vines."—SONG OF SOLOMON ii. 1.

The prevalent, growing, ominous sin of our time is Sabbath desecration. As a rule, Christian people mean to do right in this matter as in other things, but, for want of reflection, they oftentimes lend their influence the wrong way.

The head and front of the offending, is the Sunday newspaper. It is said that when burglars go prowling about at night they take with them a clever boy to climb over the transoms and open the door. The Sunday newspaper is the tuppenny door-opener for the larger forms of Sabbath desecration. Because I thus believe, I have seven or eight things to say about it.

1. The Sunday newspaper is *unnecessary;* and, if unnecessary, it ought not to be. It originated in the time of our civil war. Previously there were only two papers in the world that printed Sunday editions, the New York *Herald* and the *Alta California*. It was not strange that when our fathers and brothers were at the front and battles were being fought, we crowded about the telegraph offices and eagerly scanned the bulletins.

Then when "extras" were issued on the Sabbath,

as on other days, giving the heart-breaking lists of dead and wounded, we felt justified in getting them. Thus the wedge was entered by considerations of both mercy and necessity. But not by the wildest stretch of the imagination can the Sunday newspaper be regarded as a work of either necessity or mercy in these piping times of peace.

2. It is *unlawful*. In many of our commonwealths it is under a legal ban. In New York, however, the laws have been so adjusted as to allow it. But, inasmuch as the Supreme Court has repeatedly decided that the moral law is an organic part of our national Constitution, it may be affirmed without hesitation that this, as well as other forms of Sabbath desecration, is a distinct violation of the fundamental principles of the republic. The "sign" of God's covenant with Israel was the Sabbath. As a Christian nation we also are in covenant with God and cannot with impunity disregard his law.

3. The Sunday newspaper is *disreputable*. It is wont to present its own claims as "a great educator." This is amusing. If the claim were true it would still not excuse the offense. Our public schools are generally thought to be educational; but that does not constitute an argument for opening them on Sunday. These newspapers, however, are not an educating influence. Let me read a tabulated statement of the contents of a recent Sunday issue of several leading newspapers—the New York *Tribune, Times, Herald, Sun, Press, World, Journal* and *News*:

Murders and Assaults............	12	columns.
Adulteries.....................	7	"
Thefts, etc...................	24	"
Total of crime................	43	"

Sporting	81	columns.
Theatrical	44	"
Gossip and Fashion	77	"
Sensational	42	"
Fiction	99	"
Unclean Personals	8	"
Total of gossip (mostly disreputable).	351	"
Foreign News	47	"
Political News	113	"
Other Miscellaneous News	92	"
Editorial	39	"
Specials	199	"
Art and Literature	24	"
Religious	3¼	"
Total (chiefly) news and politics.	517¼	"
Grand total	911¼	"

The amount of religion in a Sunday newspaper is like Gratiano's "Two grains of wheat hid' in two bushels of chaff; you shall seek all day ere you find them, and when you have them they are not worth the search."

But to be more specific, here is a brief summary of the headlines in one of these Sunday papers:

Gossip of Court.—An Alleged Dramatic Shark.—Embezzlement.—A Sudden Death.—The Buzzard Gang.—A Tennessee Man in the Toils.—A Woman Burned to Death.—Vagrants.—Smuggled Goods.—A Bogus Divorce Suit.—An Eloping Husband.—A Mock Marriage Scandal.—A Chained and Beaten Wife.—Bride Arrested.—Defalcation.—Forgery.—A Stockholder Disappears.—Small-pox in Brooklyn.—Convicted of Assaulting Miss Emerson.—Mine Explosion.—Murder.—Cattle Plague.—Strangled His Wife.—Shot His Brother.—Robbed.—Killed.—Cuban

Bandits.—Deadly Canned Fruit.—Trapeze Performer's Fall.—Abhorrent Scenes in a Tropical Cemetery.—Failures.—Deadly Oleomargarine.—Gone Down at Sea.—Pacific Express Robbery.—Three Wives Living.—Suicide.—Violently Insane.—Murder Trial.—Dynamiters.—Rowdies.—He Pulled a Revolver and Threatened to Shoot Her If She Did Not Marry Him.—Desperate Murderer Arrested.—Witness Saw Clara and Traphagen in a Compromising Position.—Gossip for Ladies at the Sunday Breakfast Table.—Snubbed.—Disgrace.—An Illegitimate Child.—A Glove Fight.—Elegant Baltimore Girl for a Mistress.—Defaulting Teller.—Good Gracious!—Too Thin!—Blew Out His Brains With a Pistol.—The Waistless Dress.—The Bite of an Epileptic.—Brooklyn Tax Dodgers.

I say, therefore, the Sunday paper is disreputable. I have been told by a leading editor that it is the custom to set apart during the week all the salacious items for enlargement in the Sunday edition. It is the common sewer of all our social life, the cesspool of all shames and scandals and unmentionable things.

4. It *robs an army of employés of their needed rest.* It is estimated that since the introduction of the Sunday newspaper not less than 150,000 compositors and pressmen and others are kept at work seven days in the week, 365 days in the year. A reporter was asked, not long since, "Do you have one-seventh of your time for rest?" "No," said he, "nor one-seventy-seventh. We have no time, regularly given, that we can call our own."

It is sometimes said that it is the Monday paper that makes the Sunday work. That is a miserable evasion. If there were no Sunday issue, the preparation of the Monday number, excepting the telegraphic items, would fall on Saturday, and its publication on Monday morning.

Nor must it be overlooked that hundreds and thousands of newsboys are calling their wares on Sunday in our streets. That is their business now: and they are getting their business education for the future. To whistle up a boy and buy a newspaper for a nickel seems a matter of slight consequence. But follow it out. A Christian man in the real estate business would not think for a moment of selling a corner lot on the Lord's day. But to the newsboy the sale of his paper is relatively a matter of equal consequence; and as co-partners in the transaction, we are doing our part to train him for larger methods of Sabbath breaking in after life.

5. It *invades the Sabbath rest of a great multitude of business men.* As a people we are desperately absorbed in money-getting. Our national malady is "nervous debility." Our vital forces are under constant strain. A man with his brain in a whirl, his nerves twitching, his temper in a fever, his sleep disturbed, goes to a physician for relief. A sea voyage is prescribed. Why? Not because of any remedial virtue in sea air; but, once on the ocean, the world is shut out. The buzz of the stock ticker is unheard. Wars and revolutions may occur, but they are nothing to him. The "news" no longer frets him. If he could know what was going on in the busy world he would be as eager and perturbed as ever; but out yonder, with the infinite skies above and the boundless deep below, he has nothing to do but rest. That is precisely what God meant the Sabbath to be, an ocean voyage for the soul, a season of rest between two continents of secular toil and pleasure.

We have, therefore, no right to drag the world into our lives, as we do by means of the newspaper, on this divine day.

6. It *breaks up the home life.* Time was when in Christian families the members gathered at the family altar to worship; and after that came the reading of good books and the religious press. There was room in those days for missionary magazines; children found time to read their Sunday-school books. But how is it now? The head of the family reads his Sunday paper, and the boys and girls are waiting covetously for him to get through with it. God and heaven are crowded out. The fable of the Arab has come true. The thrusting in of the camel's nose has been followed by the thrusting out of the owner from the tent. The Sunday newspaper is responsible for the downfall of many a family altar and the breaking up of the sanctity of many a Christian home.

7. It *unfits for the sanctuary.* It is difficult to see how a man can come from the perusal of the Sunday newspaper to sing, without hypocrisy—

> This is the day the Lord hath made,
>   He calls the hours His own;
> Let heaven rejoice, let earth be glad,
>   And praise surround the throne.

Or how he can repeat the Lord's prayer: "Thy kingdom come; thy will be done on earth as it is in heaven; lead us not into temptation, but deliver us from evil," while his mind is full of the abominations of his "blanket sheet?"

One day in seven is not too much for an immortal man to set apart for sacred rest and meditation. If there is a God who hates sin; if there is a hereafter, and this life is preparatory for it, we need that portion of time for setting ourselves right with Heaven. If the adversary is ever tugging at our souls and craftily scheming to trip us up, then I submit it was a gracious act of God to set apart one day in seven, wherein we might climb to the mountain-top and think about eternal truths, breathe the pure air and be alone a little while with him. But if a man has no Sabbaths, if he allows the world to confiscate them, he must expect his spiritual nature to be dwarfed and shrivelled. His soul in its prison will cry in vain, like Sterne's starling, "I can't get out! I can't get out!"

8. It *enfeebles the conscience.* This is not a little sin, for it leads on to endless issues. Time was when a man closed his shop on Saturday night, stopped his business and went home. How is it now after twenty-five years of the Sunday newspaper? He closes his shop on Saturday night and puts an advertisement in the Sunday newspaper. He flatters himself that he is resting from toil. O no! He is doing a booming business all through the holy day. Half a million heralds are going up and down the streets, telling in flaming headlines what bargains he has to offer on the morrow. His business goes right on.

The conscience of Christian people generally has been enfeebled and debauched in this way. I can remember when there was entire unanimity among Christians as to Sabbath desecration of every sort; but we have grown accustomed to it.

> "Vice is a monster of so frightful mien
> As to be hated needs but to be seen."

That was the way we looked at it twenty five years ago.

> "Yet seen too oft, familiar with her face,
> We first endure, then pity, then embrace."

That is the condition of things to-day. We think we are growing liberal. We are simply getting loose. We are afraid of being called precisions and Puritans. But better be precisions than Parisians in this matter; far better be Puritans than profligates.

They tell us the Sunday newspaper has come to stay. Suppose it has. That is no reason why it should stay in our homes or in our hands. Sin has come to stay; so have yellow fever and cholera; but that is no reason why you should contract or foster them. In God's good time he will wipe them all out of existence as a maid shakes a napkin or wipes a platter clean. Meanwhile it is for us to be true to our consciences.

I have tried to reason with you as thoughtful men; I have tried to show the evil and why you should put it from you. Of one thing be assured, we cannot live without Sabbath rest. The promise of Isaiah is as true to-day as when it was first spoken: (Is. lviii. 13) "If thou turn away thy foot from the Sabbath, from doing thy pleasure on my holy day; and call the Sabbath a delight, holy of the Lord, honorable; and shalt honor him, not doing thine own ways, nor finding thine own pleasure, nor speaking thine own words: then shalt thou delight thyself in the Lord; and I will cause thee to ride upon the high places of the earth, and feed thee with the heritage of Jacob thy father; for the mouth of the Lord hath spoken it."

"THE FIRST AND GREAT COMMANDMENT."

"And Jesus said unto him, Thou shalt love the Lord thy God with all thy heart, and with all thy soul, and with all thy mind. This is the first and great commandment."—MATT. xxii. 37, 38.

It was Tuesday of Passion Week, "The Day of Temptations." The enemies of Jesus had compassed him about in a strenuous effort to ensnare him. The Pharisees first approached him with the question as to the payment of the capitation tax. "Is it lawful to pay tribute to Cæsar or not?" Here was a dilemma; to answer "Yes" would be to alienate his own countrymen; to answer "No" would be to antagonize the Herodians or Romanizing party. "Show me a penny," said he. On one side were the haughty features of Tiberius, on the other the inscription, *Pontifex Maximus*. How it galled them! "Whose image and superscription is this?" "Cæsar's." "Render unto Cæsar the things that are Cæsar's, and unto God the things that are God's." And they went their way.

Then came the Sadducees with an old, stale bit of casuistry. They were great quibblers. There was no room in their philosophy for the supernatural or the future life. This Jesus believed in the resurrection; they would make a *reductio ad absurdum* of his doctrine. So they propose the question of the "seven-fold widow;" to-wit, A woman, according to the Levitical law, had seven brothers as husbands, one after the other, and successively they died; then she died also; "Good Rabbi, in the resurrection whose wife shall she be?" It was a clever question, but he was equal to it. "Ye do err, not knowing the Scriptures or the power of God." What? This to the Sadducees? Not know the Scriptures? Not know the power of God? Nay, further still, they were not acquainted with the simplest of the great verities that underlie the spiritual life; that is, flesh and blood cannot inherit the kingdom. Every one to his proper conditions. "In heaven they neither marry nor are given in marriage (in the low, base sense in which the Sadducees understood it), but are as the angels of God." And they went their way.

A scribe next approached him, a professor of Biblical theology. The school to which he belonged was devoted to the analysis and exposition of the Mosaic Law. They counted and weighed its precepts, and carefully estimated their relative value. They said there were two hundred and forty-eight affirmative precepts, corresponding to the members of the body; three hundred and sixty-five negative precepts, corresponding to the veins and arteries; making a total of six hundred and thirteen, just the number of Hebrew letters in the Decalogue. Some of these were called *Kol*, or light; and others *Kobeb*, or heavy. The least of the commandments, by common consent, was that which had reference to the robbing of a bird's nest. But the important question was, Which is the greatest? Was it the injunction with respect to the breadth of fringes or phylacteries, or the prescript as to oblations or sacrifices? No point in

Rabbinical controversy was regarded as more momentous than this. It was a catch question. "Good Rabbi, which is the greatest commandment?" And Jesus pointed to the *Tephillim*, the frontlet between his eyes, on which was written, "Hear, O Israel, the Lord our God is one Lord," and asked, "What readest thou? 'Thou shalt love the Lord thy God with all thy heart and with all thy soul and with all thy mind and with all thy strength.' This is the first and great commandment. And," he continued, "the second is like unto it, 'Thou shalt love thy neighbor as thyself.'"

The Law was inscribed in two tables. The first has reference to our relations with God, and the second to our relations with our fellow-men. We have to do now with our Lord's compendium of the first table of the Law. The second can wait.

The beginning of religion is love to God. Here is a moralist who says, "I keep the Law. Thou shalt not kill, thou shalt not steal, thou shalt not commit adultery, thou shalt not lie. What more can God ask of me?" Here is a ceremonialist who says, "I worship in the beauty of holiness. I pay tithes, swing the censer and make my stated prayers. What more can be required of me?" Here is a humanitarian who says, "I try to deal kindly with all. My saint is Abu Ben Adhem. I do good as I have opportunity unto all men. Will the Lord deal hardly with one who lives in that way?"

The fact is, however, that these outward displays of goodness are the mere empty shell of religion, no more in themselves than sounding brass or a tinkling cymbal. They bear the same relation to manifestations of true piety that the flowers on a bonnet do to the sweet peas and morning glories in a cottage garden with the early dew glistening upon them. Life, life is what they lack. The buds, blossoms and fruit will take care of themselves if our religion has a living root; and the root of religion is love to God.

I. But *why should we love God?* Because he is essentially worthy of our love, the One altogether lovely: and because he is the source and centre and ultimatum of our life; our chief end being to glorify him. It is proof of our depravity that the question should arise, "Why should I love God?" The withholding of our hearts from him who created and sustained us is the very essence of sin. "Hear, O heavens, and give ear O earth; for the Lord hath spoken: 'I have nourished and brought up children, and they have rebelled against me: the ox knoweth his owner, and the ass his master's crib: but Israel doth not know, my people doth not consider. Ah, sinful nation, a people laden with iniquity; they have forsaken me!'"

> "Ah! mine iniquity
> Crimson hath been.
> Infinite! Infinite!
> Sin upon sin,
> Sin of not knowing Him,
> Sin of not loving Him,
> Infinite sin!"

II. But *how can we love God?* "Our affections are not under our control." Yes, but they are. The reason why we do not love God is because we are not acquainted with him, and we are not acquainted with him because we choose not to commune with him. We think of him as an ethereal being with whom we have little or naught to do. He is law, force, energy; a something not ourselves that worketh for righteousness; anything but a living, personal God. It is not possible under such conditions to be warmly or devotedly attached to him. The skipper of the Mary Jane will tell you that he loves his sloop; every spar and rope, every curve and angle, from keel to top-mast. But there is another Mary Jane down Cape Cod way whom he loves infinitely better and in a very d.fferent way—a tidy little woman with a babe in her arms, standing in the doorway looking out over the sea and thinking of her good man. We may admire an inanimate thing of beauty, but our affection goes out toward kindling eyes and throbbing heart and kindly hand. "As the hart panteth after the waterbrooks so panteth my soul after thee, O God. When shall I come and appear before the living God!"

If you would become acquainted with him, enter into the closet and shut to the door. "The world is too much with us." We have no time to confront the sublime truths of eternal life. We have little disposition to be alone with God. Love is like the edelweiss, which does not grow in a cottage, but on the inaccessible cliffs. Lay down your alpenstock, O weary traveller, and rest awhile; here at your feet is the fairest flower that blooms. Alas for us, if we neglect the trysting-place!

Go to the Oracles also if you would find him. Thank God for the Bible. What is it but a love-letter sent out by the King after his wandering ones? Here is a setting of his character in all its glorious attributes. Here are songs and precepts and prophecies and chronicles; but all of them centre in the glorious truth, God is love. The face of the kind

Father looks out from all its pages. Here are exceeding great and precious promises. Here are words of wooing and persuasion. The youth who went across the mountains into the far country and wasted his substance in riotous living, may perhaps have kept in a fold of his tattered cloak a letter from his father; but little heart had he to read it. But when he sat alone in the swine-field, he opened the worn parchment and read; every line seemed vibrant with love. What could he say, but—"I will arise and go"?

But if you would know God in the very fulness of his love, you must find him at Calvary. I come there a seeking sinner in the dark night; peace gone, hope abandoned, bewildered, lost, lying prone upon the verge of a bottomless abyss. I hear the sound of a breaking heart, and, looking up, see yonder the incarnation of God's love against the midnight sky—a seeking God. He has come out upon the dark mountains after me. The night has gathered about him. All the thunders of death and judgment are roaring and bellowing; all the lightnings of hell are flashing luridly over him. I reach up my trembling, helpless hand; a piercéd hand is reached down, and the two are clasped. This is the gracious at-one-ment. The seeking sinner finds the seeking God! Then the open heavens, the day-break, light and glory forever; "Son, thy sins be forgiven thee."

The secret of love toward God is in apprehending his love toward us. We love him because he first loved us. The secret is revealed beneath the cross. God so loved the world—God so loved me.

> "Shall I not love thee, Father mine?
> Shall I not love thee well?
> Not with the hope of winning heaven,
> Nor of escaping hell,

> Not for the sake of gaining aught,
>   Or earning a reward;
> But freely, fully as thyself
>   Hast loved me, O Lord."

III. What then? *The beginning of love is in the acceptance of God as he has manifested himself in Christ.* As it is written, "He that hath not the Son, hath not the Father." It is preposterous to claim loyalty to the King while rejecting his overtures through his well-beloved Son who is heir apparent to the throne. But having accepted him, what then? What is the sequel of love? Confession to begin with. It is a true saying, "They do not love who do not show their love." The Scripture speaketh on this wise: "Say not in thine heart, Who shall ascend into heaven to bring Christ down? Or, Who shall descend into the deep to bring him up again from the dead? But what saith it? The word is nigh thee, even in thy mouth and heart; that is, the word of faith—to-wit: 'If thou shalt confess with thy mouth the Lord Jesus, and shalt believe in thine heart that God has raised him from the dead, thou shalt be saved.' For with the heart man believeth unto righteousness; and with the mouth confession is made unto salvation."

Then obedience, obedience, implicit, unmurmuring and exact. "Whatsoever he saith unto you, do it." The obedience of love is not like that of servility. When Humboldt was botanizing in Central America he found it impossible to persuade his men to work as they were entering the jungle; they groaned under the burden of a basket of moss. But on their return, when their faces were set homeward, they would carry their canoes without a murmur all day long, singing by the way. Oh, how light is the labor of love! "And hereby we know that we know him, if we keep his commandments." "Ye are my friends if ye do whatsoever I command you."

Then holiness, or godliness; that is, God-likeness; the building up of character in the imitation of Christ. Be ye holy; "coy and tender to offend." In our moments of affectionate transport, we envy the privilege of Mary who poured the spikenard on the Master's feet. But to live a pure and holy life, to exemplify the Christian graces in our walk and conversation is better than spikenard, better than the fat of fed beasts, better than any offering that a soul can lay before the feet of God.

Finally, *How shall we discover whether or no we love God?*

> " 'Tis a point I long to know,
> Oft it causes anxious thought:
> Do I love my Lord or no?
> Am I his, or am I not?"

But why shall we sit moping and mourning? and why shall we question about it? Let us find out. Let us seek God face to face and set things right. Let us take the steps prerequisite to knowing and loving him. It is safe to say that none of us loves as much as he ought to; but the desire, the aspiration, is a sure token that our hearts are inclining toward him. So far so good. Let us live up to the slight measure of our love and move on. He is not an exacting God. He remembers that we are dust. He knows the trials and allurements that surround us.

I came upon the legend of an Arab, who, perishing in the desert, found a spring gushing from the sand. He drank and praised God. "There never was such water," he cried. "I will fill my leathern bottle and carry it to the king." He came at length, dusty and weary, to the royal city, presented himself in the audience room, rose from his knees and held out the water bottle. The king drank and thanked him in most gracious terms. The courtiers crowded about and begged for a draught, but in vain. When the Arab was gone, the king said, "The water was warm and insipid; but I knew the love in the traveller's heart and I saw the affectionate glow in his eyes and was grateful for it." So, good friends, there is nothing in the universe so grateful to our Father as the tribute of our poor love. Kings may lay their crowns before him, angels surround him with their anthems; but there is nothing more pleasing to him than the libations of our hearts. Love is the sublimest thing on earth, the divinest thing in heaven. Love is the highest attainment of human nature, the nearest approach to divinity; for God himself is love, and love is the fulfilling of the law.

"AND THE SECOND IS LIKE UNTO IT."

"And the second is like unto it, Thou shalt love thy neighbor as thyself."—MATT. xxii. 39.

The lawyer in this case got more than he bargained for. His purpose was to trip Jesus with the catch question, "Which is the great commandment?" The answer came without a moment's hesitation and with an emphasis and solemnity that must have made a profound impression, "Thou shalt love the Lord thy God with all thy heart and soul and mind, this is the first and great commandment." But then the Lord proceeded, "And the second is like unto it, Thou shalt love thy neighbor as thyself." The lawyer should have been familiar with the former; for was it not written in the law, "Hear, O Israel, the Lord thy God is one Lord, and thou shalt love the Lord thy God with all thy heart and soul and mind?" But this other, in the form in which it was given, was distinctly a new commandment. It was elsewhere so characterized, as when Jesus said "A new commandment give I unto you, that ye love one another." And also, "Ye have heard that it hath been said, Thou shalt love thy neighbor and hate thine enemy. But I say unto you, Love your enemies, bless them that curse you, do good to them that hate you, and pray for them which despitefully use you and persecute you."

This was putting the law upon a new basis. The Ten Commandments had been regarded as ten lofty peaks of justice, marked, like Sinai itself, by stupendous tokens of the divine Majesty; the lowering clouds, blackness, darkness, tempest, fateful lightnings with which the mountain seemed on fire, and the voice of the trumpet waxing louder and louder. But they are here given to understand that these mountains were cast up by the central fires of love. Law and love are made identical. Law proceeds from love, accomplishes its purposes and terminates in it. The sum and substance of the first table is love toward God; of the second table, love toward men.

The purpose of law is to prepare the way for the reign of love; and ultimately law will resolve itself into love and love into law. The sole remnant of the magnificence of a mediæval abbey is in granite walls and oaken beams. There were silken tapestries, once, and beautiful frescoes, and vessels of gold and silver; but only the granite and oak have resisted "the tooth of time and rasure of oblivion." Thus with the passing of the present order all will crumble save Law and Love. One is granite, the other oak; and both are destined to abide forever.

There are difficulties attending a clear understanding of this commandment, "Thou shalt love thy neighbor as thyself." They will all be made to disappear, however, by a right use of the three keywords, "Like," "As," and "Neighbor."

I. *Like;* "The second is *like* unto it." Wherein can this commandment be said to be like that, "Thou shalt love the Lord thy God?"

First—In that it proceeds from it. There is no true philanthropy which does not find its fountain in piety. There is indeed a tenderness of heart in less or greater measure among all men, but it is an open question how much of moral worth there is in a mere natural affection. Sir Walter Scott was so tender-hearted that, having broken a dog's leg by an inadvertent blow, he never ceased to feel remorse for it. Some persons can look dry-eyed on scenes of suffering that move others to ready tears. True humanity, however, is founded not upon mere sentiment, but upon principle. It proceeds from a recognition of the divine nature in every man and of the divine love toward all. A child stood at the window of a baker's shop, looking in with hungry eyes. A lady passing by took compassion on her. The little one received the purchased dainties without a word, until at parting she quaintly and pathetically said, "Be you God's wife?" There was profound philosophy at the bottom of that. All true kindness proceeds from the best and noblest—yes, from God within us.

And second—Because a true manifestation of philanthropy is the proof of love toward God. So it is written, "If a man say, I love God, and hate his neighbor, the truth is not in him." This was why Jesus denounced the Pharisees. They professed a deep piety, which they attested by tithes and frequent fasts, long prayers and broad phylacteries. "God is our Father," they said; but the Lord's reply was, "Nay; yonder is a widow whom ye have dispossessed; yonder is a man impoverished by your usury; your hands are red with blood!" He who wilfully and deliberately wrongs his neighbor can by no means be regarded as a friend of God.

II. *As;* "Thou shalt love thy neighbor *as* thyself." By this he intended to say, not that the mete or standard of love to one's neighbor is the selfishness which prevails among many, but the true self-love which should rule among all.

There is a self-love or egotism which is self-ruinous and destructive. It is said of Narcissus that, as he beheld himself in the fountain, he was so overcome by his own beauty that he died in a rapture of self-admiration. This is indeed the commonest form of suicide. Men devote themselves to wealth, pleasure and honor for the mere getting and keeping and using on self; this is miser-love, gourmand-love, Napoleonic self-love. "Let no man think of himself more highly than he ought to think." Let no man live as if he were the only soul worthy of consideration. A man living in this manner could by no possibility love his neighbor as he loves himself.

But there is another form of self-love which is right and dutiful; a true egotism which puts a right estimate on the importance of self. An old weaver in England used to make this prayer each morning, "Lord, teach me to respect myself." This was a right prayer. I am a man made in God's likeness and after his image; it is my duty to make the most of myself, not for self's sake alone, but for the sake of others and the glory of God. It is my duty to realize the vast possibilities of my life and the destiny which is divinely intended for me.

An oriental legend tells of a man who had stored away a vast quantity of wheat in expectation of famine. In the time of necessity the people besought him in vain; he would reserve his store for a higher price. Multitudes died in the streets and still his granaries were locked. At length the exigency was so great that the people were ready to pay whatever he might ask.

He opened his granaries and went in; there was nothing there but dust and crawling worms. He had overreached himself. This is the way of the selfish world. It is indeed the duty of every man to increase his stores, to fill his granaries, but only that he may disburse his wealth and distribute his possessions to the needy children of men.

III. *Neighbor.* Nach·bauer; that is, near-dweller. This word, however, does not properly characterize the thought in the Saviour's mind. The neighbor to whom he referred was distinctly not the near-dweller. For indeed vicinage has little or nothing to do with the real claims of humanity. This is a pagan conception. In the philosophy of Hierocles the relative claims of others upon a man's regard were indicated in concentric circles. The nearest circle enclosed the man himself, the next his household, the next his townsmen, the next his fellow-citizens, and the great multitude lay wholly without these circumscriptions of love. The Romans had only one word, *hostis*, by which to characterize a stranger and an enemy. To the Greeks, all but themselves were barbarians. A shipwrecked sailor on the coast of Britain was doomed without ceremony to the altar. Thus to the non-Christian thought of the world, the only neighbor was the near-dweller: the man who lived next door. There are persons in Christian communities who cherish the same idea, but it is distinctly at odds with the Christian view.

We are left in no uncertainty as to Christ's opinion at this point. A lawyer came to him on a certain occasion, asking, "Master, what shall I do to inherit eternal life?" He answered, "Thou shalt love the Lord thy God with all thy heart and soul and mind and strength, and thy neighbor as thyself.' Thereupon the lawyer, feeling some qualms of conscience and desiring to justify himself, asked, "But who is my neighbor?" And Jesus said. "*A certain man went down from Jerusalem to Jericho and fell among thieves, who stripped him of his raiment, and wounded him, and departed, leaving him half dead. And by chance there came down a certain priest that way, and when he saw him he passed by on the other side; and likewise a Levite came and looked on him and passed by on the other side. But a certain Samaritan, as he journeyed, came where he was; and when he saw him he had compassion on him, and he bound up his wounds, and took care of him. Which now of these three, thinkest thou, was neighbor to him that fell among the thieves?*" Observe, he does not directly answer the lawyer's question, "Who is my neighbor?" but tells him rather how he should be neighbor to every man: for when the lawyer answered, "He that showed mercy on him," Jesus said unto him, "Go, and do thou likewise."

> " Thy neighbor? 'Tis that wearied man
> Whose years are at their brim,
> Bent low with sickness, cares and pain:
> Go thou and comfort him.
>
> " Thy neighbor? Yonder toiling slave,
> Fetter'd in thought and limb,
> Whose hopes are all beyond the grave!
> Go thou and ransom him.'

The true Christian is a cosmopolite. He believes in the fatherhood of God, and consequently in the brotherhood of man. In pursuance of this conviction he sends out his sympathy and helpfulness not only to his kinsmen or his countrymen, but to all men everywhere, who have need of him. As it is written, "One Lord, one faith, one baptism, one God and Father of all."

The rabbis say, that once upon a time there were two affectionate brothers who tilled the same farm. On a certain night, after the gathering of the harvest, one of them said to his wife, "My brother is a lonely man, who has neither wife nor children; I will go out and carry some of my sheaves into his field." It happened that, on the same night, the other said, "My brother has wife and children, and needs the harvest more than I; I will carry some of my sheaves into his field." So the next morning their respective heaps were unchanged, and thus it happened night after night, until at length, one moonlight night, the brothers with their arms full of sheaves met midway face to face. On that spot the Temple was built, because it was esteemed to be the place where earth was nearest heaven. This is indeed the noblest attitude of man. And what a world ours would be if all men, realizing that they are children of the same God and therefore brethren of the same household, were to treat each other in this way.

And the Lord said, "On these two commandments hang all the Law and the Prophets." Love is the sum and substance of law. Love God supremely and love thy neighbor as thyself. He that doeth this law shall live by it.

If we would learn the true philosophy of the law and catch the true spirit of obedience, we must visit the cross. It is here that we discover how God loved us. "He commendeth his love toward us in that, while we were yet sinners, Christ died for us." If once we apprehend the length, breadth, depth and height of the love manifested in this supreme self-sacrifice in our behalf, we shall never need to say to ourselves again, " Thou shalt love the Lord thy God." And if once we shall perceive that Jesus here tasted death for every man—for the drunkard that reels along our streets, for the poor fetish worshipper in the far-away jungles of Africa—we shall need no more to say to ourselves, " Love thy neighbor as thyself." The God who gave Christ is the Father of all. The Christ who suffered and died is the Brother of all. To love as the Father and Son have loved is the consummation of duty. Love is the fulfilling of the Law.

ESTHER IN SHUSHAN.

"I will go in unto the king."—ESTHER iv. 16.

A group of notable dignitaries passes before us in the glamour of the far-away past.

Here is Ahasuerus, king of Persia, familiar to us as Xerxes the Great. It was he who lashed the sea because it would not obey him. He called himself the "King of kings and Lord of lords." He was cruel, capricious, magnificent; his word was irreversible law.

Here is Esther, his beautiful queen. She was a Jewess, brought up under the protection of her kinsman, Mordecai. Her exaltation to the throne was by a strange providence. She had concealed her lineage thus far, as it would appear, to avoid the finger of scorn; for the Jews were hated then as now. But, standing up among the daughters of Persia, she shone pre-eminent in beauty. Radiant as the star that sparkled in her name, she was chosen from among all.

And here is Haman, the son of Hammedatha, court favorite, villain of the play. Puffed up with a little brief authority, he will have all the people doff their bonnets as he goes by. One only refuses, the aged Mordecai. He will not "bend the pregnant hinges of the knee that thrift may follow fawning." The proud heart of Haman is filled with wrath. He puts his spies upon the old man's track. "What dost thou say? A Jew? Then we shall make a splendid reprisal." It is not enough that Mordecai shall suffer. The king is persuaded to pronounce the decree of death upon all the children of Israel within the Persian realm.

The Jewish homes of Shushan are filled with lamentation. The mourners on the housetops kneel with uplifted eyes and hands pressed together. They have learned their doom, and are praying and listening. The blast of a trumpet! The clang of horses' hoofs! A troop of heralds riding forth with parchment scrolls! They are the messengers of doom. By the Assyrian mountains, by the southern plain, by the Parthian Sea, all Israel must die.

In the open square beneath the queen's window, an old man leans on his ivory staff, uttering a low, wailing cry. At length he succeeds in attracting the queen's attention. She appears at her lattice. He tells the sorrowful story of which she in her retirement has been kept in ignorance; he entreats her to go in unto the king in behalf of her people. Useless are her protestations: "The king is at his revels; to approach him uninvited now, is death under the Persian law."—"No matter; the fate of all Israel depends upon it; and who knoweth but thou art come unto the kingdom for such a time as this?"—She pleads, resists, and yields. "I will go in unto the king; and if I perish, I perish."

The hour is come. For many days the king and his courtiers have been feasting in Shushan. The halls are filled with incense and music; the doors are defended by stolid Nubian guards. Who comes yonder along the marble walk? They start in amazement and whisper to one another. It is the queen! For a woman to intrude upon the king's revels at such a time is to incur a double certainty of death. She draws near, arrayed in her royal apparel—a vision of beauty. They stand aside, overawed, to let her pass. At the threshold of Shushan she pauses; her lips move silently in prayer; she enters and stands in the banquet hall. Yonder is the king with his favorites about him; pale, but resolute, she faces him. The destiny of her kinspeople is in the balance. Her beauty, her calm demeanor, her magnificent courage, have vanquished him. "What wilt thou, Queen Esther? It shall be done unto thee, even unto the half of my kingdom." The sceptre is stretched out; the crisis is past; Israel is saved!

And what does this signify to us? *The glory of intercession.* We are living in a world of perishing souls, who, "forever hastening to the grave, stoop downward as they run." Death has passed upon all for that all have sinned. The law has gone forth, "The soul that sinneth it shall die." Our friends, neighbors, kinsfolk, are among them, and the responsibility of their deliverance rests largely upon us.

> " I stood at the open casement
>   And looked upon the night,
> And saw the westward-going stars
>   Pass slowly out of sight.
>
> " Slowly the bright procession
>   Went down the gleaming arch,
> And my soul discerned the music
>   Of the long triumphal march;

" Till the great celestial army,
   Stretching far beyond the poles,
 Became the eternal symbol
   Of the mighty march of souls.

" Onward, forever onward,
   Red Mars led down his clan ;
 And the moon, like a veilèd maiden,
   Was riding in the van.

" And some were bright in beauty,
   And some were faint and small ;
 But these might be, in their great heights,
   The noblest of them all.

" Downward, forever downward,
   Behind earth's dusky shore,
 They passed into the unknown night,
   They passed—and were no more."

I. *Observe the bended form of this suppliant queen.* Here is the noblest attitude of human nature ; to bow before the throne of the heavenly grace in behalf of others.

To make one's calling and election sure is chronologically first and most important of all. No man can look after the spiritual welfare of others until he has attended to his personal salvation. Do the first things first. Come like the publican, beating upon your breast, and crying, " God be merciful to me a sinner." Come to the cross and the fountain filled with blood; and, by the truth of a hundred great and precious promises, he will stretch his scarred hands and say, " Thy sins be forgiven thee."

But if this were all, religion would be indeed a selfish thing. The captain of the "Algona," discharged from service, is hiding himself shamefaced somewhere. His ship went down and forty-eight of his crew and passengers went down with it ; but he swam ashore ! A man may come to heaven in that way, saved so as by fire. But, alas ! it would seem almost better to go with the outcasts. No sheaf from the harvest ; no star in one's crown. No, no ; this is not to fulfill the high vocation of a Christian life.

We have power to convert. A stupendous thought! " He that converteth a sinner from the error of his ways shall save a soul from death and hide a multitude of sins." But how ? By seasonable words which are like apples of gold in silver baskets ; by the example of an upright walk and conversation ; and by intercessory prayer. Here is where a man finds himself at his noblest and best ; on his knees interceding for men. Moses was never so great as when, after the sin of the golden calf, he threw himself upon his face on the mountain and cried, " O, this people have sinned a great sin; if thou wilt, forgive them—and if not, blot me out of thy book !" Hezekiah was never so great as when, with the tents of Sennacherib all around his city, he knelt, spread out the scornful letter of Rabshakeh and begged for their deliverance at the hands of God. Paul, the " ugly little Jew," seems of gigantic stature when he exclaims, " I could wish that myself were accursed from Christ for my brethren, my kinsmen according to the flesh." We stand reverently at the door of John Knox's closet while he p'eads, " O God, give me Scotland or I die ! " Here is our coigne of vantage in the Christian life. We can convert ! Wives can save their husbands, parents can save their children, young men can save their comrades, masters can save their servants, by the power of prayer.

> ' There is an eye that never sleeps
>   Beneath the wing of night;
> There is an ear that never shuts,
>   When sink the beams of light.
>
> " There is an arm that never tires,
>   When human strength gives way;
> There is a love that never fails,
>   When earthly loves decay.
>
> " That eye is fixed on seraph throngs;
>   That arm upholds the sky;
> That ear is filled with angels' songs;
>   That love is throned on high.
>
> " But there's a power which man can wield
>   When mortal aid is vain,
> That eye, that arm, that love to reach,
>   That listening ear to gain.
>
> " That power is prayer, which soars on high,
>   Through Jesus to the throne;
> *And moves the hand which moves the world,*
>   *To bring salvation down.*"

II. *Observe the outstretched sceptre of the King* It speaks of God's willingness to hear and answer us. We pray for ourselves with faith; we pray for our friends with misgiving. Let us rather add faith to faith when we plead for others; for certainly the good God is pleased to hear an unselfish supplication. Did not the heart of Ahasuerus respond to the petition of his beautiful queen in behalf of her people, more readily and joyously than if she had asked for the half of his kingdom or any other personal favor?

We are encouraged by great promises. Intercessory prayer falls within the circumscription of all God's assurances. No limitations are put upon it. No conditions are affixed to it. Ask, ask, and it shall be given to you; for every one that asketh, receiveth. Oh, if the multitude of half-hearted supplicants, who are pleading for their beloved, could only believe in God's willingness to hear. How many mothers there are like Rizpah who went out in the time of the barley harvest, spread sackcloth upon the barren rock, and watched beside her seven sons hanging on the gibbet; fire in heart and bludgeon in hand, keeping away the beasts of the field and the fowls of the air. But why need the wayward die? Why need the prodigal perish in his sins, when parents have power to save? God's covenant is sure; his promises are "yea" and "amen."

We are led to believe in Christ's willingness to hear intercessory prayer from the analogy of his earthly life. Did he refuse the request of Jairus who besought him for his daughter near to death? Nay; he left the feast where he was being entertained and went to the sorrowing father's house, passed through the hired mourners that were beating on their breasts, took the little, cold hand in his, saying, *Talitha, cumi;* and the child arose. Did he refuse the prayer of the Syrophœnician woman who cried, "My daughter is grievously vexed with a demon?" His disciples entreated, "Send her away, she troubleth us." But he said, "Be it unto thee even as thou wilt." Did he disregard the solicitous kindness of the four friends who carried the paralytic up the outer stairway and let him down through the roof into the midst? Nay; it is written that "when he saw *their* faith" he healed his infirmity and forgave his sin. At the gateway of Nain he had compassion on the widow who was following her son to the grave; her tears were her prayer, and he answered it. Wherever he went, the sick were brought on couches by their friends and laid along the way, and he "healed them every one." And this Jesus Christ is the same, yesterday, to-day and forever.

We are led furthermore to believe in his willingness to hear, by the fact of his own intercession. His whole life indeed was intercessory. The stretching out of his hands upon the cross was an intercessory prayer for the children of men. And in heaven he ever liveth to make intercession for us. A legend says that the angel Sandalphon waits at the outer most gates of heaven, with his feet on a ladder of light, listening. The songs of the great multitude of angels and redeemed come from above, but he heeds them not. The songs and laughter of earthly homes are all about him, but he heeds them not. He hearkens for the mother's cry in behalf of her wayward son, for the sob of a burdened heart bleeding for the lost and wandering; he bears these supplications aloft, lays them before the throne, and they turn to garlands at the feet of God.

III. *Observe the sequel.* Haman the Magnificent swings from the gallows tree; the homes of the Israelites are filled with music and laughter.

Joy is ever the sequel of unselfish toil and prayer. The delight of the Christian life is in doing for others. There is no pleasure like "the generous pleasure of kindly deeds." The Lord, at Sychar, was an hungered and his disciples went away for food. He spoke to the woman of Samaria, of the living water, and to the people of the town also who came about him. On the return of the disciples he said, "I have meat to eat that ye know not of." The cry of the body for nourishment had been hushed by his eagerness to help; the nobler passion had gotten the upper hand of it. This is the joy of the Lord, and it makes a heaven on earth.

And this is the joy of heaven too. At the close of our Civil War when Lincoln visited Richmond the slaves loosed the horses from his carriage and drew it through the streets, crying, "God bless Massa Lincoln"! There were men among them whose backs were scarred in a life-time of bondage; and he was their deliverer. Oh, there is many a Cæsarian triumph awaiting the faithful up yonder! Make to yourselves friends, that they may receive you into those everlasting habitations.

I stand by heaven's gate and see a man coming in alone. Saved; but with no souls for his hire. Saved; but with no trophies for benevolent faithfulness. O lonely, lonely man! I see another coming who has rejoiced to spend and be spent for others, and what a welcome he receives! What greeting and hand-clasping! Here are many who have come before him, saved by his faithful toil and intercession, who delight to receive him into the joy of the Lord.

Come, friends, let us cease our selfish striving for mere personal advantage, spiritual or otherwise, and busy ourselves in doing good. Let us journey by the king's highway, taking prisoners of hope with us. It was intended that every Christian should be a priest unto God. And this is a true saying, "They that be wise shall shine as the brightness of the firmament, and they that turn many to righteousness as the stars forever and ever."

ORTHODOXY.

"But speak thou the things which become sound doctrine."—TITUS ii : 1.

To begin with, orthodoxy is not "my doxy" as the common parlance puts it. If there ever was a time when a minister could say, "I am Sir Oracle, and when I ope my lips let no dog bark," that time has gone by. No man living has the right to force a formulary of belief upon another, nor has any living man the right to receive his creed at second hand. It is the business of each to make the best possible application of heart, reason, and conscience, to every proposition of faith, as each for himself must answer for his own convictions at the judgment bar of God. Prove all things; hold fast that which is good. Do your own thinking. Hear what other thinkers have to say, lend a respectful attention to the Church and council, and then determine for yourself what you will believe respecting the great problems of the endless life. Let no man take thy crown!

Still further, orthodoxy is not slavish subscription to the deliverances of the past. Of course "tradition" counts. A man would be a fool not to allow that the researches and controversies of these hundreds of years should have their proper weight. What would be thought of a farmer who, throwing aside all labor-saving inventions, should insist on ploughing with a crooked stick, threshing his grain with a flail, and grinding it with mortar and pestle? He would be independent indeed, but not bright. The creeds and deliverances of the past are labor-saving conveniences for thoughtful men. It is a true saying that a dwarf can see farther than a giant, if he stands on the giant's shoulders. No one can afford to refuse the advantage of this view-point. Climb up, friend; climb on the shoulders of the past; but when you are there, use not the giant's eyes but your own. Let creeds and catechisms and formularies be but steps upward by which you reach a magnificent coigne of vantage in your earnest quest for truth.

And further still, orthodoxy must not be regarded as the mark of a Bœotian credulity. There is a disposition on the part of some callow folk in these days to assume that all the clever people are heretics, and that loyalty to established truth is the mark of a torpid intellect. The impression is given that heresy is somehow necessary to progress—as if a locomotive could not go except on down grade with open brakes. The fact is, however, that the really progressive thinkers, who increase the world's treasure of faith, are those who give all proper deference to established facts and all due regard to the limitations of thought. It is not the wild rovers of the sea who find El Doradoes, but such as sail by chart and compass.

Orthodoxy is an honorable word. It is associated with the noblest episodes in history. It savors of the times when men loved truth better than life. It was for his loyalty to conviction that Abel was slain beside the altar. It was for his devotion to right that Abram left his country and his father's house and went forth, not knowing whither he went. It was for their orthodoxy that the three Babylonish youth were cast into the furnace of fire. The time would fail me to tell of those who in this cause had trial of cruel mockings and scourgings, yea, moreover of bonds and imprisonment; were stoned, were sawn asunder, were slain with the sword; of whom the world was not worthy. Nay, it was for his devotion to "sound doctrine" that Jesus himself set his face steadfastly towards the cross. It is an easy matter in these piping times of peace to point the finger at the word Orthodoxy and make sport of it. But there is no grander word in our vocabulary. It has been stained with blood and scarified with fire. Its joints have been drawn asunder and its flesh pulled with pincers. It is covered with honorable scars. Long life to it!

But we want a definition. What is Orthodoxy? A case came before the circuit court of Baltimore some time ago which awakened no little interest in ecclesiastical circles. A gentleman had left the bulk of his estate for the erection of an edifice for "the worship of Jesus Christ according to the Orthodox Baptist faith." The construction of the will hinged upon the meaning of the word "Orthodox." It was held by the presiding judge that, in the absence of a state church, it was not competent for the court to determine what is Orthodox and what not. In other words, that Orthodoxy is a word without a definition. It is not for us to criticise that opinion in its legal aspects, but we may venture to dissent in so far as it suggests that the word is without a very distinct significance.

It is true that the word Orthodoxy does not

occur in Scripture; but for that matter neither does creed or incarnation; but the fact is distinctly there. "The time will come," writes Paul to Timothy, "when they will not endure sound doctrine." And again in his Epistle to Titus, "Speak thou the things which become sound doctrine." Etymologically it is precisely that, *orthe doxa*, "sound doctrine."

Historically, it means loyalty to the formularies of any particular bodies. In this sense all depends upon the environment. An orthodox Mohammedan is one who believes that there is only one God and Mohammed is his prophet. An orthodox Unitarian is one who believes that Jesus of Nazareth is not the divine Son of God. An orthodox Episcopalian is one who believes in the Thirty-nine Articles. An orthodox Reformed or Presbyterian is one who believes in the system of doctrine contained in the Calvinistic symbols, such as the Canons of Dort and the Westminster Confession of Faith.

But there is a larger sense in which the word is applied to the universal fellowship of believers in Christ. *An Orthodox Christian* is one who believes in the truths which are held in common by the universal Church of Christ. We say, "I believe in the Holy Catholic Church;" that is, the Church made up of all denominations which receive the fundamentals of the gospel of Christ. There is no difficulty in understanding what this sort of Orthodoxy means, unless, indeed, there is a desire to misunderstand it.

I. *The life of Christian Orthodoxy is Christ.* He is its Alpha and Omega. He is first, last, midst and all in all. It does not follow, however, that a man is orthodox because he says he believes in Christ. This declaration may be the subterfuge of those who are constantly recreant to the fundamental truths which centre in him, or of those who repose only a partial faith in him. There are many in our time who use the name of Jesus as the specious term of an exclusively humanitarian religion. They paint his character in glowing colors, saying, "Behold him as he goes about doing good; opening blind eyes, healing the sick, comforting the sorrowing and making life sweeter and purer. What is better than to live like this? Creeds are nothing, dogma is nothing, the Scriptures are a matter of little moment. Why discuss these minor points? Let Christ be all and in all."

It is a pity to say aught against this form of belief and manner of life. Nevertheless it should be understood that Christ must not be dismembered. If we receive him at all, we must receive him every way. He offers himself not only as our Exemplar in benevolence, but as our Prophet, Priest and King. To reject his demands at any point is practically to reject him *in toto*.

(1.) He offers himself as our Priest. He stands on Calvary as our substitute to make expiation for our sin. He takes the heart out of his own bosom and lays it throbbing on the altar there. He is wounded for our transgressions and bruised for our iniquities, that by his stripes we may be healed. To deny that is to make him a deceiver. If we believe in Christ, we must believe in the atoning power of the blood that he shed for us.

(2.) He is our Prophet; that is, our Teacher in spiritual things. His Word is our court of last appeal. He has something to say as to God; as to the heinousness of sin; as to the spiritual death which follows—the worm that dieth not, the fire that is not quenched; as to life and immortality,—the resurrection body and the final judgment. If we receive Christ in sincerity, we must accept his word as a final statement of truth.

(3.) He is our King. "Ye call me Master and Lord, and ye say well, for so I am." He has much to say as to the manner of our daily life. He utters a distinct injunction as to the sacramental table: "Take, eat; do this in remembrance of me" He lays upon us a command as to the great propaganda: "Go ye, into all the world and evangelize." If we accept Christ, we should recognize his authority and should not hesitate to obey him. "Ye are my disciples if ye do whatsoever I command you." "Whatsoever he saith unto you, do it."

II. *The symbol of Christian Orthodoxy is the Bible.* The symbols of denominational Orthodoxy are the standards of the various bodies of believers in Christ. There is, however, a larger fellowship of which we say, "I believe in the Holy Catholic Church." The symbol of this larger fellowship is the Bible and the Bible only.

(1.) If it be said that Christ is enough, we answer, The Scriptures are the only authoritative source of information respecting Christ. Christ without the Scriptures is a mere name and quite meaningless except for sentimental uses. You believe in Christ? What Christ? The Christ of history. Then there is a history of Christ? Yes; the Bible. Do you mean the New Testament? No; Old Testament and New Testament. The Scriptures are Christological from beginning to end. As it takes two hemispheres to make a world, so it requires the two Testaments to make one complete record of Christ. But why must I believe in the Scriptures? Is it not enough that Christ should be everything to me? No; Christ as the incarnate Word, and the Scriptures as the written Word, make together a complete revelation—the binomial Word of God. So then, your religion is the religion of a book? Yes; the religion of the only begotten Son of God as he is reliably described in a divine book.

It is like this: You go to the Water Commissioner and say, "I want water in my house immediately; we must have it or die." "Well, don't worry," he answers. "It is an easy matter to get water there. We'll have the pipes put in right away." "Pipes? Who said anything about pipes? It's water we want." "But, my friend, you've got to get the water through the pipes. It's pipes or no water." And you submit to it. So it is the Bible or no Christ, because the Bible is the medium through which he is revealed or conveyed to us.

(2.) Let it be observed that Christ himself accepted the Scriptures as accurately revealing himself and the plan of salvation which centres in him. He was thoroughly familiar with it. He quoted from Genesis, Exodus, Leviticus, Numbers, Deuteronomy, Samuel, Kings, Chronicles, Psalms, Proverbs, Songs of Solomon, Isaiah, Jeremiah, Ezekiel, Daniel and most of the Minor Prophets. He made corroborative reference to the stories of Adam and Eve, Abel, Noah, the Flood, Abraham, the Destruction of Sodom, Lot's wife, Jacob's ladder, the Burning Bush, the Manna, the Brazen Serpent, the Queen of Sheba, Jonah in the whale's belly and other portions of the truth which have been called in question during these last days.

It is a matter of grave significance, furthermore, that Jesus himself never said a word nor gave an intimation of any sort whatever, that any portion of the Scriptures was other than absolutely trustworthy. Either he did not know as much as some of our modern destructive critics with respect to the Bible, or else he intended to convey a wrong impression, or else he believed the Scriptures to be inerrant. The conclusion is irresistible. If we accept Christ we must also accept his view of the Scriptures as the Word of God.

(3.) He commended the Scriptures to us in terms which should be decisive! "Search the Scriptures, for in them ye think ye have eternal life and these are they which testify of me." Search for yourselves with liberty of personal interpretation. Search them with the help of all the attainable lights of sound scholarship. Search them as honest men.

III. *The administrator of Christian Orthodoxy is the Holy Ghost.* Let us be thankful that we are living in a time when the Holy Ghost is more honored than formerly as the Paraclete, or constant Helper in spiritual things.

(1.) He reveals the truth of the Scriptures. Spiritual things are spiritually discerned. I stand in the wheelhouse of an ocean steamer looking in a bewildered way on the Marine Reports which are written in cipher and hieroglyphics; but presently the captain, standing by and seeing my bewilderment, makes all plain. He holds the key. So in my unaided wisdom I look upon the Scriptures and they are as if written in an unknown tongue. If I will, however, the Holy Ghost anoints my eyes and throws a light upon the pages of Scriptures, so that I see in them the treasures of truth; lo, they are full of the knowledge of God.

(2.) He takes of the things of Jesus and shows them unto us. Here I stand beside the manger, crying, "Great is the mystery of Godliness, God manifest in the flesh." He makes the incarnation clear to me. When I stand at Calvary, philosophizing as many excellent men have done with reference to the atonement, he makes it as simple as is a mother's love to the infant on her breast, saying simply, "God so loved the world." When I stand at the open grave in Joseph's garden querying, "Does death end all?" he points away to the open heavens—the living Christ and the Father's house with many mansions.

(3.) He leads us into all truth. "It is expedient that I go away," said Jesus, "for if I go not away the Paraclete will not come ; and when he is come he will lead you into all truth." If we have fallen into heresy of any sort whatever, it is simply and solely because we have not been willing that the Holy Ghost should guide us. There is a desperate and intolerable pride of human wisdom which is defiantly opposed to the work of the Holy Ghost. The promise is, "If any of you lack wisdom, let him ask of God who giveth to all men liberally and upbraideth not; and it shall be given him."

It is my hope that as the result of this meditation, we shall think a little more kindly of Orthodoxy. Of late it has been the fashion to deride it. The new school of thinkers have smeared its face with phosphorus, crowned it with cap and bells, and put it in the stocks to be gazed at. But, moved by the love of truth, devotion to principle, and fealty to God, let us uncover and do obeisance as we pass by.

We are grieved just now for the sorrows of the Armenians. Their homes have been burned, their villages destroyed, their liberties taken away, their wives and daughters dishonored, and a hundred thousand of them have been butchered in cold blood. And why? Is it not all unnecessary? Did not the Sultan long ago make them a most reasonable proposition? "You shall be treated with all due consideration, if only you will utter the formula, 'God is God and Mohammed is his Prophet.' Nay, if you will only lift your finger in token of assent to it." But, blessed be God, they would not! There is a spirit in man. They would not accept life on such contemptible terms. They preferred to die rather than surrender their convictions of truth. That is Orthodoxy. And in the long run, when right and expediency shall have ended their strife and the light of eternity shall shine upon nations and individual lives, it will be found that Orthodoxy was worth dying for. *Sto pro veritate.* Have your convictions. Is there a sense of duty and assurance of truth deep at the centre of your soul? Then by your hope of eternal blessedness stand for it!

"HE IS APPREHENDED IN THE GARDEN."

Judas then, having received a band of men and officers from the chief priests and Pharisees, cometh thither with lanterns and torches and weapons."
—JNO. xviii. 3.

On a moonlight night in a garden just outside the walls of Jerusalem was gathered the most historic group that ever came together on earth. If the Czar of Russia, Queen Victoria, the Mikado, the Emperor of China, the War Lord of Germany and the President of the United States were all to meet in conference they would not form such an historic assemblage as this. The central figure in this group is Jesus of Nazareth, claiming to be Emmanuel,—that is, God with us. He bears no outward mark to distinguish him from other men, and yet all the great problems of subsequent centuries were destined to revolve about him. He has just come from a stupendous struggle under the shadow of the olive trees, where the purple cup of death was pressed to his lips; the marks of that conflict are still upon him. Near by are John and James, the Sons of Thunder; Peter, the Man of Rock; and the other disciples, with a single exception. One is missing; where is he?

On the same memorable night the door of the high priest's palace in Jerusalem was flung open and a strange company issued from it. In front was Judas, the missing one of the twelve; then came scribes, members of the Sanhedrin, soldiers and others. They were armed with swords and staves and carried lanterns; for, though it was the time of the paschal moon, they were going to the heights beyond the Kedron to search for a malefactor, and there were many lurking places there. As this company passed along the streets, they were joined by many of the people; they passed out at the north gate, down into the dark valley of the Kedron, up the slope of Olivet, with the moon shining on their faces, until they reached the garden. Here let us pause and observe them; for they constitute a typical company of the enemies of Christ. We have their counterpart in these days.

I. *Judas, the man of Kerioth.* He has no friends. There are indeed those who would mitigate his guilt by representing that he simply wished, in the betrayal of Christ, to precipitate the setting up of his earthly throne; but there is nothing in this. He was a wilful, deliberate betrayer of his Lord; a rebel against the truth and righteousness of the kingdom of God. In brief, he was a hypocrite. The word means, "under a mask." A hypocrite is not one who unwittingly deceives himself and others, but one who, like Judas, steals the livery of heaven to serve the devil in. The punishment is measured by the guilt. Dante leads us down through his series of hells until he comes to the deepest, darkest place of torture, the sea of ice, where he shows us Judas transfixed in unimaginable pain. We may not penetrate the mysteries of the unseen world as boldly as the poet does; but we recall the significant words of Jesus, "It were better for that man had he never been born." For the better understanding of that word, let us see Judas in the hall Gazith bargaining, under the malignant inspiration of envy and covetousness, to deliver his Lord for thirty pieces of silver. Let us see him a little later when his treason had been consummated, returning to the temple, his face distorted with a tragic remorse, flinging down at the feet of the rabbis those blood-stained pieces of silver, with the cry, "I have betrayed innocent blood!" Let us then go out to the cliff above the Valley of Hinnom and see his body swinging from yonder tree in the night wind. So shall we, perhaps, gain a measurable apprehension of the significance of that sentence, "It were better for him had he never been born."

And the lesson is sincerity. Let us be true to our convictions. "To counterfeit is death." Let us be what we seem to be. Lord Bacon says, "An ill man is always ill, but he is worst who pretends to be a saint." The original meaning of the word sincere is said to be, "tried by the sun." Honesty is transparency. Let us see that all our graces are translucent, inasmuch as presently we must stand in our true characters in the light of the countenance of God.

II. Close after Judas follow *the Rabbis*. And what an opportunity was theirs! They were the religious teachers who, having special charge of the oracles, should have been familiar with messianic prophecy. They were the leaders of the people, the makers of public sentiment. At this juncture it would appear, had they been so disposed, they might have swung all Jewry into line with the redemptive purposes of God. But, alas! two things were in the way:

(1) Pride; the pride of intellect. They had made such acquisitions in rabbinical lore that they were unwilling to be taught by any man, and least of all by this Nazarene carpenter! They saw him standing in Solomon's Porch with the people gathered about him, touching with an unparalleled boldness the great spiritual problems which had defied all the wisdom of the schools. "Is not this the son of Joseph?" they asked. "And whence hath this man letters?" "Shall he teach us?"

> "A little learning is a dangerous thing;
> Drink deep or taste not the Pierian spring."

But, unfortunately for us, we cannot drink deep; we can only at the best wet our lips at the Pierian springs. Pride ill becomes the wisest among us. "He who knows his own ignorance," said Socrates, "is on the way to knowing more." And when we stop to reflect, how preposterous is our assumption of wisdom in the presence of the omniscient One. The light of our intellect is as the infinitesimal spark in the eye of a snail to the glory of the noonday sun that shrivels it.

(2) Prejudice. They had their own opinions of Messiah. He must come wearing a crown, and show himself, by outward pomp and circumstance, worthy to restore the glory to Israel. A thoughtful reference to their oracles would have corrected this misconception, but unfortunately "a man convinced against his will is of the same opinion still." Prejudice is like a jaundiced eye; all things look yellow to it; the sea, the verdant fields, the overarching sky, all yellow, because the eye itself is so. God save us from pride and prejudice. If we would make a voyage, we must begin by hoisting the anchor. If we would attain to

truth, we must cut loose from all ill-formed prejudgments, hold ourselves open to convictions, and be willing to see. The same Jesus who taught in Solomon's Porch is still teaching among us. He who rightly apprehends the value of wisdom and sincerely desires to acquire it, will lend a listening ear despite the confusing clamor from within and without, saying, "If this be truth, I will receive it."

III. Then *the Soldiers*. There is something to be said for them; for they were under orders and accustomed to obey. Had any of them desired to befriend Christ, he would have found circumstances greatly against him. But what of that? Are not circumstances against us all?

(1) Are we not all under the constraint of heredity? The blood of long generations of sinners is in our veins; but this furnishes no excuse for ill-doing. Nero was the son of a father who drove over a beggar in Appia Via, struck out a soldier's eye in a quarrel in the forum, and killed a freedman for failing to drink enough to please him. Thus the heir-apparent to the Roman throne inherited the disposition of a tiger; was he then to blame for it? Aye; greatly to blame for giving way to it. We are all alike under the curse of such inheritance. One man has intemperance running hot in his blood, another licentiousness, another avarice; and others still inherit the less conspicuous, but not less heinous, vices. A large part of the serious business of our life is to fight against our ancestors. The man who excuses himself for giving way to an evil disposition on the ground of heredity is a coward. It was bad enough for Adam to throw the blame of his transgression on his wife; it is incomparably worse and meaner for one

to blame his forbears. The thing to do is to make a brave struggle and triumph over an evil heredity. And, blessed be God, this is possible, has been proven to be possible ten thousand times ten thousand times. Here is the key to Samson's riddle: "Out of the eater is come forth meat, and out of the strong is come forth sweetness."

(2) Environment. No man finds it easy to live a righteous life or build up a noble character. There are difficulties all about him and obstacles ever in the way. But the mark of true greatness is to overcome them and rise above them. One of the best men I have ever known, was born in the slums of New York of parents who were no better than they ought to be. His home was next door to a distillery; and he has told me that when he was a lad of eight years, it was no uncommon thing for him to lie down under the mash tubs where he could catch the intoxicating drippings, and be carried home by his mother at evening sodden with drink. But there came a time in his early manhood when he determined that neither heredity nor environment should get the better of him; but that, by the grace of God, he would prove himself a man. To-day he is one of the most successful ministers of Christ.

(3) Habit. As if it were not enough that our ancestors and companions should be against us, we bind ourselves with fetters and manacles; and true manliness becomes more and more difficult as the years pass on. But the comforting thought is that God stands ready with his sovereign and omnipotent relief, and there is no living man who cannot, thus reinforced, break these bands of habit as Samson broke the green withes wherewith they bound him.

No man can excuse himself for sin, by saying, "I cannot help it." By God's grace he can help it.

> "———Toil on;
> In hope o'ercome the steeps God set for thee,
> For past the Alpine summits of great toil lieth thine Italy."

No doubt the soldiers who went out against Jesus on that memorable night would have found it difficult to resist the current of opposition to Christ; but that it was not impossible is proven by the fact that one, who was probably one of their number—the centurion to whom was assigned the task of superintending the crucifixion of Jesus—was himself convicted and convinced and moved to say, "Verily, this was the Son of God."

IV. Then came *the People*; a rabble made up from the multitude who are gathered from all directions to attend the feast. There were traders, shepherds, vine dressers, camel-drivers, artisans, all sorts and conditions of men. They correspond to the lapsed masses of our time—the unchurched multitudes, who fall in impulsively with every popular movement, except that which impels toward acceptance of divine grace in the gospel of Christ. Where is the trouble?

(1) They do not think. They do not stop to consider seriously the great problems and the verities which center in Christ. The common sin of every age is heedlessness. "For want of a nail, the shoe was lost; for want of a shoe, the horse was lost; for want of a horse, the rider was lost; for want of a rider, the kingdom was lost.' The average man is so busy with the common cares of life—the bread-and-butter work, the gaining of a livelihood, the winning

of a competence—that the greater matters of truth and righteousness are little or nothing to him.

(2) They run with the multitude, doing as others do. When Napoleon returned from his Austrian campaign, he was received with bonfires and huzzas. One of his marshals remarking upon the devotion of the people to his cause, he replied "Yes; but they would follow me just as eagerly to prison and the guillotine." And the sequel proved it. So is it ever. Those who to-day receive the Christ at the city gates with shouts of "Hosanna! Hosanna to the Son of David!" will to-morrow fall in with the rabble who cry, "Crucify him! crucify him!"

Let us have the courage, good friends, to stand by ourselves while the multitude surges by. Let us do our own thinking. Let us read our Bibles for ourselves with the light which the Holy Spirit gives us. Let us gaze with our own eyes at the cross, until the eye affecteth the heart and we believe in him. It is written that when Jesus was dying on the cross, "The people stood beholding." The coldness of that word makes us shiver. They stood beholding with dull eyes, while the heart of the Saviour yonder on the cross was breaking under the burden of their sins. O, if they had known! And they would have known, had they stopped to reflect, had they been willing to reason for themselves. Yet, our condemnation under like conditions is greater than theirs. "O foolish Galatians, who hath bewitched you, that ye should not obey the truth, before whose eyes Jesus Christ hath been evidently set forth, crucified among you?"

But while we have been taking counsel together, the band has entered the garden. They are peering, lantern in hand, here and there into the dense shadows.

Lo, yonder he stands; pale, worn, with a forecast of the last agony upon him. The torchlight falls weirdly on his face. "Whom seek ye?" "Jesus of Nazareth" "I am he." They lead him away to judgment and thence to the cross.

The three hours of vicarious pain are over; the Galilean is dead!

Time passes; and by the banks of the Tigris, worsted in a vain struggle against the increasing power of the gospel and wounded unto death, Julian the Apostate clutches the earth and cries, "Galilean, thou hast conquered!"

Time passes; and Constantine marching back from Saxa-Rubra, where he won his famous victory against the old herdsman emperor, plants the red cross banner of Jesus in the Forum at Rome.

Time passes; and under the oaks of Britain, beside the cromlechs, the missionary Augustine preaches the gospel to the Druid worshippers.

Time passes; and Columbus plants the red cross banner on the shores of the new world, christening it *San Salvador*, "Land of the Saviour."

Time passes; and missionaries are going everywhere, their feet beautiful upon the mountains, to carry into the regions of darkness and the habitations of death the unsearchable riches of the gospel of Christ.

Time passes; and the world grows brighter and brighter, and the day approaches when the clouds above shall part asunder, and he whose right it is to reign, shall come to be king over all and blessed forever. In that day his faithful friends shall rejoice at his appearing, and they that pierced him shall behold him. Let us be getting ready, friends, for the coronation.

> "All hail the power of Jesus' name!
>   Let angels prostrate fall;
> Bring forth the royal diadem,
>   And crown Him Lord of all.
>
> Sinners, whose love can ne'er forget
>   The wormwood and the gall,
> Go, spread your trophies at His feet,
>   And crown Him Lord of all.
>
> O that with yonder sacred throng,
>   We at His feet may fall;
> We'll join the everlasting song,
>   And crown Him Lord of all."

HOW DAVID THOUGHT OF THE FORGIVENESS OF SIN.

"Blessed is he whose transgression is forgiven, whose sin is covered." —Ps. xxxii. 1. "Even as David also describeth the blessedness of the man unto whom God imputeth righteousness without works, saying, Blessed are they whose iniquities are forgiven, and whose sins are covered."— ROMANS iv. 6, 7.

We have a peculiar expression here, known as the "plural of emphasis." In like manner when the Hebrews wished to name the greatest of monsters they said, *Behemoth*, a plural word meaning "beasts." So the words of the Psalmist would be more accurately rendered, "O the blessednesses of the man whose transgression is forgiven." The singular number would not express it. Joy upon joy! Numberless pleasures! O the felicities of the pardoned soul!

The Apostle Paul attributes this saying to David. Some of the higher critics insist that David had nothing to do with it. But we old-fashioned folk must be permitted to believe that Paul was probably as familiar with correct Biblical exegesis as those who take issue with him. And particularly since the higher critics have nothing to proceed upon except what they call "internal evidence"—that is, David could not have written this Psalm because it does not sound like him. Aye, but it does. The internal evidence is what convinces us of the Davidic authorship of this saying. The ring of David's voice is in it; the twang of David's harp-string is in it. He knew sin and he knew the burden of sin. It may be that when he wrote this rhapsody he had in mind the matter of Uriah and Bathsheba. It rested as an intolerable burden on his soul; it stained his hands blood red; it ploughed furrows of remorse across his brow. He could not sleep; the furies sat about him in the watches of the night, pointing their fingers and whispering, "Uriah!" "Bathsheba!" What should he do? What could he do but cry unto the Lord in his trouble, "Have mercy upon me according to thy loving kindness, and according unto the multitude of thy tender mercies blot out my transgressions; for against thee, thee only, have I sinned, and done this evil in thy sight?" Did God hear? God always hears. There is nothing in the universe so sweet to him as the cry of a returning prodigal. So David sings, "This poor man cried, and the Lord heard and saved him out of all his trouble. O that men would praise the Lord for his goodness and for his wonderful works to the children of men."

And it was meet and proper that Paul should echo this; for his was a similar experience. His sin was ever before him. He could not forget how he had held the garments of those who stoned Stephen;—that upturned, pleading face, that last prayer, "Lay not this sin to their charge." He could not forget the deeds of blood committed, when, as a zealot of the Sanhedrin, he went hither and yon breathing out slaughter against God's little ones; when in pursuit of his inquisition he rode down the Damascus highway and saw in a sudden flash of light the face so marred, yet divinely beautiful, and heard the voice, "I am Jesus whom thou persecutest." It is anguish to remember this, and anguish to know that the "motions of sin" are still in his members. "O wretched man," he cries, "who shall deliver me from the body of this death?" And then he continues, "Thanks be to God through our Lord Jesus Christ!" His regret for the past is swallowed up in his blissful experience of God's pardoning grace: "Who shall separate me from the love of Christ? I am persuaded that neither death, nor life, nor angels, nor principalities, nor powers, nor things present, nor things to come, nor height, nor depth, nor any other creature shall be able to separate me from the love of God which is in Christ Jesus my Lord."

"I believe in the forgiveness of sins;" so the Church professes in her historic creed. So sing the innumerable multitude of the redeemed in heaven, "I believe in the forgiveness of sins."

> "O! may the sweet, the blissful theme
> Fill every heart and tongue,
> Till strangers love Thy charming name,
> And join the sacred song!"

It is a vast subject; too great for a single discourse. It will answer our purpose merely to inquire what David thought about it. He uses four significant expressions for the forgiveness of sin.

I. He speaks of it as "*covering*." "Blessed is the man whose sin is covered." This expression is the equivalent of erased or blotted out. So Peter said to the multitude in Solomon's Porch, "Repent and be converted, that your sins may be blotted out, when the times of refreshing shall come from the presence of the Lord."

In those days the writing was frequently done on wax tablets; it was an easy matter, therefore, to erase it. The accounts were kept in that way. If a man came in to square his account, the stylus was simply drawn over the tablet and the score vanished; it was covered, and thus erased or blotted out.

In the interest of justice a strict account is kept of every man. We read of a memorial book in which our sins are all written down. We may forget them; indeed we do forget them nearly all. But the ledger will be opened on the judgment day; sins innumerable that had passed from remembrance will be exposed to view; destiny will be determined by that record. If no payment has been made in our behalf, then the uttermost farthing will be required of us. If we are forgiven, it will be only because our indebtedness has been paid by our Lord Jesus Christ. He holds the stylus in his pierced hand, awaiting our word of prayer that he may erase it. If faith speaks the word, lo, it is done!

> "Jesus paid it all,
> All to Him I owe."

II. David also speaks of the forgiveness of sin as a *cleansing*. "Purge me with hyssop, and I shall be clean; wash me, and I shall be whiter than snow." The response to this prayer is in the assurance of the gospel: "The blood of Jesus Christ, the Son of God, cleanseth us from all sin."

The finer instincts of our nature grasp the fact that sin is uncleanness. One of the Greek philosophers expressed the wish that, in the interest of sincerity, a window might be placed in the breast of every man. But there are few, if any, of us who would be willing to have it so. One of the best of modern Christians has said, "If the secret imaginations of my heart were known, I should be ashamed to pass along the street, lest the children should make sport of me and the very dogs bark at me." At times this repugnant aspect of sin forces itself upon us ; but we are loath to dwell upon it.

One of the significant types of sin is leprosy, not because of the incurableness of that malady, but rather of its uncleanness. There are other mortal diseases, but there is none that so utterly excludes the patient from all fellowship of men. Let a leper be found in the Chinese quarter of New York City to-day, and he is hurried away to a lone island in the harbor, to dwell there in a secluded hut where none shall approach him. It is written of Naaman the Syrian, " He was a great man with his master, and honorable ; he was also a mighty man of valor, but he was a leper." What mattered it if his was the arrow that smote through the joints of Ahab's armor, or tha the had often-times distinguished himself on the high places of the field ? He would fain have traded places with the meanest of the cringing slaves in his kitchen, if only those white spots might be taken from him. The Jew who was infected with this disease must needs go apart from his fellows, and stand afar off, with his finger upon his lips, crying, " Unclean ! unclean !" This is the significant type by which the inspired writers are wont to characterize the repulsiveness of sin. But a fountain has been opened for uncleanness, in the blood of Jesus Christ : " Come now, saith the Lord, and let us reason together ; though your sins be as scarlet, they shall be as white as snow ; though they be red like crimson, they shall be as wool."

III. Again the Psalmist speaks of forgiveness as a *removing*. "He hath not dealt with us after our sins, nor rewarded us according to our iniquities; for as the heaven is high above the earth, so great is his mercy toward them that fear him; as far as the east is from the west, so far hath he removed our transgressions from us." In like manner Hosea says, "O Israel, return unto the Lord your God, and say, Take away our iniquity and receive us graciously; so will we render the calves of our lips."

Sin is here conceived of as a burden. So Cain, fleeing from his brother's blood, cried out, "My punishment is greater than I can bear." But God in the gospel of Christ has made known his willingness to lift the burden and carry it away. The Christian in the "Pilgrim's Progress" went through great difficulty "because of the load upon his back," until he came to the cross; and at the foot of the cross was the sepulchre; and when he came there, his burden was loosed from off his shoulder and "began to tumble and so continued to do until it came to the mouth of the sepulchre, where it fell in and he saw it no more. Then was he glad and blithesome, and said with a merry heart, 'He hath given me rest by his sorrow and life by his death.'"

On Yom Kippur, the great Day of Atonement, the scapegoat was brought to the door of the tabernacle and the high priest laid his hands upon its head, so signifying that the sins of the people were laid there; then the scapegoat was led by the hand of a fit man out into the land of Azazel. The people stood, shading their eyes, and saw the fit man lead the goat over the hills and far away. It was gone, and their sins were gone with it! So is the sinner's burden laid upon the heart of Christ at Calvary, and Christ's heart breaks under it.

> " My faith would lay her hand
> On that dear head of Thine,
> While like a penitent I stand
> And there confess my sin."

How far is our sin removed by this loving kindness of our Lord? Mark the great distance: "As far as the east is from the west, so far hath he removed our transgressions from us." We may measure the distance from north to south, but not from east to west. The sailor who sets out with his prow pointed westward may sail on and on and round and round forever. So our sins are removed infinitely from us.

IV. But the most significant figure which David uses to designate the forgiveness of sin is *"forgetting."* His prayer is, "O Lord, remember not the sins of my youth;" and again, "O Lord, remember not against us our former iniquities; let thy tender mercies prevent us." And God's answer is in these words, "I will be merciful unto thee, and thine iniquities will I remember no more against thee." An "Act of Oblivion" is passed upon our sins. They shall never more be recalled or cast up against us.

In Hebrew and Arabic "to forget" is expressed by the phrase "to cast behind one's back." Thus if an oriental ruler desires to rid himself of his Prime Minister, he "casts him behind his back;" that is, out of his sight. He thinks no more of him. This is precisely what God, in his infinite mercy, does with our sins. Up to the moment of forgiveness they are before his face, as it is written: "He hath set our secret sins in the light of his countenance"—the light beyond the brightest glory of the sun. But when he forgives, he puts our iniquities behind his back and so stands between us and them forever.

We find an expression of like emphasis in the words of Micah, "Thou wilt turn again and have compassion; thou wilt cast the sins of the people into the depths of the sea." Was the prophet thinking of a stone that goes down, down into the depths forever? Or shall we find the similitude in a burial at sea, where the shotted, shrouded burden slips from the plank and with a momentary splash disappears from view? Nay, not so; for there shall be a resurrection, the sea shall give up its dead; but the sin that is forgiven shall be seen no more forever.

In 1862 the British ship Enrica was fitted out as a Confederate cruiser, to be commanded by Captain Raphael Semmes. Her crew and armament were British; and she carried a British flag to use when occasion required it. In the course of the next two years she destroyed sixty-six American vessels and millions upon millions of property. The "Alabama Claims" have been settled in just arbitration; but the merchant marine of America has never recovered from the blow. The Alabama never entered a southern port, but cruised to and fro, capturing and burning everywhere. At length, early in the summer of 1864, she put into the harbor of Cherbourg, France, for repairs. The Kearsarge, commanded by Captain Winslow, which had long been pursuing her, anchored at the entrance of the harbor. A meeting was inevitable. On the 19th day of June they joined battle seven miles out. They were at close quarters for an hour, firing shot and shell into each other; then the Alabama began to settle; she quivered like a living thing and went down, down, fathoms down, among the coral and sea-weed and slimy crawling things on the bottom of the sea. There she has lain ever since; there she will lie until the end of time; her iron rusting, her timbers rotting, the fishes swimming through her port holes. There is no resurrection for her. So God sends our sins down, down, to the bottom of the sea, never to be seen again, never to be heard of, never to be remembered.

The ancients speak of a river called Lethe, flowing through hell. The dead drank of it and forgot the past. It is not we, however, who drink of Lethe. We shall remember our sins, but only to praise the God who has forgiven them. We shall look upon the pit out of which we are delivered, and call upon our souls and all that is within us to bless his holy name. Nay, it is God who drinks of Lethe; he forgets, he remembers our sins no more against us.

Let it be observed that the forgiveness here vouchsafed to us is only for Jesus' sake. There is no word in Scripture to encourage hope otherwise. "There is none other name under heaven given among men whereby we must be saved." The atonement of the cross furnishes the only theory of pardon which ever has been suggested. The false religions are utterly devoid of any hint of the forgiveness of sin. This is the glory of our religion. The world believes in Karma, the doctrine of retribution. "Whatsoever a man soweth, that shall he also reap." It makes one shiver to think of this philosophy of irrevocable death. It was fifty years ago, or thereabouts, when Professor Webster, of Harvard University, was tried for murder. The man who sat in judgment on that occasion was Chief Justice Shaw, who had been the college friend of the prisoner at the bar. When the jury returned with its verdict of "Guilty," the judge was so overcome that tears poured over his cheeks and he could not speak. At length he arose to pronounce the death sentence, saying, "The law must have its course." Thanks be to God, the law need not have its course at the Great Assize, "for what the law could not do in that it was weak through the flesh" —our sinful flesh—"God, sending his own Son in the likeness of sinful flesh, hath done for us." We believe that through Jesus Christ there is forgiveness with God.

But only through faith in him. Faith is the hand stretched out to appropriate the unspeakable gift. We shall probably agree that the strangling swimmer who deliberately refuses to grasp the rope thrown to him deserves to drown; that the Jew who would not eat of the manna that lay around his feet, plenteous and white as hoar frost, deserved to starve; that the man who will not dip up the water of the fountain and drink, deserves to perish of thirst. The great salvation is offered to us on the sole condition of faith; "He that believeth on the Lord Jesus Christ shall be saved, and he that believeth not shall be damned;" that is, he who takes Christ to be the propitiation of his sin shall live through him, but he who prefers to his own sins forever shall have his way. Who then, shall complain? And how shall we escape if we neglect so great salvation? Let us accept Christ, therefore, and be grateful. Only believe! Only believe! And let our lives show that we believe in Christ, and that in him we have received the forgiveness of sin.

THE GOLDEN WEDGE.

"Therefore, the children of Israel could not stand, but turned their backs before their enemies."— JOSH. vii. 12.

The siege of Jericho was a singular performance. In all the history of military tactics there was nothing like it. It was never known that a city should be reduced by the simple tramp, tramping of a multitude, in profound silence, and then a final blast of rams' horns. It was manifestly the Lord's doing, and marvellous in all the people's eyes. And, inasmuch as God had planned the siege, and reduced the city without any man's aid, it was obviously his right to affix any conditions whatsoever to the triumph that might please him. He said, accordingly, "There must be no looting, no plunder now." He was not going to have the army of Israel develop into a mere mob of marauders. That would do for pagan nations, but not for the people of God. He said that the city itself should be devoted to destruction; it must be utterly burned up, and the gold and the silver must be consecrated to the house of God; but there should be no plunder. And so they went into Jericho.

Out in his tent on the hillside that night, in full sight of the smoke that still rose from the burning city, was a soldier who had in his possession a Babylonish garment, a purse that contained two hundred shekels of silver, and a golden wedge. He was all alone; and he digged a hole in the ground, and kneeled down and, folding up that precious Babylonish garment, and looking around him to see if any one was watching him, he put it there. And he opened the purse, and counted out the two hundred shekels of silver, and replaced them, and placed it also there. And the wedge of gold—how his eyes sparkled as he laid it with the silver, and buried it! And he looked about him, and said, "None seeth me." But the eyes that "run to and fro through all the earth, beholding the evil and the good," were all the while looking down upon him.

The next morning it was proposed to take yonder fortress that lay three thousand feet higher up the mountain road that led into the Holy Land. A squad of soldiers was sent up to reconnoitre, and they came back and said, "We need not send the army up there; it will be enough to send two or three regiments. It is only a small garrison; we can easily overcome it." So in the camp they watched the men going up, and heard in the distance the sound of conflict; but soon they saw their warriors come flying down like a flock of sheep, for their hearts had melted like water within them. Joshua, the man of battle, stood by, wondering; he called the roll, and asked, "Were ye overcome? Did some great disaster fall upon you?" But they were all there except thirty-six. They had not been overwhelmed by numbers, or by superior strength. What was it, then, that struck them with that sudden panic, and sent them fleeing down the hillside? Joshua, overwhelmed with shame, fell down upon his face, and cried out, "Alas, that Israel should have done this! That an army of Israel should ever have failed to take the little fortress of Ai! What will the Canaanites say of it? And what shall be said for the name of the Lord, our God?" Then a voice said to him, "Rise up! Stand upon thy feet! Why liest thou here, mourning and lamenting? There is a golden wedge in the camp. One of thy soldiers hath taken of the devoted, the unclean thing. Find it; punish him; for, therefore, Israel hath not been able to stand before the enemy, but hath turned his back upon him." And it was proclaimed throughout the camp that there was a malefactor who had taken plunder, and that he was to be found out.

That was a terrible night for Achan. He lay in his tent, with the Babylonish garment, and the golden wedge, and the purse of shekels buried beneath him, and tossed, sleepless, like guilty Macbeth. O, if he would only arise now, and get down upon his knees, and make a clean breast of the whole matter before God! O, if he would only leave his tent, and fall before Joshua, and confess all! "But," he said to himself, "may be these are unfounded qualms of mind. I shall never be found out."

The next morning the lot was taken, and the black stone fell to the tribe of Judah; and the rabbis say that every man in Judah then drew his sword, and vowed that the malefactor should die. The ballot was cast again, and the black stone fell to the clan of the Zerahites; again, and the black stone fell to the family of Zabdi; again, and Achan trembled to the centre of his heart—for the black stone was in his hand! What shall be done to the man who by his sin has endangered all Israel, and put God's people to an open shame? It was at the very beginning of the theocracy, and an exemplary punishment must be inflicted upon him. He was taken out and stoned to death, and his tent was burned. Then went the army of Israel forward, and Ai fell, and the people went in to possess the land.

I preached here a little while ago on the secret of success. But success is a very extraordinary thing. I doubt if there is a man or woman here who feels that he or she has achieved it. I want to say something to you now about the secret of failure; and that will touch every one of us.

As to the Church, I know how gloriously the blessing of Heaven has rested upon the Church all along the ages. The eleven men that came down the outer stairway from that upper room have come to be four hundred millions of people, scattered all over the world, in more or less close connection with the Church of God. It is a wonderful history—the history of the universal Church of Christ. It is a wonderful success—when we look at it from this standpoint of our lower life. But O! it is the colossal failure of all the history of the universe, when we look at it from the standpoint of the ideal, and the possible, and the divinely-intended. "Go ye," said the Master, to the people who were assembled upon the Mount of Ascension,—" Go ye into all the world, and preach the Gospel to every creature ; and, lo! I am with you alway, even unto the end of the world." If they had only heeded ! There was a command— "Go ye ! " There was a promise—" Lo ! I am with you." Omniscience marked out the campaign. Omnipotence was pledged to the ultimate triumph. Yet here we are, after the lapse of eighteen weary centuries, still watching the heavens, and wondering when the Lord will come. "O Lord, how long? how long?"

What is the trouble? Sin in the camp. The Church of God is not what it ought to be. But for the sin of the Church, the conquest of the world would have been accomplished long centuries ago. If you want to transmit an electric current and produce a tremendous power by it, you must be very careful that the wires along which the power passes shall be thoroughly insulated. There must be no loss of power by contact with foreign things. I can place you on an insulated stool, and turn a current of electricity upon you; and if you will not touch anything, but hold yourself aloof from everything that could possibly conduct the power away from you, I will fill you so full of electricity that it will go sparkling in electric flashes from your finger tips. There will be convulsions of power and earthquakes of energy within you. O! if the Church had only stood there—"Come out from the world, and be ye separate, saith the Lord: for I have chosen you to be an holy priesthood, a peculiar people. Put away the unclean thing from among you." That is the injunction which God is ever addressing to his militant Church. If you want to reduce Buddhism; if you want to conquer Islam; if you want to destroy Confucianism; if you want to save the nations who are worshipping Fetish idols in the darkness of death, put away the unclean thing from you. "Loose thyself from thy bands; shake thyself from the dust, O captive daughter of Jerusalem." Let God energize thee. Then shalt thou be God's people, and God himself shall be thy God.

But now as to the individual Christian—for it is not a matter of great consequence to speak of the

Church in the abstract, or en masse. The Church is what we individual Christians make it. From one standpoint, it is a wonder that you are as good a Christian man as you are. That is to be said to your credit. "For we wrestle not against flesh and blood, but against principalities and powers, against spiritual wickedness in high places." We are constantly opposed by the world, and the flesh, and the devil; and it is a wonder to me that we Christian people are half as good as we are reputed to be. What was it that Baxter said? "I am not what I ought to be; I am not what I hope to be; I am not what I mean to be; but by the grace of God I am what I am!"

So you have made a success of it, if you look at the Christian life from the lower levels; but if you occupy the standpoint of the ideal and the possible, O, what a colossal failure you and I have made of it! "Ye are the light of the world. A city that is set on a hill cannot be hid. Let your light so shine before men that they may see your good works, and glorify God." How is it that you have been thwarted in your best resolutions? How is it that you have risen in the morning, and made your prayer of consecration, and gone out to meet the world, and come back defeated, as the soldiers of Israel came back along that mountain road from Ai? And then you have kneeled down to say, as David did—"Have mercy upon me, O God, according to thy loving kindness, and according to the multitude of thy tender mercies blot out my transgressions; for I have sinned." How is it that when you have made your best resolutions you have, after all, come to say with Paul: "I find a law in my members, so that the good that I would, I do not; and the evil that I would not, that I do; who shall deliver me from the body of this death?" There it is—the corpse tied to the swimmer's neck, and he strangling and struggling for his life. But who shall deliver me from this sin, this very body of death?

That is the trouble with us—the old, the darling sin, the long-cherished habit, that is continually getting the better of us. It seems a little matter. In one of the fairy tales that we used to read when we were children, there was a princess immured in a dungeon, who after a while found a secret passage, and crept along in the dark until she came within sight of an open door, and made her way toward it. But here was a spider's thread. She paused, and drew it aside, and there was another; and she paused, and drew that aside, and there was another; and presently she was in the meshes of a million spiders' threads. And she sat down and wept, and gave up the struggle. That is the story of many a Christian life. The little sin, year after year, loved and cherished—the darling sin—enmeshes and destroys us.

But here is a word also for those who never have professed to be the followers of Christ. I give the average man who does not love the Lord Jesus Christ credit for many excellent hopes and purposes and earnest resolutions. We cannot get rid of the fact that we were made in the likeness of God. You may not have prayed this morning. It is probable that there is a man in this congregation who did not have the grace, after sleeping in God's arms all night, and being cared for by his providence, to get down before him this morning and say, "I thank you." But no matter how far you have wandered from God, you know that you were born of God; you feel stirring within you the impulses of your better nature. I believe in total depravity, but not in any such sense as that the man who is depraved has nothing that is naturally good in him. You may be a kind husband, an intelligent father, a good neighbor, and a loyal citizen; you may be a good man, as men go, and looked at from the earthly standpoint; but if you look at yourself from the standpoint of the ideal and the possible, your life has been a lamentable failure, and you have met with a stupendous defeat. You are not what you ought to be.

A man came to me recently, and said, "I am in a little trouble, and I want to talk with you. Now, don't tell me to repent, and think I come to you as a sinner, because I am not a sinner;" and I opened my eyes, for that is a very extraordinary thing—"I am not a sinner, and I don't need to repent; but I am just dead weary of a life of mere self-gratification. I have got enough of this world's goods; I have a surplus of energy, and I am doing nothing for anybody, and I am just weary of living this way." Defeated, thwarted, tired out! Why is it? What is the matter? Sin! Sin! Paralyzing, debilitating, unnerving, unmanning sin! If you don't get rid of it, my brother, it will be the death of you. Sin kills. It ruins us while we are going on toward eternity. It meets us at every step. It lays upon our hearts a burden beyond what we are able to bear, and ultimately consigns us to spiritual and eternal death— or else there is not a word of truth in that old-fashioned Book of ours.

You may have seen the instrument of torture in the castle of Nuremberg, that is called "The Virgin." Her arms were open, and the victim of the Inquisition was commanded to embrace her. As he obeyed, a knife pierced his eye, a knife pierced his temple, a knife pierced his breast, knives pierced him everywhere. That was quick death. It is not always so sudden, but sin is sure death.

What is needed? Up! Consecrate yourselves! Get rid of sin, as you love life! Get rid of the old sin that has been accumulating upon you in the mislived past! How will you get rid of it? You cannot wash your hands, like Pilate, in a basin of water and get rid of it. The laver stood before the altar. The cross of Jesus Christ is both laver and altar. A fountain gushes out from the rock beneath the cross —"a fountain opened for all uncleanness." Come, my friend; you have failed everywhere else. You know your infirmity. You know you will be thwarted and defeated if you keep on this way. Come, and kneel down here at Calvary. "Come, now, saith the Lord; let us reason together. Though your sins are as scarlet, they shall be white as snow; though they be red like crimson, they shall be as wool." "The blood of Jesus Christ, the only begotten Son of God, cleanseth us from all sin." It is the old message; but, my brother, it is the message of life to you.

And having done that, what then? Christians all, now, let us see to it that we cherish no sin henceforth and forever; that we bury no golden wedges in our tent. When Madagascar became a Christian island, and the Hovas surrendered to Christ, the Queen was baptized, and there was a solemn day of consecration, in which the great image was brought from the temple, and the smaller idols were brought from the Hovas' homes, a great bonfire was made, and the idolatry of the island was burned up. But there was something wrong. The Queen herself, long afterwards, came to the missionaries and took from her neck a little black image, only three inches long, which she had still cherished, and worn as an amulet there. The royal idol! The darling sin! Not until that was surrendered, could she become a Christian Queen. Not until the last idol was burned, was the Island of Madagascar given to Christ. Let us surrender all. Let us consecrate all. Let us not touch the unclean thing. The secret of failure is devotion to any sin. The secret of success is—

> "Here, Lord, I give myself away,
> 'Tis all that I can do."

The secret of success is insulation from the world; consecration to truth, and goodness, to the love of Jesus Christ, and the service of God.

www.ingramcontent.com/pod-product-compliance
Lightning Source LLC
Chambersburg PA
CBHW032044220426
43664CB00008B/851